D1601110

Regional Studies

Number Twelve
ESSAYS ON THE AMERICAN WEST
sponsored by the
Elma Dill Russell Spencer Foundation

Regional Studies

The Interplay of Land and People

EDITED BY GLEN E. LICH

TEXAS A&M UNIVERSITY PRESS, COLLEGE STATION, TEXAS

The paper used in this book meets the minimum requirements
of the American National Standard for Permanence of Paper
for Printed Library Materials, Z39.48–1984.
Binding materials have been chosen for durability.

Library of Congress Cataloging-in-Publication Data
Regional studies : the interplay of land and people / edited by Glen E. Lich.
   —1st ed.
    p. cm.
   Based on papers from a symposium held at Baylor University in 1987.
   ISBN 0-89096-477-7
   1. Texas—Civilization—20th century—Congresses. 2. Regionalism—Texas—
Congresses. 3. Human geography—Texas—Congresses. 4. Texas—Rural condi-
tions—Congresses. I. Lich, Glen E., 1948–.
F391.2.R44 1992
976.4'06—dc20   91-4133
                                                  CIP

Contents

Maps

Tables

Preface
Glen E. Lich

Even though the term *regional studies* and the idea of regionalism are not new, many questions attend the development of regional studies in universities, colleges, and high schools. This volume addresses itself therefore to the underlying meanings of regionalism and regional studies, forms of regionalism, and perspectives on the theory, the practice, and—occasionally—the history of the concept and methods.

The volume grows from a 1987 Baylor University symposium on the concepts and applications of regionalism. The three-day conference included twelve plenary presentations, one library exhibit, two museum exhibits, folk demonstrations, and a field trip on "Geology and Urban Growth" conducted by O. T. Hayward, a member of the Regional Studies Council at Baylor.

Professor Thomas L. Charlton, chairman of the council, asked the speakers to consider the methods available for the study of regions and the ways those methods can draw on each other, as well as ways in which the integrative study of regions can deepen understanding of community and nation. What makes one know that a region is a region, and how is it different from others? What are the tests of evidence of regionalism? What boundaries have meaning—political, geophysical, economic, cultural, psychological, ethnic, linguistic? When ways are discovered to study life within a region, are there special problems in reporting findings?

Methodology and interdisciplinarity are the themes that connect the series of papers on the interplay of land and people.

Questions like these guided planning for the conference at Baylor University, much as they guided the planning of a preceding conference, nearly forty years earlier, when Professor Merrill Jensen of the University of Wisconsin prepared a list of "propositions" for a symposium on "Regionalism in America." In the late 1940s, Jensen was part of a committee organized at Madison to administer a grant of funds from the Rockefeller Foundation. He carried the group's charge to "encourage research and teaching in the field of American civilization" to a brilliant conclusion when he coordinated a symposium in 1949 on American regionalism. Motivated both by a desire to deepen understanding of the "Wisconsin region" and by a conviction that regional study was relevant to the way scholars needed to study the nation as a whole, Jensen concluded that structures for such innovative and highly interconnected studies were not lacking, but that terms shifted so greatly in relation to physical, economic, political, and temporal variables that comprehensive national studies with the depth presumed possible in regional studies were as difficult to execute as they were necessary for national policy planners. While some of his older colleagues mused about the prospects of the university as an additional "branch of government," Jensen edited the symposium proceedings into a small volume that suggested some possibilities for national studies organized on a regional basis and susceptible of simultaneous enlargement and concentration in the study of regions and the nation.[1]

As Jensen explained in the introduction to *Regionalism in America*, "the concept of 'region' means different things to different academic disciplines, to administrators of state and federal governments, and to administrators of great industrial and financial organizations. "In other words," he concluded, "the nature of a 'region' varies with the needs, purposes, and standards of those using the concept."[2]

Jensen began with general and conceptual considerations. His papers show that he looked at concepts of regionalism, the history of regions, the development of regional character in America, and some systematic, comparative applications of regional concepts. One is hardly surprised to see that he started with definitions, but what is perhaps important is that he picked comparison and contrast as the first step toward a definition of *regionalism*. From comparison and contrast of *regions*, he went on to cite comparison and contrast of disciplinary definitions and methods.

I want to emphasize that point because I think our survival as regional studies scholars depends on it.

We may have varied reactions to Jensen's views, but the truth is that when the Baylor scholars confronted the opportunity of planning a symposium on "Regionalism: Concepts and Applications," they made much the same list, at least at the start. And I think that is because what were the basics then are still the basics today. A folklorist, a linguist, or a composition teacher, happening upon some predecessor's notes from four decades ago, might confront a broader generation gap.

Not that there hasn't been growth. But often the progress has been isolated, and until fairly recently it was hard to learn if someone else had already invented whatever it was we were still struggling to build. With the exception of folklore, regional studies publications have been picked up in bibliographies mainly on the basis of content or location, but not method. If you cared about the Cumberland or the Mississippi Delta, you found Lynwood Montell and William Ferris. But if you wanted to study and write something other than a folk life study of your land that like Isak Dinesen's Africa "had not its like in all the world" but yet was "the strong and refined essence of a continent," few of our teachers could point to appropriate models.[3] Perhaps that is one reason that, with the exception of Frederick Leubke's systematic coverage of the Great Plains, folklorists dominated regional studies in the United States until the late 1980s.

When I think of the service that women's studies conferences, courses, and bibliographies have afforded precisely in this way of putting scholars from a variety of disciplines in touch with each other methodologically and theoretically, I feel doubled respect for such approaches and eagerness for the advance of regional studies. A recent bibliography, such as Michael Steiner's and Clarence Mondale's *Regions and Regionalism in the United States: A Source Book for the Humanities and Social Sciences* (New York: Garland, 1988) does much to close those gaps, as do increasingly multi- and interdisciplinary interpretations—the so-called "new regional studies"—such as John R. Borchert's *America's Northern Heartland: An Economic and Historical Geography of the Upper Midwest* (Minneapolis: University of Minnesota Press, 1987); William E. Mallory's and Paul Simpson-Housley's *Geography and Literature: A Meeting of the Disciplines* (Syracuse: Syracuse University Press, 1987); James H. Madison's *Heart Land* (Bloomington: Indiana University Press, 1988); Michael P. Malone's and Richard W. Etulain's *The American West: A Twentieth-Century History* (Lincoln: University of Nebraska Press, 1989); James P. Shortridge's *The Middle West: Its Meaning in American Culture* (Lawrence: University of Kansas Press, 1989); and Andrew R. L. Clayton's and Peter S. Onuf's *The Midwest and the Nation: Rethinking the History of an American Region* (Bloomington: Indiana University Press, 1990).

If we in regional studies can develop the networks that our colleagues in American, women's, folk, or interdisciplinary studies have developed, we can enjoy some of the comparative perspectives that seem to have been high on Jensen's list of concepts and that are central goals of this volume.

The volume is arranged in three parts. The first part includes two complementary views from William Ferris and Terry Jordan, along with a panoramic methodology by Howard Lamar for the comparative study of regions.

The second part applies multidisciplinary considerations to the study of regionalism and economics, politics, culture, religion, gender, and language. Each of these chapters moves up and down the macro-micro scale in presenting perspectives on regionalism, and each appeals for new or broader applications, as in Charles Hamm's conclusion on the exchange between regions and the people who study them.

The third part of the book points toward three closely integrated goals: the study of variables in regionalism; approaches to regions writ large and regions writ small; and a final appeal for integration and comparative perspectives, whether implicit or explicit.

Thus, these papers come a full circle, as did the planners of the symposium, in their intent to place the study of regionalism within the wide parameters of the history of the concept, its significance in Western thought, and its many and varied manifestations. The important questions about regionalism as a phenomenon, the extent to which regional thought unifies other thought, the extent to which regionalism detracts from efforts to synthesize knowledge and to consider the unity of all thought—these are questions with which this book invites the reader to grapple.

Notes

1.   While this Wisconsin model and the proceedings of the symposium in 1949 (see note 2) at the University of Wisconsin were studied by the Regional Studies Council and by the new director of the Program for Regional Studies, the North Carolina regional studies heritage, represented by Howard W. Odum and Rupert B. Vance in the 1920s—with its dual aspects of study and policy—could also have served as a historical model for Baylor's program; see Daniel Joseph Singal, *The War Within: From Victorian to Modernist Thought in the South, 1919–1945* (Chapel Hill: University of North Carolina Press, 1982). What is particularly interesting in the Singal study is, of course, his argument that the tendency in the 1920s toward regional studies in academia paralleled a shift in scholarly thinking from Victorian to Modernist—elitist to deterministic—concepts of culture (see pp. 4–5, 136–37).

2.   Merrill Jensen, ed., *Regionalism in America* (1951; rpt., Madison: University of Wisconsin Press, 1965), pp. vii-viii.

3.   Isak Dinesen, *Out of Africa* (New York: Vintage, 1985), p. 3.

Acknowledgments

More than fifty people at Baylor University deserve credit for the national symposium from which this volume grew. Hardworking committees fashioned the program, built exhibits, coordinated local arrangements, and developed public relations. The staffs of the Institute for Oral History, the Texas Collection, the Strecker Museum, and the Regional Studies Program warrant great appreciation. The program itself was the work of Thomas L. Charlton, Dean William F. Cooper, Kent Keeth, Calvin B. Smith, and David Stricklin. Active support came from all twelve members of the Regional Studies Council.

I was a newcomer on the scene. But in those early months I developed a debt of gratitude to the contributors and to Alta Lane, O. T. Hayward, David Lintz, Lois Myers, Jaclyn Jeffrey, David Stricklin, Richard Veit, Ellen Brown, Tom Lawrence, Leslie Nichols Dievernich, Jenny Civa, Ed Griffin, Fred Luebke, Lou Rodenberger, Sandra Myres, Ingeborg McCoy, Don Yoder, and Michael Steiner, as well as to the fifty others.

Publication of the book was made possible by Baylor University's president, Herbert H. Reynolds, and John S. Belew, vice-president for academic affairs. Financial support was provided by a grant from Procter and Gamble. The editing was greatly facilitated by this grant and also by the hard work of my assistant Doug McGrath, my wife Lera, and our children James, Stephen, and Elizabeth.

G. E. L.

Part I Concepts

Despite long-standing assumptions that regionalism loses its
validity as the world grows smaller, the concept endures with
remarkable variety and vitality. Whether defined by geographic
or political boundaries, or by culture, economy, language, or
religion, regionalism continues to offer new and fundamental
challenges to theoreticians and practitioners in a multitude of
fields.

1 Region as Art
William R. Ferris

The study of regionalism is the study of the relation between people and the places in which they live. Such study can be approached from the outside, as anthropologists often do, entering cultures and places foreign to their own, or from the inside, as artists and writers have often done.

The ultimate ethnographer is the artist who writes of what he or she knows, feels, smells, sees, and hears from childhood. The approach to regionalism from within or from without has traditionally implied an essential difference in tools and perspectives. The anthropologist, the sociologist, the historian, the literary critic, all view region and its culture through a lens of prevailing theories within their respective disciplines. Each asks certain questions that yield certain answers. Each establishes a "distance" between himself or herself and the subject. Maintaining this distance establishes a focus and raises and resolves questions for the scholar.

The artist, in contrast, seeks to dissolve distance and to establish a "oneness" with the subject. He or she becomes the character, the place, and thereby animates it through imagination and drama.

Both the scholar and artist in their own ways study regionalism and the relation of people to the places in which they live. Their approaches are essentially different and have been so as long as we can judge. In his *Poetics* Aristotle comments on how poorly the poet describes his own craft, while the critic who cannot write poetry describes it with eloquence. Each has a distinctive role, and together they are complementary in their respective creation and study of poetry. If we substitute *regionalism* for *poetry,* the distinctions between the approaches of scholar and artist to its study are strikingly similar to those Aristotle describes.

Our comparison of region to poetry is a romantic notion and one I make without shame or apology. To understand region and its power over people, we must recognize that the whole is far greater than the sum of its parts. Geography, history, and literature all offer insights, but our attachment to places is an emotional, irrational force that is revealed in the romantic vision of nature and man's relation to it. Both figuratively and literally the romantic seeks to become one with nature. Walt Whitman celebrated this union in *Leaves of Grass:*

A child said, What is the grass? fetching it to me with full hands;
 . . .
I guess it is the handkerchief of the Lord . . .
What do you think has become of the young and old men?
And what do you think has become of the women and children?
They are alive and well somewhere,
The smallest sprout shows there is really no death.[1]

The romantic view of the union of man and nature has persisted as a central theme in the American literary tradition, much as Mark Twain's selection of the Mississippi River as quintessential place signaled the growth of American fiction.

American oral tradition—American folklore—parallels literary tradition and is often mined by writers in shaping their fiction. Twain acknowledges at the opening of *Huckleberry Finn* that he has listened carefully to the regional dialects of both white and black speakers and uses these dialects to distinguish characters in his novel: "In this book a number of dialects are used, to wit: the Missouri Negro dialect; the extremist form of the backwoods South-Western dialect; the ordinary 'Pike-County' dialect; and four modified varieties of this last. The shadings have not been done in a haphazard fashion, or by guesswork; but painstakingly, and with the trustworthy guidance and support of personal familiarity with these several forms of speech."[2] Twain also makes extensive use of superstition and folk belief throughout the novel.

The Mississippi, we might argue, is as much a character in the novel as are Huck and Jim. Huck and Jim move in and out of dramas on land and retreat to shelter on their raft. By night and day they witness the river's beauty and discover each other while floating down its waters.

Similar talismanic power of place is developed in William Faulkner's fictional Yoknapatawpha County. Faulkner's world elicits a mix of both love and hatred from Mississippi characters like Quentin Compson who declares to Shreve, his Canadian roommate at Harvard, "I dont hate it, . . . I dont hate it, . . . *I dont hate it . . . I dont. I dont! I dont hate it! I dont hate it!*"[3] Shreve questions Quentin insistently: *"Tell about the South. What's it like there. What do they do there. Why do they live there. Why do they live at all?"*[4] Shreve's questions probe, and Quentin answers from the heart. These are questions and answers we must consider in the study of regionalism. We must balance both the inner and outer approaches to the study. While we consider history, anthropology, and other fields as they relate to region, we must never lose sight of Quentin wrestling with his region. Like Jacob's match with the angel, it is a struggle that cannot be won, but without it our knowledge is incomplete.

While we admire the powerful vision of Twain and Faulkner, those of us who labor in the vineyards of academia must deal with the basic question of how we define a region and then, having defined it, how we engage in study that does the world justice.

One can begin with a three-part definition. The first and perhaps clearest statement of the region is geographical. We can, for example, map the Confederate states and show an easily defined territory which we call "the South."

A second definition, then, of the South might embrace the southern "diaspora." White and black working-class southerners left the region throughout this century and settled in northern and western urban areas. Mississippi Delta blacks relocated on the south and west sides of Chicago, while Appalachian whites moved to Cincinnati and Indianapolis. These communities preserved their southern roots through traditions such as blues, country music, and white and black "soul" foods.

New York Times music critic Robert Palmer once interviewed Muddy Waters at his home in Chicago, and after the interview Waters invited Palmer to view his garden in the back yard. There Palmer discovered, growing in Chicago soil, okra, corn, cotton, and other crops that Waters had transplanted from the world he knew as a farm laborer on Stovall's Plantation in the Mississippi Delta. He had recreated his "postage stamp" of southern soil in another land. Waters likewise also transplanted blues from the cotton fields to the Chicago ghetto.

Muddy Waters's journey from the South to the North, from country to city, parallels the lives of southern expatriate writers such as Richard Wright and Tennessee Williams. Like Joyce, these writers fled the nets of family, religion, and politics to create their arts. From their homes in Paris and New York, respectively, Wright and Williams mined their southern homeland for their writings.

These writers and many others like them formed an expatriate community which, like the northern neighborhoods of working-class white and black southerners, was in effect a "South outside the South." Whether for racial, economic, or artistic reasons, they could not "go home." These expatriate worlds were in many ways more intensely southern than the communities left behind.

The region remembered and recreated is then a very real and true extension of the geographic place mapped earlier.

The third and perhaps most interesting definition is revealed in the global world of myth, literature, music, architecture, and popular culture which some regions in particular engender throughout the world. Interest in a region like the South or like Tibet or Isak Dinesen's Africa intensifies as the distance from the region increases. In the Soviet Union, for example, an edition of fifty thousand copies of William Faulkner's *The Unvan-quished* goes out of print in less than a week, while in Japan young musicians master blues and country music styles for performance in local clubs.

A geographic spread of land, migrations of working-class and expatriate artists, and the mythic world abroad all may define a place as a region.

Like the Great Books Program that Robert Hutchins and Mortimer Adler created at the University of Chicago, regional studies programs bridge academic disciplines through a holistic view of a single topic. Rather than Western intellectual history, such programs focus on the culture of a place and its people. Like a patchwork quilt, successive studies of that union of people and place reveal colorful, dramatic views of the region in ways never before possible, eventually offering a comprehensive statement about the region and its people.

To study a region is to open academic doors and minds to the community of which the university is a part. We both draw on that community for our study and return the fruits of our labor to her citizens. For too long academic institutions developed an ivory tower view of education as isolated from their community and culture. A clear pecking order developed in which the term *region* connoted local or parochial visions of education. Southern universities looked northeast to the Ivy League as the nation's seat of learning and culture. The Ivy League in turn looked cross the Atlantic to Oxford and Cambridge for inspiration.

What was lost in this model was American culture. The study of regionalism is in fact a discovery of America through her regions. This work is best understood within the context of American studies. From the classic models of New England Yankee culture, southern antebellum worlds, and the western cowboy and Indian, a more complex view of our regions has steadily developed. In the sixties Afro-American studies emerged as a field and reshaped our understanding of American and especially the southern rural and northern urban worlds of which blacks are a major part. In the seventies the study of American culture further deepened through new fields of women's and ethnic studies, each of which staked out new territory and significantly expanded our understanding of the nation. The eighties will be seen as the moment when regional studies emerged as a catalyst for further reshaping the traditional definition of American culture.

Regionalism views culture as a living library of human and natural resources from which to draw. By bridging academic fields and by bridging inner and outer worlds, the study approximates a holistic vision of knowledge. Rather than isolating people and studies within highly specialized disciplines, the study of region has redefined learning in a medieval sense. The guardian angel of this process, as Eudora Welty suggests in her *Place in Fiction,* is sense of place. The study of place suggests common themes that link literature, history, music, art, and other fields into a richly textured view of American culture.[5]

In studying regionalism we view a mirrored image of ourselves and use that image as a central theme of higher education. Such study helps us to live with and understand the places in which we live. Our artists have long understood that this is the fire through which they must walk to be whole, to be true to their craft. We follow a similar course in addressing place and its relation to our lives.

Our study of regionalism demands that we bridge inside and outside views of our culture and become one with it. We must merge the dancer with the dance, the singer with the song, the painter with the painting.

Notes

1.   Walt Whitman, "Song of Myself," in Louis Untermeyer, ed., *Modern American Poetry* (New York: 1958), pp. 46–47.

2.   Mark Twain, *The Adventures of Huckleberry Finn* (New York: Norton, 1977), p. 2.

3.   William Faulkner, *Absalom, Absalom!* (New York: Random House, 1936), p. 378.

4.   Faulkner, *Absalom, Absalom!* p. 174.

5.   Eudora Welty, *Place in Fiction* (New York: House of Books, 1957).

2   The Concept and Method
Terry G. Jordan

I come both to celebrate regions and, more importantly, to issue some words of caution from the perspective of a geographer. There was a time when the regional concept and method—that is, research into regionalism—dominated the discipline of geography. As late as the 1950s, the study of regions was said to constitute the core of my chosen field and to represent the logical culmination of the geographer's art. Many if not most practitioners believed that the face of the earth could be marked off into areas of distinctive character, that the land and its inhabitants tend to be divided into a mosaic of more or less homogeneous spatial units. Geographers sought in their scholarship to create a sound, comparable world pattern of regions. Some approached the problem through the analytical method, beginning with the entire world and dividing it into spatial subclasses on the basis of a number of principles, creating a logical division. Others chose a synthetic approach, beginning with the smallest homogeneous units on the local level and working up to larger regions grouped on the basis of properties.

It was once even fashionable to speak of "natural" regions, based analytically in physical environmental features such as terrain, climate, and vegetation. In an era of environmental determinism, these natural regions served as the most fitting framework for the study of human adaptation to the forces of nature. Geographers of the time were so convinced that environment shaped culture as to suggest that economic regions, which were easily defined through census statistics, would reveal the existence of the natural regions, whose extent was more difficult to ascertain. Once discovered, the natural regions could be classified into types, following the precepts of science.

Regions were believed to be real entities, "more or less tangible," and geographers saw as one of their noblest tasks the study of the nature, extent, and causes of regions.[1] Indeed, regions were proper subjects of research precisely because they were viewed as real. If two geographers proposed different regional divisions for some part of the earth's surface, then the normal result was an argument about who was right and who was wrong. The underlying assumption was rarely questioned.

We geographers came by these notions honestly. The concept of region is ancient; the word itself derives from Latin *regio,* the straight line traced

8

by the augur's staff when he delimited the regions of the sky. Almost every language has a word for region, suggesting that the concept may be a universal, inborn human way of looking at the earth.

Unfortunately, I come bearing bad news for students of regionalism. After two millennia of using, misusing, and reusing the concept, geographers have concluded that regions do not exist. Now, we can either try to make the best of these unhappy tidings, or we can adjourn to one of the many beer halls lining the banks of the Brazos and try to drown our disappointment. I feel certain that most of us want to stay on and try to muddle through this little problem.

You see, the revised wisdom of the discipline of geography informs us that no two traits—no two cultural phenomena, no two aspects of the physical environment—have the same spatial distribution. Each possesses a unique geography. Many traits exhibit a somewhat similar distribution, but no two are identical. Therefore it follows that no two places on the earth's surface are alike. Every place enjoys its own particular character and personality. In short, the world, geographically, is chaotic—far more than we ever admit in the classroom or even in our scholarly works.

The geographical focus upon regions, this house of shards, collapsed around about 1960, blown down by a zephyr emanating from a young, confident group of geographers who offered a mathematical, theoretical study of process, based in models, as an alternative. They promised us, eventually, that we could have universal laws of human spatial behavior, if only we followed them. The trouble was, by placing a premium on universal principles, they lost all interest in the differences among places, retaining no use for specialism by area, for regionalism. We were also encouraged to embrace this new age by happenings in certain other academic disciplines; most notably anthropology and linguistics. Physical anthropologists, beginning in the nineteenth century, had identified a number of races and subraces of humankind. They believed that many physical traits covaried within discreet breeding populations, producing homogeneities that could be detected through research. These races and subraces were even given names by the anthropologists, such as "Negroid," "Nordic," "Alpine," and "Lapponoid." The character, origin, and behavioral attributes of races became a major field of anthropological research. Then, rather abruptly, the most respected journals, like *Current Anthropology,* started printing articles with titles such as "On the Non-Existence of Human Races." Quickly and noisily, the concept of race was abandoned, replaced by a far more complex view of how human heredity functions.

Meanwhile, kindred problems surfaced among linguists studying dialects of American English. They had discovered the alarming truth that no two words or pronunciations, when mapped, displayed the same geographical distribution. Drawing dialect boundaries became an arbitrary exercise, and the task seemed to become more difficult with increasing distance from the Atlantic. One linguist surveyed the South and found two dialects; another, using the same evidence, found five. In the end, one brave linguist wondered whether dialects existed at all. Chaos was loose in another of the halls of academia.

No doubt similar unpleasantness occurred in some other disciplines. Had historians not been so casual in their use of the word *period,* neglecting formally to elevate it to the status of a concrete entity, then they, too, would have endured such a debacle, for period is the historical equivalent of region, race, and dialect. As it happened, there were only a few caustic criticisms of "scissors-and-paste historians" who studied periods, collecting "all the extant testimony about a certain limited group of events," in the vain hope "that something will come out of it."[2] Scientific historians, it was said, studied problems, while those who dealt with periods were concerned with mere description. Regional geographers were similarly accused of dealing only in description, not analysis.

On the defensive and in retreat, the regionalists argued that many features, though not geographically identical, displayed a general spatial coincidence or covariance, implying causal relationships and regional identities. Too, they claimed, the limited territorial framework of the region offered a manageable unit in which the causal interplay of factors might conveniently be studied. Their model-building critics replied harshly that even total spatial correlation provided wholly inadequate evidence or understanding of cause and effect, that focusing upon a region in fact prevents consideration of causal forces lying outside the area. Regional geography, they said, was amorphous and pointless, knowing no laws and seeking no end beyond description. Only by studying processes in a problem-oriented, systematic manner could understanding be attained. Thus the regional concept and method, wounded by the inherent spatial chaos in the world, by the discovery that regions were abstractions, suffered the added indignity of not being able to explain that lack of order.

One might expect that, after so devastating an attack, the concept of region would have disappeared from the scholarly literature, as race did in anthropology. Well, I am pleased to say that geographers continued to make abundant use of the regional concept, although there was a decline in the 1960s and 1970s. Nor are geographers alone in their use of regionalism, for geologists, biologists, economists, and linguists also employ the concept. My edition of *Webster's New Collegiate Dictionary* devotes fourteen lines to the word *region,* noting that even physicians use terms such as "the region of the heart." When you consider that the same dictionary awards only nine lines to its grossly inaccurate definition of the word *ge-*

ography, it becomes clear that the regional concept has nicely survived its demotion to the status of abstraction. Indeed, some universities that lack a department of geography have one named "regional science."

What explains this remarkable persistence of a concept many geographers sought to kill? Well, even if regions are abstractions and do not exist; even if, indeed, every place is unique, the concept of regionalism remains useful. How else are we to deal with the obvious fact that Central Texas is different from the American Midwest or the Mexican plateau? We can easily accommodate regionalism simply by avoiding the trap of believing that regions are real. All that is necessary is for us to accept the region as a *classification system,* a geographical generalization. Classification is a time-tested way to handle the chaos of the actual world, to convert the continuum of reality into the stairsteps of "types." In fact, this view of regions as classifications has been implicit in the writings of some geographers for a century or more.

In this manner we can lump the array of unique places into regional types for convenience. Classifications usefully serve the purposes of teaching, research, and application of knowledge. Regions, then, are not an end in themselves, but merely descriptive and analytical tools. They offer a useful framework for handling large amounts of diverse information, for logical simplification. They facilitate systems analysis by providing the level of deliberate imprecision needed for investigation. The human mind cannot cope with chaos, and devices such as regions allow us to avoid such no-win confrontations.

Caution must be exercised, however, in the development of regional or any other types of classification. It is important to realize that, for any data base, an infinite number of classifications can be devised. Nor is any single classification best for all purposes. For example, one of the most popular regional classifications of climate types in use in geography classrooms today was specifically designed sixty years ago to illustrate the influence of climate upon natural vegetation. It is, in other words, a climate classification keyed to that specific purpose and to no other purpose. Even so, geography students continue to memorize these types of climate as if they were real, with no inkling of the original purpose of the classification. That is an example of the worst abuse of the regional concept.

I stress this point again. Whatever regional classification you devise *must be designed for a particular purpose.* There is no "best" regional classification. You must also realize that even with purpose-specific regional classifications, subjectivity is always present—in the number of classes you create, in the numerical borders you select to separate classes, in the rank order of your defining criteria, in the very selection of the traits that form the basis of the classification.

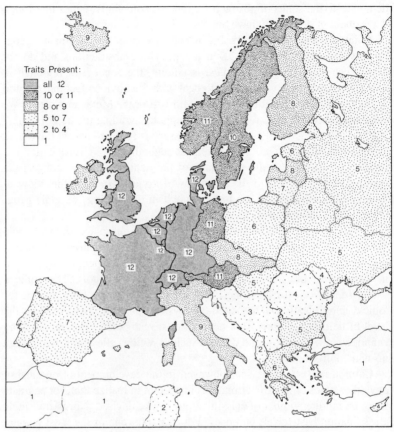

Map 2.1. The European culture region, defined on the basis of the twelve traits listed in the text. *Source:* Jordan, 1988, p. 14.

Map 2.2 (facing page). A regional classification of Europe, based on selected east-west, north-south, and core-periphery contrasts. *Source:* Jordan, 1988, pp. 401–402.

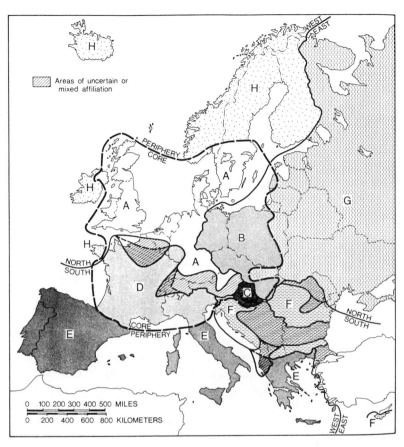

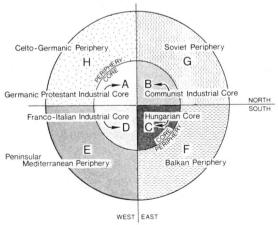

An example is in order. Let us assume that I wish to demonstrate to a group of undergraduate geography students that Europe possesses coherence as a human/cultural geographical unit. I would then select traits that demonstrate that unity, producing a map of a "European culture region" (see map 2.1). I could choose two or twenty or two hundred traits that demonstrate Europe as a region.[3] In fact, I selected twelve traits that I felt were significant in the regional definition of Europe. These were: Christianity, Indo-European languages, the Caucasian race, high health standards, a well-educated population, a well-fed population, a below-average birth rate, a high annual income per capita, a dominantly urban population, industrialized economies, freely elected governments, and a dense transportation network. With this classification I make the point that in many important respects Europeans are different from other inhabitants of the Old World, that in the human sense Europe is different from Africa and Asia. The classification also illustrates another point I wish to emphasize to my class—that the transition from European to non-European is gradual in the spatial sense, that the human Europe lacks sharp boundaries. The students busily copy the map, knowing that this sort of truth has a way of showing up on examinations.

Then, later in the semester, I wish to make a quite different point: namely that, while Europe is in many ways a cultural unit, it displays major internal contrasts. Now my point is that Europe consists of many subcultures and contrasted environments.[4] To drive that point home, I devise a regional classification designed specifically for the purpose (see map 2.2). The resultant map looks rather different from the earlier one. It shows a different pattern, one revealing: East versus West (as reflected in such contrasts as totalitarianism versus democracy, Satem versus Centum languages, harsh versus mild winters, and Orthodoxy versus Western Christianity); North versus South (as is seen in Germanic versus Romance languages, Protestantism versus Catholicism, cloudy versus sunny climates, presence versus absence of viticulture, and certain other features); and core versus periphery (as revealed in dense versus sparse populations, industrial versus agricultural economies, low versus moderate birth rates, substantial versus minimal acid rain, and the like).

Sensing that the ground had shifted somewhat beneath them, the diligent undergraduates would once more commence a frenzied scribbling and sketching, realizing that Professor Jordan was again dispensing the stuff of final exams. Perhaps only much later, certainly not in this century, a few of them might realize that the good professor had used two regional classifications of the same area to demonstrate two apparently contradictory points. At that juncture in their lives they could finally come to grips with the chaos out there that I have been describing. This realization normally comes at around age forty-five or fifty and is often sufficient to trigger mid-life crisis. Certainly I would never use the word *chaos* to undergraduates, for our entire educational system, from kindergarten through college, is carefully designed to generalize genuine chaos into artificial order. That is, in fact, a fine definition of education, and perhaps of research as well.

The failure to recognize that regions are abstractions, that in them we deal merely with categories within classifications, can detract from our ability to synthesize knowledge and diminish our capacity to investigate cause-and-effect relationships. The minute you begin thinking of a region as a real entity, you have compromised your ability as a scholar, teacher, or planner. In this context, perhaps the worst violators are those who have not arrived at their regional definition objectively and purposefully by means of classification, but instead subjectively though impressions or intuition. Such regions are not only unreal, but lack even the diagnostic potential of classifications. They may be art but lack scholarly value.

Equally hazardous is the tendency to consider regions in isolation. They should never be taken out of their worldwide context, because of the inter-connectedness of things. Interconnectedness is the sinister companion of chaos. Our educational system is similarly silent about it, since the human mind is not equal to the battle. It, too, can cause the onset of midlife crisis.

I now need to make things still a bit more complicated, quite aside from chaotic interconnections. I must report that geographers have discovered three different kinds of regions, that the regional concept is a trinity of sorts. The type I have been talking about up to now is called a *formal region,* an area that displays homogeneity of one or more traits. Simplest are the formal regions based upon a single defining trait. For example, one can devise regions for the United States based upon the national origin of the population. While you might imagine that such regions are very simple to devise and that a minimum of arbitrariness is involved, in fact many decisions have to be made. Should only the largest origin group in each area be shown, or should you try also to show the presence of others? Should some attempt be made to indicate whether the largest group en-joyed an absolute majority or merely a plurality? The classification shown here includes such a scheme of differentiation. Should the statistical units be states, or should we resort to the much more detailed county level (see map 2.3)? Do better ways exist to show the distribution of ethnic groups? For example, if you seek a map of German ethnicity, the national origin data, which place the German-Swiss in a different category from those de-rived from Germany proper, might be misleading. A map based upon the distribution of German-language newspapers might be better. Should the groups be subdivided? Should we use Spanish ancestry or subdivide it into Mexican, Puerto Rican, Cuban, and the like?

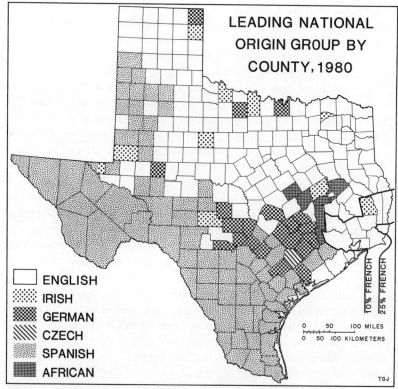

LEADING NATIONAL ORIGIN GROUP BY COUNTY, 1980

ENGLISH
IRISH
GERMAN
CZECH
SPANISH
AFRICAN

10% FRENCH
25% FRENCH

0   50   100 MILES
0   50   100 KILOMETERS

TGJ

Map 2.3. A county-level classification of national origin group. Persons wholly or partially of the ancestry indicated are included. *Source:* 1980 U.S. census computer tapes.

The point is, that even when a regional classification is designed to show only one trait, there are many hard choices and decisions to be made. It is crucial that one understand that every change in defining criteria, no matter how small, changes the extent of the regions in the classification. The map of regions changes, kaleidoscopelike, before our eyes as we jiggle the defining data.

Formal regions can also be devised on the basis of multiple traits. Traditionally, this has been the most common use of the formal region concept. The previously shown map of a twelve-trait Europe is an example. Another is my effort of twenty years ago to demonstrate that antebellum Texas had been divided culturally and economically between lower southern planters and upper southern yeoman farmers.[5] (see map 2.4). I chose six criteria: leading region of birth of population, the local importance of slavery, cotton cultivation, wheat cultivation, the selection of draft ani-

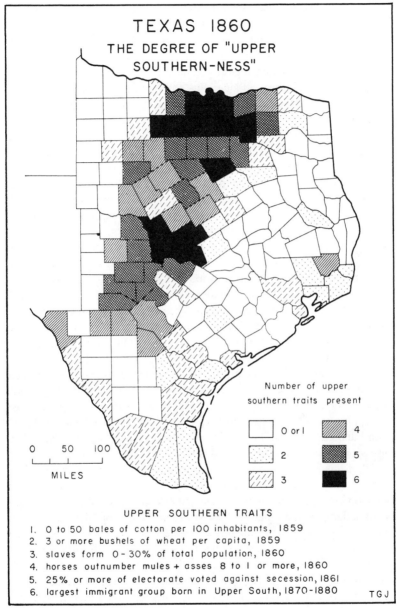

TEXAS 1860
THE DEGREE OF "UPPER
SOUTHERN-NESS"

Number of upper
southern traits present

☐	0 or 1	▨	4
⬚	2	▨	5
▨	3	■	6

0   50   100
MILES

UPPER SOUTHERN TRAITS

1. 0 to 50 bales of cotton per 100 inhabitants, 1859
2. 3 or more bushels of wheat per capita, 1859
3. slaves form 0-30% of total population, 1860
4. horses outnumber mules + asses 8 to 1 or more, 1860
5. 25% or more of electorate voted against secession, 1861
6. largest immigrant group born in Upper South, 1870-1880

TGJ

Map 2.4. A regional classification revealing hill southern yeoman influence in Texas. *Source:* Jordan, 1967, p. 689.

mals, and the vote on secession from the Union. Several things become evident from the map of the hill southern region of Texas which are true of all multitrait formal regions. First, a core-periphery pattern is revealed. Upper southern traits are purest in a core zone and weaken gradually as one approaches the plantation region. Second, the statistical breaking points are more or less arbitrary, although this problem can be lessened by choosing the statewide average as the division, as I did for the percentage of slaves in the population. Third, six is an arbitrary number of defining traits.

An example from another part of the world will illustrate the difference that criteria number and selection can cause. Let us say that I am devising a regional classification of the Eastern Hemisphere. I start with six criteria. One region that appears on my map is characterized by: monotheism, patriarchal families, swarthy Caucasians, sunny climates with summer drought, a cuisine including shish kebab, and coffeehouses as a male social institution. At this point, the region includes Greeks, Turks, and Arabs, among others. Only if I add a more specific religious criterion than monotheism will the Greeks be separated from this unholy trinity. Only if I provide a linguistic criterion will Arab and Turk go their different ways.

The boundaries of formal regions are always fuzzy; outliers and enclaves further complicate the situation. The more defining criteria you add, the smaller the core and the broader the periphery. That, of course, is a function of no two traits having the same distribution. At the same time, it often happens that the borders of different traits are at least parallel and in proximity to each other (see map 2.5). Such bundles of isolines are often used as generalized regional boundaries. In this case, they might provide the basis for a dialect border in Texas. But be aware that even by this stage of mapping much generalization has already occurred. Isoglosses are based upon hundreds of local interviews, and many such data points end up on the "wrong" side of the generalized isogloss.[6]

All of this leads to another rather important point. Let us suppose that, being young and foolish, you seek the *total region,* a formal compage based on all observable traits, human and environmental alike. This might be something on the order of "the American South" or "the West." I am here to tell you that such a quest is a fool's errand. Attempts to define total formal regions can only result either in gross statistical distortion and departure from reality or a map so infernally complicated that you will have a visual image of chaos. All of the problems I have listed become magnified with each added trait. A totality of traits will yield total frustration. Formal regions are classifications, and no sane person has ever attempted a classification of total reality.

Well, after some generations of flagellating ourselves with formal regions, we geographers had an inspired idea. Instead of devising these

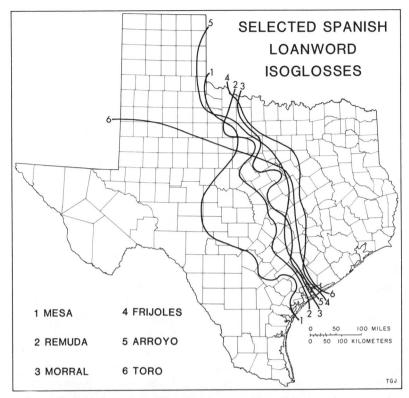

SELECTED SPANISH
LOANWORD
ISOGLOSSES

1 MESA   4 FRIJOLES

2 REMUDA   5 ARROYO

3 MORRAL   6 TORO

0   50   100 MILES
0   50 100 KILOMETERS

TGJ

Map 2.5. These six Spanish loanwords used in Texan English
demonstrate similar distributions, producing a bundle of isoglosses. *Source:* Jordan, Bean, and Holmes, 1984, p. 101, and
Atwood, 1962.

flawed abstractions in the privacy of our ivory towers, we would go to that
ultimate source of truth and amusement—the People. That is, we would
ask the real people out there in the world to tell us what regions they perceived to exist. Every human being, we learned, possesses *mental maps.*
Thus was born the *vernacular region,* the second major type.

The essential difference between the vernacular and formal regions is
that, in the former type, we deal with a broadly perceived regional self-
consciousness. That is, the inhabitants believe that the region exists. They
have a name for it and know they reside within its limits. By questionnaire,
interview, or the use of regional names listed in telephone directories in the
names of business and governmental agencies, we can discover these vernacular regions and map them. In two decades of frenzied activity, we
charted these previously unexplored lands, our mouths agape like latter-

day Magellans and Columbuses. We laid bare the collective regional schemes of the masses. Wilbur Zelinsky, for example, mapped the vernacular West, South, Midwest, North, and East by simple reference to the white pages of telephone directories.[7] Other geographers, more provincial than the cosmopolitan Zelinsky, focused on smaller areas. I myself, the epitome of the plodding *paisano,* surveyed Texas, discovering wondrous regions with names such as Big Country, Golden Triangle, Heart of Texas, and Metroplex.[8] The search goes on, and each year brings more articles on vernacular regions.

We have not yet paused to determine exactly what value or meaning can be attached to these popular, self-conscious expressions of regionalism. A superficial analysis yields some disturbing facts about vernacular regions, though. First, they exist at all different scales in a series of wild overlays and overlaps. A person might simultaneously report that they live in the Southwest, Central Texas, and the Heart of Texas. In other words, many different expressions of regionalism exist in each person's mind. There is no single regional scheme to be discovered on the vernacular level; rather, there are many. Second, these popular perceptions change through time, often rather rapidly. Third, no two persons have the same mental map. Chaos rears its ugly head once more. Even worse, there is often no logic or reason behind these vernacular regions. When analyzed objectively, many demonstrate little or no homogeneity that might explain their perceived existence. In truth, they are even more artificial and abstract than the formal regions devised by professional geographers. They, too, do not exist. They are figments of the collective imagination. Bear in mind that the common people who told you about these vernacular regions also believe that Elvis Presley is alive and living with Natalie Wood on a South Pacific desert island.

The third type of region recognized by geographers is called *functional.* It differs rather fundamentally from the other types. A functional region is an area that has been organized to function politically, socially, or economically. A city is a functional region, as are a state, independent country, precinct, school district, church diocese and parish, farm, market area for a product, Federal Reserve bank district, or land use planning area. Most functional regions have clearly marked borders.

Functional regions also have *nodes,* or central points where the functions are coordinated, directed, or dispensed. Examples of such nodes are city halls, capital cities, precinct voting places, church buildings, farmsteads, and factories. The difference between formal and functional regions can be seen in a simple example. Imagine a valley full of farms. Each farm consists of a strip of land reaching from the center up to the adjacent ridge crest. Farmsteads are at the front of the farms, lined up along a road that bisects the valley. On each farm, the slope of the land becomes steeper toward the rear. On the level land, near the road, wheat is raised on each farm. With increasing slope toward the rear are belts of vineyards, pasture, and forest. In this situation, both formal and functional regions exist. Each farm constitutes a functional region, each land use zone a formal region.

Not all functional regions have clearly defined borders. A good example is a daily newspaper's trade area. The node for the paper would be the plant where it is produced. Every morning, trucks move out of the plant to distribute the paper throughout the city. The newspaper may have a sales area extending into the city's suburbs, local bedroom communities, nearby towns, and rural areas. There its sales area overlaps the sales territories of competing newspapers published in other cities. It would be futile to try to define borders for such a process. How would you draw a sales area boundary for the *New York Times?* Its Sunday edition is sold in some quantity even in California, thousands of miles from its node.

Clearly, the functional region is not abstract, like the formal or vernacular types. However, the value of functional regions to the study of regionalism or sectionalism may be rather minimal. The biggest problem is that functional regions are not based upon any sort of internal homogeneity and generally do not possess a distinctive character. The state of Texas provides an excellent example of this problem. Texas houses two major and very different cultures—Anglo-American and Latin-American. Northern and southern sections belong to fundamentally contrasting peoples, and Texas' functioning as a state does not fully suppress these differences. Therefore, the concept of Texas is of minimal value to the understanding of regionalism. Indeed, it may well hinder our understanding, because the very presence of Texas has led misguided people, including a geographer or two, to speak of the typical Texan or to think in terms of a Texan culture. Perhaps the most revealing demonstration of the irrationality of functional regions is the map of independent states in Africa.

Another confusing aspect of functional regions is that a bewildering array of them exist, at different scales, overlaid and overlapped like vernacular regions. Sometimes the lack of correspondence is truly bewildering. The Dallas Independent School District, for example, does not coincide with the city limits of Dallas. Again, behold chaos.

At the same time, we need to be aware that powerfully functioning regions, especially independent states, can act to create cultural homogeneity within their borders, causing formal and functional regions to become kindred. An example would be the central and eastern European tendency in this century to forcibly expel ethnic minorities. Were Texas to enact and rigorously enforce an "English only" language law, the linguistic geography of the state might change.

We also need to know that functional regions can influence vernacular regions. The Abilene news media, for example, have for years promoted and disseminated the notion that Abilene and surrounding areas are called "Big Country." The functional region served by the Abilene media thus becomes the vernacular region perceived to exist by the population at large.

The elusive, mysterious character of regions has led the discipline of geography alternately to worship and damn them. When the abstract nature of formal regions was finally fully realized, many geographers moved away from regional studies. From about 1960 to the late 1970s, regional geography experienced a marked decline. Some academic departments stopped offering regional courses altogether. In retrospect, that was a mistake on our part. Many of us had given up on regions, but academia had not. As a result, many geography departments were abolished, their function assumed by regional study institutes or departments of regional science. Geographers, it turned out, could not abolish regions in the manner in which anthropologists had done away with races. About a decade ago, we returned to our senses, and regionalism was restored. Some of us had never abandoned the concept, and we could now come out of the closet. I am happy to report that regional geography is again thriving, although we are often forced to operate, as at Baylor, without a department of geography.

Why have geographers returned to the regional concept? It is, I believe, because we recognize that, for all its shortcomings and potential traps, it offers a useful and valuable way to come to grips with the chaotic world. We know we can more closely approach an understanding of spatial reality through this method.

One of the recent expressions of what is being accomplished in geography through the regional approach has been demonstrated by the so-called "humanistic" movement in the discipline. The humanistic geographers, in particular phenomenologists, fully appreciate the complexity and irrationality of the real world. Indeed, they revel in it. They are now attempting in their studies to convey the holistic sense of what they variously call the essence or personality of place. Recognizing that places are unique, they are seeking to capture those elusive qualities in print, fully aware that their impressions are subjective, a condition they believe is unavoidable. The humanists may in time replace the word *region* with *place*. If so, place will also become an elusive, wild thing that does not like to be pressed between the pages of a book.

Be warned, however, that if you delve into the works of the phenomenological place seekers, into this new land of the lotus eaters, you will encounter a strange jargon and, sometimes, sentences that boggle the mind. One of the more notorious passages, from a recent book, admonishes us to "let those things which show themselves show themselves from the very way in which they show themselves."[9] Clearly the phenomenological approach to regionalism is not for those with weak stomachs.

What, then, should be the principal tasks of scholars—geographers and nongeographers alike—who are intrigued by spatial variations and choose to employ the regional concept? First and foremost, we must continue to use the simplifications of reality generated by the regional classifications to teach students about the world, while avoiding lapses into pure description. We must continue to employ more complicated regional classifications to probe cause-and-effect relationships and to chart the course of geographical change through time. Many of the most basic questions remained unanswered. For example, is sectionalism in the United States diminishing as we all become more alike? This so-called *convergence hypothesis* has been widely proclaimed as a truth, but it remains unproven. In fact, one study by a cultural geographer, Roger W. Stump, indicated that precisely the opposite is occurring—that American regions are more pronounced today than at the beginning of the century. His evidence was based upon religious membership, and he found, for example, that the South was more purely Baptist today than in 1900, the Great Basin more purely Mormon, the upper Midwest more purely Lutheran. The complex migrational movements have had almost no religious impact, for within a short time, migrants convert to the locally dominant church.[10] This scenario might be called the *divergence* model. Give us ten years and we can make a Texan out of almost anyone.

What I am saying is that our present state of ignorance is considerable. Let us, without misusing the concept or method, classify regions, bottle the essence of place, chart spatial perceptions and regional consciousness. Maybe we can make a little headway against chaos. Perhaps we can unravel a few of the strands of interconnectedness. I hope and trust that the essays in this volume will help stimulate that kind of scholarly work.

Notes

1.   Robert B. Hall, "The Geographic Region: A Résumé," *Annals of the Association of American Geographers* 25 (1935): 122–36.

2.   Charles A. Fisher, "Wither Regional Geography?" *Geography* 55 (1970): 373–89.

3.   Terry G. Jordan, *The European Culture Area: A Systematic Geography,* 2nd ed. (New York: Harper and Row, 1988), p. 14.

4.   Ibid., pp. 401–402.

5.   Terry G. Jordan, "The Imprint of the Upper and Lower South on
          Mid-Nineteenth-Century Texas," *Annals of the Association of
          American Geographers* 57 (1967): 667–90.
6.   Terry G. Jordan, John L. Bean, Jr., and William M. Holmes,
          Texas: A Geography (Boulder, Colo.: Westview Press, 1984), p.
          101; E. Bagby Atwood, *The Regional Vocabulary of Texas* (Aus-
          tin: University of Texas Press, 1962).
7.   Wilbur Zelinsky, "North America's Vernacular Regions," *Annals
          of the Association of American Geographers* 70 (1980): 1–16.
8.   Terry G. Jordan, "Perceptual Regions in Texas," *Geographical
          Review* 68 (1978): 293–307.
9.   David Seamon and Robert Mugerauer, eds., *Dwelling, Place and
          Environment: Towards a Phenomenology of Person and World*
          (Dordrecht, Netherlands: Martinus Nijhoff, 1985), p. 71.
10.   Terry G. Jordan and Lester Rowntree, *The Human Mosaic: The-
          matic Introduction to Cultural Geography,* 5th ed. (New York:
          Harper Collins, 1990), p. 193.

3   Regionalism and the Broad Methodological Problem

Howard R. Lamar

In 1982 Professor Richard W. Van Orman of Purdue University at Calumet surveyed teachers of courses on the history of the American West to ask which historian and which book they felt had been most influential in shaping their concept of the West. Of the seventy-two who replied, the majority identified Walter Prescott Webb as the most influential historian, and his *The Great Plains* as the most important book. They also indicated that current textbooks followed Webb's ideas more closely than they did those of Frederick Jackson Turner.[1]

That finding has many implications, and certainly one of the most obvious is that the Great Plains as a regional concept has been accepted by historians and the public as both a useful geographic entity and a sensible way of treating sociocultural and economic topics at the subnational level. As Frederick C. Luebke has observed, the Great Plains exists in the minds of persons "even minimally knowledgeable about the United States."[2] Naturally not everyone has accepted Webb's Great Plains concept. Fred A. Shannon's devastating critique of the way Webb embraced many quite distinctive geographic and economic areas in his definition of a single region is well known.[3] Others have faulted Webb for ignoring the large number and variety of ethnic groups that in some plains areas constituted the majority of the population.[4] Biographers of Webb have wondered aloud whether he was a romantic who created the Great Plains and its subculture out of whole cloth.[5] Therein lies the first methodological problem facing the student of regionalism: what is merely perceived and what is real when one discusses region and regionalism? That leads immediately to the second problem: why is the perceived region or regional culture sometimes a more powerful concept than the actual geographic region?

Although there is much to quarrel within Webb's approach to the Great Plains, he did hit on a fundamental characteristic of a people living in a particular place over time: inevitably they try to rationalize the landscape and the social and economic conditions in which they find themselves.[6] The image could be either favorable or negative, and it could equally well be more inaccurate than accurate, but a sense of distinctive place and/or community—or what is lacking to prevent that sense—usually comes sooner or later.[7]

The student of region faces yet another problem in identifying the impetus or source for the regional concept. Gene M. Gressley highlighted this problem in his 1979 essay, "Regionalism and the Twentieth-Century West," which noted that "to many Westerners regionalism is essentially administrative regionalism imposed from Washington." He goes on to say: "Contemporary Westerners define regionalism in terms of multi-purpose river-basin developments, soil conservation districts, and bureaucrats running about the western landscape in the guise of scientists and conservationists, dictating what the West should do about its resources."[8] Indeed, Gressley concludes that western leaders associate regional planning with depression. "Regionalism and economic failure are indelibly inscribed on the western mentality," he writes, and one result has been that voluntary regionalism has not gotten very far. "With a strong bias for decentralization, inherited from the nineteenth century, western citizens feared any loss of influence as a total abdication of their future."[9]

Thus we come quickly to the basic methodological problem: what defines a region—a unique environment and its adaptive human inhabitants, as Webb suggested? Or is it the culture of the immigrant settlers, as Luebke suggests?[10] Or is it an outside, threatening group, such as the federal government, which believes that an area has such distinctive problems that it requires special policies and legislation to resolve them? If, in addition to the above, there is a conscious will to be a region, based on a shared sense of place and experiences over time and sustained by writers and public leaders, how does one evaluate all of these factors in relation to one another?

Certainly one answer is to take a comparative approach. It should be stated at the outset that this is hardly an original idea. More than thirty years ago Paul F. Sharp pioneered in comparative history by comparing the frontiers (as stage, process, and place) of Australia, Canada, and the United States. If we think of these frontiers as regions at a certain stage of development, then we can observe what was common or distinctive about each.[11] Building on Sharp's work, Jerome O. Steffen noted that some frontiers, such as those characterized by a rural, self-sufficient farming economy and society, were very different, because of their isolation, whereas commercially oriented frontiers, such as those devoted to fur trading and mining, always had an intimate relationship to a metropole where the product was handled and from whence supplies were sent into the field.[12]

Steffen focused on another basic issue as well: namely, that a frontier cannot be defined except in some kind of relationship to a nation or to an international political or economic nexus. This is also true for the regional concept, for it takes its definition from the fact that it is part of something larger—most often a nation.

The virtues of the comparative approach are many, but it can be overdone. In 1967, Earl Pomeroy told the Western History Association that, while the territories of the United States deserve to be compared to emerging colonies in Africa and Asia, social scientists have usually directed their studies of comparative development toward a predestined end, and therefore the comparative approach was not "an ideal star to hitch our covered wagon to." Instead, Pomeroy suggested that we compare the way a particular activity or social process is pursued in the West with the way it is pursued elsewhere. For example, he urged his audience to compare various groups of English-speaking farmers in several countries or areas of the world to see how each had adapted and evolved. [13]

In 1981 Leonard M. Thompson and I, in cooperation with eight other authors, four of whom had written about the southern African frontier and four of whom were students of the North American frontier, compared the experiences of the two frontiers to see if we could find what was common and what was unique. [14] By defining frontiers as zones of interpenetration in which neither the native inhabitants nor the intruding Europeans had yet established true hegemony, we were really talking about the existence of two or more cultural regions in one area.

Thus far I have defined region as an appealing concept (Webb's *The Great Plains*); as a useful administrative approach; as a negative, local reaction to policies imposed from the outside; as an "insider" image of one's local area; and as a developing area whose experiences can be compared to similar developing areas. In a sense all of these approaches deal with holistic units. They lack detailed depth and do not acknowledge the degrees of complexity and the multiple factors that some scholars may feel is necessary in serious regional studies.

One way, of course, to achieve depth of analysis is to follow the methods of the French *annales* school of historians. Certainly, exhaustive studies of a local area or community done from a large number of angles or approaches is one way to gain intimate knowledge and understanding of a people and a place. Two excellent examples of in-depth studies of American communities are Richard White's fine study of a Puget Sound county in the Pacific Northwest and John M. Faragher's charming but total history of Sugar Creek, Illinois, a Sangamon County frontier community. [15] Obviously, there are difficulties in applying the *annales* school approach to a vast region like the Great Plains, or to studying each of its communities as Faragher did Sugar Creek.

As a way out of this dilemma William Cronon has suggested—with others—that to study regional history we need the "layered look." That is, we need to identify and study a series of overlapping entities which, taken together, define a region, but in each of which there would be a different set of components or factors. [16] There would be, for example, an "environ-

mental layer," a federal-regional relations layer, and an urban-rural relations area (a concept R. R. Dykstra developed brilliantly in his *The Cattle
Towns*), among many others.[17] These would be complemented by demographic, ethnographic, and economic studies and by investigating transportation and communication systems and analyses of regional literature,
public rhetoric, and art.

All of the above problems and challenges came to mind in 1984 when
Richard Etulain and Gerald Nash of the University of New Mexico asked
me to write an essay evaluating the uses and promises of the comparative
approach to recent western American history for a volume on approaches
to twentieth-century western history. One good place to start, it seemed,
was to compare western regions; and from there it was but a short step to
consider the most famous and vivid of the regional concepts—that of the
Great Plains. Further, it seemed to make sense to compare a major episode
or a distinct period that occurred simultaneously in the Great Plains and in
the Prairie Provinces of Manitoba, Saskatchewan, and Alberta, these three
provinces having correctly been identified as parts of the larger Great
Plains environment.

Moreover, both the American and Canadian plains were characterized
by wheat-raising and cattle-raising economies. Both were more rural than
urban, and both had a significant mix of an older Anglo-American population and a large varied immigrant population from northern and central
Europe. But most important, both areas had endured severe drought and
depression between 1929 and 1941. However, even a superficial analysis
soon revealed that this vast area had produced not one "Dust Bowl" in the
1930s, but three. Thus, it was necessary to compare all three subregions.
But, following the precepts of the "layered" approach, it was also clear that
each state or province constituted a sociopolitical and cultural mini-region,
and to ignore these geographic and political units was to miss a major com-
ponent in assessing the history of the region.

The most famous of the "Dust Bowl" areas was found in the southern
plains. It embraced the Oklahoma and Texas Panhandles, northeastern
New Mexico, southeastern Colorado, and roughly the western third of
Kansas. During the 1930s it had come to have the unenviable reputation—
given to it in part by journalists—of being *the* American "Dust Bowl." The
second was a less well known but equally severe "Dust Bowl" in the northern plains, which included part of North and South Dakota and eastern
Montana. As will be suggested later, some experts believe that this area
may have suffered more than the southern plains region. The third was the
so-called Palliser's Triangle of the Canadian Prairie Provinces. This Canadian "Dust Bowl" centered on Saskatchewan and southeastern Alberta just
above western North Dakota and eastern Montana.

Most historians agree that the combination of drought in a largely one-crop economy of wheat and grain, low prices for what grain was produced, the collapse of the market due to national and international economic depression, and lack of any alternative forms of employment made the "dirty thirties" the grimmest and most critical decade in the history of the Great Plains states and the Prairie Provinces.[18] One would expect that almost identical problems in similar areas would provoke at least similar if not identical responses. But each of these three regions had different social, economic, and political responses to drought and depression. Thus, it seems logical that by comparing these responses one could gain further insight into the factors that produced distinctiveness and, perhaps equally important, ascertain which area actually suffered the most. The approach may also supply a partial explanation for why historians and other writers treating the depression years in each of these regions told such different stories and stressed such different themes. A comparative approach might even identify what has been missing or neglected in the history of one region as opposed to another.

There have been many excellent monographs and general studies of the Great Plains and the Prairie Provinces, and especially of the years during which they suffered from drought and depression.[19] In seeking to develop a comparative approach, this essay builds on those findings. And because it is impossible to compare everything, the essay focuses first on the changing perceptions, internally and externally, of one state or province in each of the three "Dust Bowls"—North Dakota, Kansas, and Saskatchewan—and then notes how each state or province responded politically to drought and depression. And finally, it seems important to note what basic social and political changes occurred as a result of a decade of economic and environmental hardship.[20]

If we look at what the first explorer-scientists said about the three regions under consideration, it is striking how uniformly negative they were. In 1820, after his trek up to the Platte and South Platte rivers to the base of the Rocky Mountains and his return via the Arkansas River, Major Stephen H. Long labeled much of the central and southern plains a "Great American Desert."[21] Thirty-seven years later, Lieutenant Gouverneur Kemble Warren concluded that the present western portions of North and South Dakota were not fit for agriculture. The tracts beyond the ninety-seventh meridian, he wrote, "must ever be occupied by a pastoral people, whether civilized or savage."[22] That same year, 1857, John Palliser, heading a British royal expedition to report on the Canadian Prairie Provinces, reported that a triangular section of land (lying in present-day Saskatchewan and Alberta) was unfit for agriculture. Palliser's Triangle, as it was soon labeled on maps of Canada, came to be seen as Canada's Great American Desert.[23]

As anyone familiar with the history of the American and Canadian plains regions knows, the negative image of the explorer-scientists was dramatically reversed in the late 1870s and early 1880s.[24] Many parts became both a wheat belt and a cattle-raising frontier. In Canada, immigrants from the British Isles and later from central and eastern Europe poured into the prairie provinces up to the early 1890s, and then after a hiatus, more came in the first three decades of the twentieth century.[25] In Dakota Territory, Scandinavian and German-Russian immigrants joined Anglo-American settlers who had come largely from the northern tier of states to the east. Meanwhile, a very large number of German immigrants came to Nebraska and to a lesser extent to Kansas.[26]

When drought and economic depression hit all three areas in the 1890s, similar agrarian populist protests occurred in both Canada and the United States. But these disastrous years were followed by a new boom in the 1900s that, with fluctuations, lasted until the end of World War I. A severe postwar drop in agricultural prices combined with the overextension of credit for the purchase of farmlands and agricultural machinery resulted in a moderate depression in the plains states that lasted throughout the 1920s. And again, as is well known, the 1929 Wall Street crash ushered in a decade of extreme economic depression coupled with severe drought in the 1930s.

In North Dakota, even before drought or depression in the 1890s, the wheat economy had come under the control of the railroads. Farmers had come to regard the Northern Pacific (and later the Great Northern as well) and the grain merchants, bankers, and millers of Minneapolis and St. Paul as their enemies. The sense of being an exploited "colony" added to the bitterness of the Populist protests in the state during the 1890s. That protest continued in another guise when reform-minded Progressives seized control of the state government between 1900 and 1914. North Dakotans thought of themselves as politically radical when they built state-owned elevators and chartered a state bank to defy the St. Paul milling and railroad interests.[27] Protest continued through the war years and into the 1920s in the form of the Non-Partisan League and the Farmers' Union movement.

Two of North Dakota's most prominent historians, Elwyn B. Robinson and D. Jerome Tweton, have noted that between 1915 and 1945 the state's population developed a negative image of themselves and their state.[28] Its citizens also resented, as any rural population would, the image of the farmer as a backward, uneducated hayseed whose problems were largely his own fault. This was especially galling to North Dakotans because, despite the "homestead" image associated with the settlement of the Great Plains, they were engaged in commercial wheat farming on relatively large farms and were, or aspired to be, middle-class entrepreneurs.[29] They also knew that their prosperity depended on the price their grain brought in a very competitive world market.

Although there is no precise way of measuring such a phenomenon, it seems that a profound general psychological depression already existed when the very real economic depression and the extremes in weather came to North Dakota in the 1930s. This despairing attitude is captured in the diary of Ann Marie Low, the teenage daughter of an able farmer-rancher in central North Dakota in 1928. "Now times are hard, prices low, and this year we are hailed out. . . . Come to think of it, Dad never plays his violin anymore."[30]

Certainly the conditions that plagued North Dakota in the 1930s were grim enough to break the strongest spirit. Between 1929 and 1931 drought conditions were so bad in the northwestern section of the state that more than 50 percent of the farmers there needed relief.[31] The state escaped drought in 1932, but 1933 was "the fourth driest year ever recorded," and 1934 was "the driest year yet on record."[32] In May of that year a vast dust storm arose on the northern plains and traveled eastward to scatter dust all the way to New York and Washington, D.C. Dust storms that came early in 1935 were alleviated by timely rain in the summer; but then came a plague of grasshoppers. In 1936 North Dakota experienced a combination of blizzards in winter and summer drought with hundred-degree heat that was devastating. The rainfall for the next three years (1937, 1938, and 1939) was below normal, but at least the extreme conditions of 1934 and 1936 did not return.[33] Buttressing their accounts with tragic, telling statistics, historians of North Dakota's depression years note that the state produced only two normal wheat crops between 1929 and 1941 and that the per capita income for North Dakota was less than half that of the average for the nation during the 1930s.[34]

These conditions, juxtaposed with a general sense of alienation, negation, and despair, shaped North Dakota's response not only to drought and the depression but to the government relief programs designed to lessen their impact. Elwyn B. Robinson has noted that although North Dakotans had long had a liberal and progressive outlook and believed in cooperative farm efforts, they "resented the loss of freedom" implied by "aid and direction from the federal government." Rather than help, it seemed to "accentuate North Dakota's dependent status."[35] Thus, the state remained Republican in its politics, except in voting for Franklin D. Roosevelt in the national elections of 1932 and 1936. It had no major New Deal newspapers, nor did it have any "single leader in the State, Democrat or Republican," who "was a consistent supporter of the New Deal."[36]

Moreover, North Dakota's best-known and most outspoken governor, William Langer, increased his popularity by using his authority to place a

moratorium on foreclosures and to force a rise in wheat prices by threatening a statewide embargo on shipments, but did not really address larger
questions on reform in land use and agricultural production.[37] As did most
state governments, North Dakota pursued a policy of retrenchment during
the depression, although it looks as if Langer kept a larger state bureaucracy in office (perhaps one source of his political power) than was perhaps
the case in other plains states.

Altogether the federal government spent 266 million dollars in North
Dakota between 1934 and 1940. "Relief," writes Robinson, "soon became
the biggest business in the state."[38] But even these efforts did not stop
losses of farms, prevent a large exodus of citizens, or restore prosperity. It
appears that North Dakota, in the long tradition of distrusting outsiders,
resisted both the New Deal and most prospects of change in these years.

At one level, then, I have identified a regional attitude, except that most
often its unit of expression was the state and its regional voice was political
although the crises were social and economic. At the same time the state,
with a reputation for radical solutions to its economic problems, did not
now have either a formula or the resources to improve things. A regional
attitude of long standing prevented North Dakota from cooperating with
the federal government or with other states.[39] At the same time there is
evidence that a genuine and positive camaraderie developed among North
Dakotans working in the local offices of New Deal agencies and programs.[40] Still, it is important to remember, if one is to understand regionalism, that it is often the state and not the region that best articulates regional views, and these views are often expressed in political terms by
political leaders rather than by cultural leaders or persons stressing an environmental approach.

In the so-called Dust Bowl area of the southern plains of which southwestern Kansas was a part, it looks as if its inhabitants were more passive
and fatalistic about their environment and their lot in life. Donald Worster
has called their attitude a "next year philosophy" that supposed that Provi-
dence and not "Washington would see them come out all right."[41] This
attitude may have stemmed from the fact that many southern plains settlers
were from the South. Moreover, recent research has suggested that compared with the settlers of North Dakota or Nebraska, they were recent arrivals and had arrived in the Dust Bowl area only after having lost jobs or
having been displaced from an older farming or industrial area.[42] In contrast to the situation in North Dakota, many had farms that were too small
to support a family decently, and so they depended on part-time work in
the oil industry and on other nonagricultural jobs.

While the southern plains people had a distrust of the East and the outsider—we should remember that both Kansas and Texas had been major

sources of Populist protest in the 1890s—they do not appear to have resisted federal largess and outside help as much as North Dakotans did. While Kansas's very able governor, Alf Landon, hated the New Deal and constantly urged a return to individual initiative and a free market to solve all economic problems, he also got as much help from the federal government as he possibly could. Indeed, it was supremely ironic that Landon's success as a Republican governor during the depression was due, in part, to his influence in Democratic Washington. It was partly through using the New Deal as both a source of help and a proven enemy that he became so nationally visible that he was the Republican party's choice to run against Roosevelt in the 1936 election![43] But here again a sense of region is expressed in terms of the state's needs—and by no less a person than its governor.

Three other factors distinguish the southern plains experience during the depression from that of North Dakota. First, oil was discovered in the Dust Bowl area in the 1930s, and as depressed as the oil market was, developing the new wells provided an alternative source of income for some Dust Bowl inhabitants that was completely missing in North Dakota.[44] In the perspective of time, it looks as if the famous Dust Bowl was less severely hit than were North and South Dakota.

The second distinguishing feature of the southern plains drought and depression area was that if affected portions of five very different states: Kansas, Colorado, New Mexico, Oklahoma, and Texas. That meant these were five different local responses, again due in part to who controlled the state government in a given state. For example, Kansans, seeing themselves as living in a unique state with a strong governor and an able delegation in Congress, tried to handle their economic and drought problems at the state level in fairly traditional political ways. Landon even played down the drought in Kansas as something temporary—like the hard times of the 1890s.[45]

The third distinguishing factor was that the federal government chose to make the southern plains Dust Bowl the national symbol of what was wrong with farming in the Great Plains. Here in Soil Conservation District No. 6, New Deal agencies tried to move people off submarginal lands, introduce new forms of agriculture, practice conservation, and, according to some, completely reorder the lives of its inhabitants.[46] Yet despite all the efforts to provide reform as well as relief, Donald Worster concludes in *Dust Bowl* that no really basic changes occurred in the southern plains region. "The failure of adaptation," he writes, "may be the region's most important value—as a model from which we can learn about the ecological insensitivity of our culture."[47]

On the other hand, historians of the New Deal often cast the federal government as the Dust Bowl hero, arguing that a dedicated set of bureau-crats and experts worked near-miracles there.[48] Even so, with the coming of World War II and the return of good weather and economic prosperity to the Great Plains, the efforts and successes of the New Deal in the Great Plains have been especially downplayed by local historians. In Donald R. McCoy's full biography, *Landon of Kansas* (1966), for example, there is coverage of drought and depression, but the index has no entries for *depression, New Deal,* or *relief.* These things are seen as temporary annoy-ances rather than significant events.[49]

In Kenneth S. Davis's *Kansas: A Bicentennial History* (1976), the words *Dust Bowl, depression, drought,* and *dry farming* are not to be found in the index; yet one of Davis's major themes is that weather is a key deter-minant of the Kansan's personality.[50] Somewhat as Robinson and Tweton did for North Dakota, Davis concludes that during the 1920s and 1930s Kansans began to have a negative image of their state. Certainly it devel-oped into a national image during its teetotaling, puritanical,and moralistic years. At the same time he found that its citizens have retained a deep love for the state and an overwhelming pride about any Kansan who makes his mark. In the view of Kansans, Dwight D. Eisenhower, a Kansan, defeated Hitler. That perception created such a positive feeling that Davis believes it largely destroyed the old negative image after 1945.[51]

From this discussion it seems obvious that if we are to develop better methodologies for studying regionalism, it is imperative to look at feelings about one's state and its relation both to the local inhabitants and to the federal government. This is particularly important because, as several his-torians have noted, the western states never had to deal with the federal government in any significant way that affected the everyday lives of the people until the New Deal.[52] Certainly the fact that this was a traumatic first encounter helps to explain the resistance and negative responses ex-emplified in North Dakota, in Kansas, and in Oklahoma, where "Alfalfa Bill" Murray fought the New Deal tooth and nail, and in Texas, where Governor Miriam A. ("Ma") Ferguson and her husband put up an equally stiff resistance while she was in the governor's chair in 1933–34.

For a regionalist, then, it would make sense to focus on the drought and depression decade not so much in terms of the New Deal programs but in terms of a region developing a heightened self-consciousness due to an outside force symbolizing threat and change.

Turning to the Canadian Prairie Provinces, let us look in particular at Saskatchewan, which in the 1930s was devoted almost exclusively to wheat raising and was thus even more vulnerable to international price col-lapse and drought than many of the plains states. Historians of the Prairie Provinces such as Gerald Friesen argue, in fact, that Saskatchewan suffered more from drought, blizzard, dust storms, and severe economic depression than either the southern or northern plains in the United States.[53] As had been the case in the two American states, there was a massive exodus of people to cities, especially to Vancouver in British Columbia.

How did Saskatchewan respond to drought and depression? In the beginning the central government at Ottawa said that relief was strictly a provincial affair. In turn, the provinces said that it was the bailiwick of the local municipality.[54] Ottawa eventually provided some relief to farmers, but it was the provinces that had to handle the crisis. If Canadian prairie historians are correct, out of that challenge came a new sense of community, a revival of local pride and, most important, a sense that Manitoba, Alberta, and Saskatchewan now formed a true region. In fact, the Prairie Provinces found a depression decade "as important in the development of a regional society as the era of the pioneer."[55]

The prairie historians, Friesen among them, also pursue another theme in depth, and that is the story of relief. They have particularly emphasized how young unemployed men were treated, how food was handed out, and how clothing, fuel, and money were provided. There is a sense of a society that seems missing in the North Dakota and Kansas narratives; however, it is to be found in the accounts of *national* New Deal historians.[56]

During the 1930s it also appears that the provinces had to pummel the Ottawa government into action, for there was no "New Deal" at the national level in Canada. Fortunately, all three Prairie Provinces chose able premiers during the 1930s and kept them in office a long time. And partly because of the depression the Conservative party lost out to the Liberals only to have the latter eventually replaced in Saskatchewan when a farmer-labor coalition, the Co-operative Commonwealth Federation, or CCF, took over. Meanwhile, in neighboring Alberta, the Social Credit Party assumed power.[57]

Both of these parties, while devoted to the task of improving the economy, were at the same time interested in limiting the excesses of capitalism and seeking social legislation that would guarantee security for its citizens in both good times and bad. These themes are epitomized in Friesen's description of the Co-operative Commonwealth Federation of Saskatchewan:

> The CCF was prairie Canada's version of socialism; it was an alliance of farmers, laborers, and professionals who shared a deep faith in British parliamentary institutions and an abiding distrust of the competitive market economy; it was quite willing to mix private enterprise with state ownership, but it would not, given the opportunity, permit the market to dictate the availability of health and education services, to bankrupt thousands of family homes, or to

develop provincial resources in such a manner that the people did
not benefit. It was an indigenous response to long-term urban and
class issues as well as to the immediate crisis of the agricultural
depression.

The CCF was a movement, at times radical, at times moderate in
outlook, seeking economic security and the amelioration of social
injustice.[58]

Put another way, the trauma of the depression defeated the Conservatives
and spawned a new party that tried to address the more fundamental social
and economic issues plaguing the Prairie Provinces.

In neighboring Alberta, the United Farmers were in power until 1935,
and although they claimed to speak for the farmers, they proved unable to
cope with the problems brought on by drought and depression. By 1935,
William Aberhart, a fundamentalist Baptist who, in addition to being a
high school principal, ran the Bible Institute and had a popular Sunday
radio broadcast that is said to have had 350,000 listeners, succeeded as the
first premier representing a new group called the Social Credit party.[59]

The Social Credit party took its ideas and name from the economic doctrines of C. H. Douglas, an English engineer. At the risk of oversimplifi-
cation, Douglas and Aberhart's Social Credit philosophy argued that modern technology has produced an era of great plenty and leisure, so the
resulting riches and free time should be distributed throughout the economy as unearned income.[60] In some sense it resembled the Townsend Plan
and the Technocrats in California, who argued that all senior citizens de-
served a certain amount to spend each month.[61] Social Credit should probably also acknowledge a certain indebtedness to Henry George's concept
of the unearned increment, for George's ideas had been popular in Canada.

In contrast, no major new parties emerged in the plains states in the
1930s. There were many brief radical responses such as the Farmers' Hol-
iday Association, as well as anti-Roosevelt groups. The Non-Partisan
League and the Farmers' Union movement in North Dakota and elsewhere
seem closer in nature to the new provincial parties, but they did not replace
either the Democrats or the Republicans.[62] In fact, in the national election
of 1952 the members of the Nonpartisan League and the Farmers' Union
began to move into the two national parties. What is more important is
why the Plains states received government help unwillingly and resisted
reform while the Canadian provinces helped themselves and reformed
themselves.

Moreover, at the end of the depression American states hated regional
planning, although they accepted certain programs that were obviously
wise and beneficial to them. The Prairie Provinces, on the other hand, now

seem to celebrate the fact that adversity had created a sense of region, a new sense of community, that it had founded new political parties and enacted social security measures. In discussing the 1930s its historians and social scientists focus on family, culture, and ethnic groups, as well as on government. They actually stress the coming of social services. In a sampling of standard histories of North Dakota and Kansas, on the other hand, the Social Security Act of 1935, surely one of the most significant pieces of legislation in this century, is either not mentioned, or is covered in a few sentences.[63]

In searching for some explanation of these different perceptions of what was happening and what was important in the drought and depression years, certainly one clue is that Canadians did not confuse the mores and values of the frontier period with those of the later period. Indeed, some Canadian histories say frankly that prairie farmers did not see themselves as pioneers or rugged individualists, whereas these frontier characteristics were constantly featured as ways for Americans to master drought and depression. Such an attitude is seen in Lawrence Svobida's *An Empire of Dust*.[64] The attitude is also shown by the fact that New Deal propagandists spent much time explaining that it was now too late for pioneering and rugged self-sufficiency.[65] Thus, a frontier syndrome—what Kenneth Davis in his history of Kansas calls a nineteenth-century "mindset"—created serious obstacles for handling economic and environmental crises at the state, regional, or national level.

Certainly a worthwhile comparative approach would be to explore the themes Canadian historians have stressed about the 1930s as opposed to those American scholars have emphasized. One might profitably ask if the words *region, rural, party, union,* and *relief* mean the same for the historians of the two countries. Curiously, relief camps in Canada were considered an abomination and a general failure—indeed, some of them do seem to have resembled prisoner-of-war camps. On the other hand, American government camps for transient labor received good press, and the accomplishments of the Civilian Conservation Corps have been highly praised.[66] Although the evidence is quite fragmentary, it appears that the cooperation between government, farmers, and university experts was greater in Canada than in the Great Plains, although Governor Landon of Kansas apparently worked closely with university experts in agriculture during the 1930s.[67] One possible answer is that many of the dedicated young New Dealers were also arrogant and patronizing, thus making reform proposals seem even more alarming.[68]

And finally it should be noted that for many years the depression in Canada has been a major concern for Canadian historians, as well as a subject for the best novelists—James H. Gray and Margaret Laurence, among others. Only recently have historians like Donald Worster, Paul Bonnifield, and Douglas Hurt given full scholarly attention to specific areas, while Frederick Luebke and Richard Lowitt have treated the decade in a more general way.[69]

If we approach regional history using many disciplines and many techniques, probe layer by layer and state by state, and seek meaningful comparisons, I believe that regional studies can become one of the most effective means of understanding both ourselves and our extraordinarily pluralistic nation that we have yet attempted.

Notes

1.   Telephone conversation with Richard A. Van Orman, Sept. 20, 1988.
2.   Frederick C. Luebke, "Regionalism and the Great Plains: Problems of Concept and Method," *Western Historical Quarterly* 15 (Jan., 1984): 27.
3.   Fred A. Shannon, "An Appraisal of Walter Prescott Webb's *The Great Plains: A Study in Institutions and Environment*," *Critiques of Research in the Social Sciences* (New York: Social Science Research Council, 1940).
4.   Frederick C. Luebke, "Ethnic Group Settlement on the Great Plains," *Western Historical Quarterly* 7 (Oct., 1977): 405–30.
5.   Gregory M. Tobin, *The Making of a History: Walter Prescott Webb and the Great Plains* (Austin: University of Texas Press, 1976).
6.   Robert V. Hine, *Community on the American Frontier: Separate But Not Alone* (Norman: University of Oklahoma Press, 1980), addresses this question, but Webb's *Great Plains* and Robert G. Athearn's *The Mythic West in Twentieth-Century America* (Lawrence: University Press of Kansas, 1986) are both classic examples of the rationalizing process.
7.   A "sense of place" is brilliantly treated in C. Vann Woodward, *The Burden of Southern History* (Baton Rouge: Louisiana State University Press, 1960), pp. 3–26 and throughout. See also Gavin Wright, *The Political Economy of the Cotton South: Households, Markets and Wealth in the Nineteenth Century* (New York: Norton, 1978), pp. 158–84, in which he argues that the South, incorrectly and therefore disastrously, perceived that it had to continue its cotton economy and culture after the Civil War.

8. Gene M. Gressley, "Regionalism and the Twentieth-Century West," in *The American West: New Perspectives, New Dimensions,* ed. Jerome O. Steffen (Norman: University of Oklahoma Press, 1979), p. 199.
9. Ibid., pp. 200–201.
10. Luebke, "Regionalism and the Great Plains," pp. 32–34.
11. Paul F. Sharp, "Three Frontiers: Some Comparative Studies of Canadian, American, and Australian Settlement," *Pacific Historical Review* 24 (Nov., 1955).
12. Jerome O. Steffen, *Comparative Frontiers: A Proposal for Studying the American West* (Norman: University of Oklahoma Press, 1980), pp. ix-xix, spells out Steffen's thesis about cosmopolitan and insular frontiers.
13. Earl Pomeroy, "The West and New Nations in Other Continents," in *Reflections of American Historians,* ed. John Alexander Carroll (Tucson: University of Arizona Press, 1969), pp. 237–61, especially p. 252.
14. Howard Lamar and Leonard Thompson, eds., *The Frontier in History: North America and Southern Africa Compared* (New Haven, Conn.: Yale University Press, 1981).
15. Richard White, *Land Use, Environment, and Social Change: The Shaping of Island County, Washington* (Seattle: University of Washington Press, 1980); John M. Faragher, *Sugar-Creek: Life on the Illinois Prairie* (New Haven, Conn.: Yale University Press, 1986). Both have Merle E. Curti's *The Making of an American Community* (1959) and in-depth histories of towns in colonial New England as models.
16. Conversation with William Cronon, Sept. 20, 1987, New Haven, Conn.
17. R. R. Dykstra, *The Cattle Towns* (New York: Athenaeum, 1979).
18. This is a main theme in R. D. Francis and H. Ganzevoort, eds., *The Dirty Thirties in Prairie Canada* (Vancouver, Canada: Tantalus Research, 1973).
19. Besides Webb, *The Great Plains,* see Fred A. Shannon, *The Farmer's Last Frontier: Agriculture, 1860–1897* (New York: Holt, Rinehart and Winston, 1945); James C. Malin, *The Grassland of North America: Prolegomena to Its History* (Lawrence, Kansas: by the author, 1947); and Carl Frederick Kraenzel, *The Great Plains in Transition* (Norman: University of Oklahoma Press, 1952); Howard W. Ottoson et al., *Land and People of the*

Northern Plains Transition Area (Lincoln: University of Nebraska Press, 1979). Other books and articles by Blouet and Luebke should also be consulted.

Gerald Friesen, *The Canadian Prairies: A History* (Toronto, Canada: University of Toronto Press, 1984), contains extensive footnotes reflecting the latest scholarship, as well as a convenient bibliographical essay on pp. 505–509.

References to recent scholarship on the specific "Dust Bowls" being discussed appear later in this paper.

The most recent general histories of the West that cover the depression and drought years are Athearn, *The Mythic West* and Richard Lowitt, *The New Deal and the West* (Bloomington: Indiana University Press, 1984), in which considerable coverage is devoted to the Great Plains.

20.   Portions of the following pages have been adapted and abridged from my essay, "Comparing Depressions: The Great Plains and the Canadian Prairie Experiences, 1929–1941," in *The Twentieth-Century West: Historical Interpretations,* ed. Gerald D. Nash and Richard W. Etulain, pp. 175–206 (Albuquerque: University of New Mexico Press, 1989), with the kind permission of the University of New Mexico Press.

21.   Edwin James, *Account of an Expedition from Pittsburgh to the Rocky Mountains, 1819–1829,* in *Early Western Travels, 1748–1863,* ed. Reuben G. Thwaites (Cleveland: A. H. Clark Company, 1905), p. 174.

22.   Lieutenant G. K. Warren, *Exploration in the Dacota Country in the Year 1855,* Senate Executive Document No. 76, 34th Congress, 1st Session (1856), pp. 21–22. Warren's map appeared in 1857.

23.   *The Papers of the Palliser Expedition, 1857–1860,* edited with an introduction by Irene M. Spry (Toronto, Canada: The Champlain Society, 1968).

24.   Gilbert C. Fite, *The Farmer's Frontier, 1865–1890* (New York: Holt, Rinehart and Winston, 1966); and James G. Snell, "The Frontier Sweeps Northwest: American Perceptions of the British American Prairie West at the Point of Canadian Expansion (Circa 1870)," *Western Historical Quarterly* 11 (Oct., 1980): 381–400.

25.   Friesen, *The Canadian Prairies,* chs. 11–13.

26.   Luebke, "Ethnic Group Settlement," pp. 405–406, 413–14, 417–18.

27.   Elwyn B. Robinson, *The Themes of North Dakota History* (Grand Forks: University of North Dakota Department of History, 1959), pp. 6–9.

28.   Elwyn B. Robinson, *History of North Dakota* (Lincoln: University of Nebraska Press, 1966); and D. Jerome Tweton and Theodore B. Jelliff, *North Dakota: The Heritage of a People* (Fargo, N.D.: Institute for Regional Studies, 1976).

29.   Many writers have noted the larger size of North Dakota farms and the commercial approach. See Robinson, *Themes of North Dakota History*, p. 11; and Harry C. McDean, "Federal Farm Policy and the Dust Bowl: The Half-Right Solution," *North Dakota History* 47 (Winter, 1980): 21–30. McDean draws compelling contrasts between northern plains and southern plains methods of farming and the difference in the makeup and attitudes of the farming population of the two regions.

30.   Ann Marie Low, *Dust Bowl Diary* (Lincoln: University of Nebraska Press, 1984), p. 13.

31.   Robinson, *North Dakota*, p. 398.

32.   Ibid.

33.   Robinson, p. 399.

34.   Ibid., pp. 399–400; Robert P. Wilkins and Wynona Huchette Wilkins, *North Dakota: A Bicentennial History* (New York: Norton, 1979), p. 102.

35.   Robinson, *North Dakota*, p. 397.

36.   Ibid.

37.   Wilkins and Wilkins, *North Dakota*, pp. 114–19.

38.   Robinson, *North Dakota*, 407–408.

39.   This theme is also explored in Athearn, *The Mythic West*, pp. 99–101.

40.   This positive view is suggested in Tweton and Jelliff, *North Dakota*, ch. 17.

41.   Donald Worster, *Dust Bowl: The Southern Plains in the 1930s* (New York: Oxford University Press, 1979), p. 28.

42.   McDean, "Federal Farm Policy and the Dust Bowl," pp. 21, 30, and nn. 50–53 (p. 30).

43.   Donald R. McCoy, *Landon of Kansas* (Lincoln: University of Nebraska Press, 1966), pp. 118–19, 140–43, 164, 174, 197–201, and 334.

44.   Paul Bonnifield, *Dust Bowl: Men, Dirt and Depression* (Albuquerque: University of New Mexico Press, 1979), pp. 37–38, 98.

45.   Landon argued that individual initiative, increased consumption,
             and a free market, not a new system, were the keys to recovery.
46.   Bonnifield, *Dust Bowl,* pp. 177, 180; Lawrence Svobida, *An
             Empire of Dust* (Caldwell, Idaho: Caxton Printers, 1940), p. 57.
             (A new edition of Svobida with a new foreword by R. Douglas
             Hurt has a different title: *Farming the Dust Bowl: A First-Hand
             Account from Kansas* [Lawrence: University Press of Kansas,
             1986]).
47.   Worster, *Dust Bowl,* p. 4.
48.   Elise Broach, "The Unsettling Frontier: New Deal Resettlement
             and the Turnerian Legacy," research paper, Yale University, May,
             1987. I am grateful to Ms. Broach for allowing me to cite her
             paper, which traces the speeches and radio broadcasts of Rexford
             G. Tugwell and other New Deal officials involved in agricultural
             reform and resettlement policies.
49.   See the index in McCoy, *Landon of Kansas.*
50.   See index in Kenneth S. Davis, *Kansas: A Bicentennial History*
             (New York: W. W. Norton, 1976).
51.   Davis, *Kansas,* p. 195.
52.   This is a theme in Athearn, *The Mythic West,* pp. 99–101, and in
             McCoy, *Landon of Kansas,* p. 300.
53.   Gerald Friesen, *The Canadian Prairies,* pp. 382–89.
54.   Alma Lawton, "Relief Administration in Saskatoon During the
             Depression," *Saskatchewan History* 22 (Spring, 1969): 42.
55.   Friesen, *The Canadian Prairies,* p. 382.
56.   Friesen, "The Depression, 1930–40," ch. 15 of *The Canadian
             Prairies,* pp. 382–417. There are, of course, significant excep-
             tions. See, for example, Donald W. Whisenhunt, "The Transient
             in the Depression," *Red River Valley Historical Review* 1
             (Spring, 1974): 7–20; Athearn, *The Mythic West,* pp. 111–12;
             Lowitt, *The New Deal and the West,* pp. 21, 142, 184–85.
57.   P. A. Russell, "The Co-operative Government's Response to the
             Depression, 1930–1934," *Saskatchewan History* 24 (Autumn,
             1971): 81–82, 86–100.
58.   Friesen, *The Canadian Prairies,* p. 409. See also Peter R. Sin-
             clair, "The Saskatchewan CCF: Ascent to Power and the Decline
             of Socialism," *The Canadian Historical Review* 54 (Dec., 1973),
             419–33.
59.   Friesen, *The Canadian Prairies,* p. 410; John A. Irving, *The So-
             cial Credit Movement in Alberta* (Toronto, Canada: University of
             Toronto Press, 1959); Seymour M. Lipset, *Agrarian Socialism*
             (Berkeley: University of California Press, 1959); C. B. Mc-

Pherson, *Democracy in Alberta: Social Credit and the Party System* (Toronto, Canada: University of Toronto Press, 1960); and David Elliot, "William Aberhart: Right or Left?" in *Dirty Thirties,* ed. Francis and Ganzevoort, pp. 11–32.

60. Friesen, *The Canadian Prairies,* pp. 412–15.

61. Lowitt, *The New Deal and the West,* p. 172; and Robert S. McElvane, *The Great Depression: America, 1921–1941* (New York: Times Books, 1984), pp. 236, 241–43.

62. Robinson, *Themes of North Dakota History,* p. 8.

63. Robinson, *North Dakota,* pp. 470–74; and Tweton and Jelliff, *North Dakota,* pp. 185–93. The Social Security Act of 1935 is well covered in McCoy, *Landon of Kansas,* but that was partly because Landon opposed an act written by Democrats. The act is mentioned twice in Worster, *Dust Bowl,* pp. 134–37, and in Lowitt, *The New Deal and the West,* pp. 133, 187. It is not an index item in Hurt, *Dust Bowl.*

64. John W. Bennett and Seena B. Kohl, writing in A. W. Rasporich, ed., *Western Canada: Past and Present* (Calgary, Alberta, Canada: McClelland and Stewart West, University of Calgary, 1975), on pp. 9, 15, and 17, assert that the stress on individualism in Canada came from academics and not from the residents themselves. See also Friesen, *The Canadian Prairies,* p. 382; and Svobida, *An Empire of Dust,* which in the introduction suggests a pioneering approach. See also Bonnifield, *Dust Bowl,* pp. 185–86.

65. See note 48.

66. Lorne A. Brown, "Unemployment Relief Camps in Saskatchewan, 1933–36," *Saskatchewan History* 23 (autumn, 1970): 81–83, 90–98. In contrast, the CCC was called the most popular New Deal agency in Idaho according to Athearn, *The Mythic West,* pp. 97–98. In Lowitt, *The New Deal and the West,* transient camps are praised (p. 24), as is the CCC's role in conservation efforts (pp. 58, 224); they are also commended for implementing the Taylor Grazing Act of 1934 (p. 68). See also Kenneth E. Hendrickson, Jr., "The Civilian Conservation Corps in the Southwestern States," in *The Depression in the Southwest,* ed. Donald W. Whisenhunt (Port Washington, N.Y.: Kennikat Press, 1980), pp. 3–25.

67. Friesen, *The Canadian Prairies,* pp. 391–92. According to Friesen, "what is surprising and even inspiring in retrospect is the determination of the farm and community in the southern prairies to confront the Depression head on and defeat it. Scientists,

administrators and farmers contributed a great deal to the ultimate recovery of the agricultural economy." Friesen, *The Canadian Prairies,* p. 389. See McCoy, *Landon of Kansas,* p. 177.

68.	Arrogant and insensitive bureaucrats are a major theme in Low,
Dust Bowl Diary, and in Bonnifield, *Dust Bowl.*

68.	In addition to Friesen's excellent *The Canadian Prairies,* see W.
L. Morton, *Manitoba: A History* (Toronto, Canada: University of
Toronto Press, 1967).

69.	James H. Gray, *The Winter Years: The Depression on the Prai-
ries;* the fictional work of Sinclair Ross, *As for Me and My
House;* Margaret Laurence, *The Stone Angel;* and W. O. Mitchell, *Who Has Seen the Wind* create rich images of prairie life
even in depression. Counterparts seem lacking in fiction about
the American Great Plains. On the other hand, it is clear that a
new and most promising era of scholarship about the southern
plains during the depression has arrived with the publication of
Paul Bonnifield's *Dust Bowl: Men, Dirt and Depression* in 1979;
Donald Worster's *Dust Bowl: The Southern Plains in the 1930s*
in 1979; and R. Douglas Hurt's *The Dust Bowl: An Agricultural
and Social History,* in 1981. The existence of the Center for
Great Plains Studies in Lincoln, Nebraska, and the ongoing publication of the *Great Plains Quarterly,* along with an increased
interest in the history of the West in the twentieth century, are all
causes for optimism. In addition to centers for studies of the individual plains states, the founding of the Regional Studies Center at Baylor University in 1987, dedicated to a truly broad and
comparative study of regionalism, is cause for even greater optimism.

Part II. Applications

Focusing on theoretical and practical applications of regionalism, these chapters delve into meanings of regionalism, perspectives on the study of regions and regionalism, and the value of regions as laboratories for teaching and interdisciplinary research. Some papers argue convergence, while other emphasize divergence of regions.

4   The Economics and Politics of Regionalism

Ann R. Markusen

To the average American, the word *regionalism* brings to mind vivid and picturesque local customs—Cajun music, New England clam chowder, California Zen, Appalachian bluegrass, and Rocky Mountain highs. Our chief connotation of *regionalism* is one of highly differentiated and traditional cultures which have survived the homogenization of television and extraordinary rates of internal migration. But rarely do these powerful images of regional uniqueness come with an explicit recognition of the economic and political forces that divide one region from another.

Yet economic cleavages, both past and present, have been major factors in shaping differential regional development. Equally significant is the role of the American political structure in engendering regionalism. Indeed, many perceived cultural differences are the legacy of distinctive economic experiences, often conflictual, which have created regional self-consciousness and antagonism.

In this paper, I lay out a number of ways in which regions can be distinguished from one another economically, in each case with a number of examples from American history or contemporary regionalism. Then I examine the ways in which American political structure cultivates regionalism, while often blunting its political effectiveness. Again, I offer a number of illustrations drawn from the American experience, where regional antagonisms arising from economic disparities were fueled by political structures. My purpose is to stress the significance of economic and political forces, in addition to geographic and cultural forces, as shapers of regionalism.

The Economic Origins of Regionalism

How a society organizes it economic life—the way it combines its natural resources with human labor and technology—may be highly differentiated across territory. At the most general level, variations in economic organization can be characterized as "modes of production." In our part of North America, at least three such systems have existed since the Middle Ages: the Native American hunting, gathering, and agricultural society; southern slavery; and capitalism. When brought face to face over contiguous boundaries, differential needs arising from these sharp differences in modes have

47

prompted bloody regional conflicts. Indeed, much of the regional structure and sentiment we live with today dates from encounters between protagonists of different modes that took place in earlier centuries.

Conflicts between regional Native American cultures and European intruders in the sixteenth through the eighteenth centuries illustrate both the start and the early differentiation of such structures and sentiments. In the Northeast, French and later English traders fashioned exchange relationships with the Huron and Iroquois in which Indian labor was used to harvest the furs. Further south, the English companies, eyeing rich agricultural land, forcibly displaced Native American farmers and set off a centuries-long east-west conflict and genocide. On the West Coast, the Spaniards forced Native Americans into servitude to supply labor for missions, outposts, and ranches.[1]

Each of these conflicts was over the ownership and employment of resources and labor. The victory was more or less determined by the differential technologies available to each. Although our myths of the settlement of the virgin wilderness do not often encourage us to acknowledge these first full-scale American regional conflicts, they left permanent imprints on American regional structure. Much of the political geography of the United States can be explained by this clash between nascent European capitalism and Native American "primitive communism."

The borders of many territories and states were originally established as frontiers between white and Indian territories. Many of these borders, as in the Northwest Territory, followed topographical features that could easily be defended militarily—riverbeds, lakefronts, and mountain crests. The result is an American landscape in which natural ecological units, like river basins, are unnaturally severed by such political boundaries.

American landownership and settlement patterns were also profoundly shaped by the clash between Native Americans and Europeans. Early settlements in all regions had an important defensive function which often dictated their placement and size. Many important interior towns had their origins as Indian trading posts or forts, and the prevalence of small homesteads in the interior resulted from the necessity to compensate a poor man's militia for its services in ridding the territory of Indians.[2] Only in California, where Indian resistance was easily broken and Indian labor appropriated, were large landholdings possible. This difference between landholding patterns in California and the rest of the country persists today in the highly differentiated structure of agriculture—immense corporate farms in the former, and smaller, family-owned farms in the midwestern and plains states.[3]

A second era of regional bellicosity that left deep marks on the American political and cultural landscape was, of course, the War Between the States. Two modes of production, one based on slave labor and one on wage labor, produced irreconcilable demands and divergent growth dynamics which led to bloody conflict. The South—heavily dependent upon slaves, cotton, new soils, export markets, and manufactured imports—demanded free trade, government land sales, and the extension of slavery into the territories. The North, with its booming wage labor manufacturing and smallholder agriculture, demanded tariffs, homesteading, and nonextension. Economic elites in both regions built a political program around these economic ends and developed respective ideologies that galvanized less privileged segments of the population around their sectionalist platforms.

Disparate modes of production also affected the outcome of the conflict. With its diversified agriculture and large numbers of skilled workers, the North found arming and supplying troops relatively easy. Because of the dynamism of its economy over the previous thirty years, the North had ten times as many factories and workers and twice as many rail lines as the South. The South, in contrast, found its manufacturing capacity woefully underdeveloped, its supply lines easily disrupted, and its overseas markets difficult to reach under conditions of siege. Furthermore, its labor force of two million slaves could not be mustered into military service, whereas many workers in the North fought on the Union side.[4]

The Civil War era was the single most influential force shaping American regionalism. First of all, the post-Reconstruction compromise, which left slaves free to own their own labor power but preserved ownership of all land in the hands of former slaveholders, forced upon the South a unique and highly inefficient agricultural system which left the region underdeveloped economically until well into the postwar period.[5] Recent disparities between "frostbelt" and Sunbelt growth rates can be traced to this phenomenon—not until the postwar period could the resulting cheaper, less well-organized, and more racially divided southern work force act as a magnet for mobile capital. But once unleashed, the region boomed as profit-squeezed northern companies moved south. In addition, many aspects of southern regionalism that we think of as political or cultural—the region's one-party politics, its unique version of racism, its predilection for evangelical and fundamentalist religions, its residual culture of defeatism[6]—are the progeny of that tumultuous midcentury conflict between two modes of production.

Since that time, capitalism has been the dominant mode of production in the United States. In many ways, capitalism is more ubiquitous than previous modes, eliminating the isolation and variation that existed in medieval Europe and among Native American groups. In the United States, for instance, we have no significant regional linguistic differences, in contrast to the many Indian tongues once spoken here or to the plurality of modern European languages. But capitalism has introduced its own forms of regional economic disparity, several of which have been, and continue to be, important regional differentiators.

First, class structure may be unevenly distributed across a territory. An example in the United States is the heavy concentration of working-class people in the coal-mining areas of Appalachia, recently dramatized in John Sayles's *Matewan*. When both owners and managers operate from outside the region, a distinctive social life and culture is apt to emerge. In advanced industrial countries, instances of geographical class segregation are few, although breakthroughs in communications technologies, which permit corporations to control worldwide production sites from a remote headquarters, may increase their incidence in the future.[7]

More common is the region whose class structure is skewed, or distinctive for its mixture of subclasses. Regions with high proportions of small business or individual entrepreneurs in their class structures, such as the American farm belt, have evolved with distinctive identities. In another variant, some regions have a high proportion of skilled unionized workers, as in the industrial Northeast, or high proportions of low-skilled, nonunionized workers, as in portions of the Southwest.

In addition to the fact of class presence, regions may also be differentiated by labor system, particularly the ways in which surplus is extracted from the labor force. Managers may choose to seek profits above labor costs in two ways: one, by increasing the amount of machinery each worker uses, so that productivity goes up without compensation wage increases, the typical, and indeed more successful strategy. But in some cases, it appears easier simply to suppress the wages of workers, extend their hours, and/or intensify the amount of work that they must do in a given period. Where the second system is chosen, both wages and productivity remain low, production continues to be highly labor-intensive, and the regional economy exhibits little dynamism.

Such was the case in the Appalachian coalfields through the 1930s. Small, competitively pressured operators found it easier to control wages through the devices of scrip, the company store, and unpredictable work schedules than by mechanizing the mines.[8] As a result, in the coal communities a culture evolved that differed from that of their millworker counterparts in the youthful factories of the North. The inevitable restructuring, which came in the 1940s, left acute problems of employment in its wake and fed the extraordinary outmigration of Appalachian folk through the 1950s.

Outside ownership is often a leavening factor in regionalism based on class segregation. In the Appalachian case, the success of mining areas in developing their own militant, distinctive cultures was facilitated by the absence of owners and even managers from community life. Where local elites are more closely tied to a dominant industry's management, local politics are more conflictual—and regional solidarity may be more difficult to achieve. In their absence, people's common troubles can be more easily attributed to the venality of outside interests, and a strong self-identity emerges.

A third source of regional differentiation occurs when one region is primarily a producer and another makes its living by financing, shipping, and distributing the product of the other. In this case, the concerns and cultures of each region grow to be congruent with the major livelihoods of each. Regional antagonisms are easily ignited in such a case because the prosperity of one region may imply the impoverishment of the other. An outstanding instance was the late nineteenth-century Populist challenge to the eastern establishment. Western and southern farmers, and their communities, found themselves allied against a powerful ensemble of grain dealers, railroads, and bankers based in the East. The market power of the latter, which enabled them to squeeze the producers through high freight rates, low grain prices, and high interest rates, created an enduring regional animosity.

A fourth economic differentiator is sectoral specialization—the simple fact that in different regions, with their differing natural endowments, different industrial structures evolve. Regional economies in the United States have traditionally been, and continue to be, highly structured production complexes centered on unique commodity groups, like automobiles in southeastern Michigan, steel in southwestern Pennsylvania, electronics in Silicon Valley, aerospace in Los Angeles, oil in the west south-central region, textiles on the eastern Piedmont, chemicals in the Gulf region, and, of course, agriculture, fishing, and forestry in many areas.

It is not simply the existence of such sectoral differentiation, but rather the way these sectoral complexes compare to those of other regions and respond to the disruptive events of the world economy as a whole that gives regions their character and shapes their economic life. Individual sectors display differential rates of change in growth of jobs and output, depending upon their position in the world market and their profitability at different points in their evolution. These sectoral peculiarities may carry entire regions with them, so that even in a period of relative prosperity, a particular region suffers dramatically from capital disinvestment. In the 1980s, for instance, the oil states of Texas, Oklahoma, and Louisiana suffered severe setbacks from the downside of the energy crises, while the military-led aerospace buildup has quickened the economies of heavily defense-dependent areas like southern California.

Sectoral specialization is most apt to produce antagonism when regions occupy sequential positions in the exchange process, especially if market power is uneven. For instance, if one region produces raw material sold by small firms to another region where purchases are controlled by a few large buyers, then the latter's monopoly power may systematically impoverish the former. In the Appalachian case, underdevelopment was intensified because relatively small coal operators for decades faced oligopolistic steel companies and utilities who kept the price of coal at a minimum. Or, it may be the selling region that holds the advantage. In the 1970s, successful political organizing in energy-producing states led to the adoption of severance taxes and other levies, which energy-consuming states claimed were exploitative and hampered the profitability of their energy-fueled industries.

Yet another source of regional economic disparity is the differential in the maturation of class conflict across regions. In some regions where antagonistic class conflicts erupted, institutions have evolved to manage and arbitrate these conflicts. The innovations of labor unions, collective bargaining, and a social welfare state are now deeply entrenched in certain regions of the United States, particularly the manufacturing belt of the Northeast and Midwest and on the West Coast. Unlike most other advanced industrial countries, where such institutions are ubiquitous, the United States has regions that lack them almost entirely, a legacy of the Civil War and the incomplete incorporation of the southern economy into a truly capitalistic regime.

As a result, regions in the United States have produced dramatically different wage and tax structures, or what we euphemistically call regional "business climates." In recent decades, regions with differentially developed institutions of class conflict find themselves competing over the same sectors, such as textile, clothing, shoes, and simple machining, subject to greater competitive pressure to seek out low-cost production sites. Regional antagonisms may arise in this case, as the more developed region struggles to preserve these institutions by demanding their imposition on the less developed region. Examples are the Northeast's and Midwest's so far unsuccessful demands for federal welfare takeover and for labor law reform. On the other hand, the recipient region, in this case the Old South, will fight to preserve the low-cost environment which is finally helping to industrialize its agricultural hinterland.

A final source of economic differentiation is disparity in growth dynamics. When one region, for reasons of resource depletion or industrial obsolescence, finds its entire economy going downhill, it will have special needs for adjustment and development. These demands are apt to be brought to the federal government, since resources within the region are already stressed. But other regions may be experiencing quite different growth dynamics which produce unique claims on the same national resources. Thus, divergent growth experiences may lead to regional antagonism.

For instance, in the 1970s, the Northeast was experiencing severe structural change which resulted in city fiscal crises, rising unemployment, and greater welfare roles. The region organized to demand a redistribution of federal funds in favor of regions with such problems of decline. But at the same time, both the South and the West were coping with the relatively new phenomenon of economic boom. Their problems were very different: how to house and provide public services for a migration-swollen population, how to protect an increasingly fragile environment from the ravages of industrialization, and how to manage new conflicts internally between old and new land uses. They were not sympathetic with the problems of the Northeast, their old rival, and lobbied fairly successfully in the nation's capital to prevent such redistribution.

Any or all of these aspects of economic differentiation may be present in any historical instance of regionalism. I am not suggesting that economic forces are the sole shapers of regionalism. Indeed, preexisting regional politics and cultures often determine the possibilities for a region's economic life within the context of a broader evolutionary process. I am trying to correct an omission in the regional literature generally, whereby the economic origins of regional disparity and conflict are submerged in an analysis that gives central ground to natural and cultural factors.

Nor are the economic distinctions themselves the most interesting facet. Rather, it is the way in which developing differences in territorial economies generate regional antagonisms that gives us the key to American regionalism. Two regions may coexist peacefully for decades with highly differentiated economic structures. And in at least two historical instances, powerful regional antipathies were subdued in the formation of a national alliance or program that incorporated their disparate demands. One was the Populist movement, where regional configurations gave way to a national class-based politics, a product of excellent leadership and good, if ultimately unsuccessful, strategy. The second was the New Deal era, when Roosevelt masterminded a coalition that brought northeastern urban workers, blacks, and liberals together with southern and western agriculturalists to transcend the strict north-south party divisions that had persisted since the Civil War. Whether regional economic differences turn into outbreaks of regionalism, or, in the example of the New Deal, into transregional co-operation, is heavily dependent upon the existing political apparatus, as well as on leadership and context.

The Political Dimension of Regionalism

Central to the study of regionalism in its conflictual, competitive guise is the question of the state. In the United States, the structure of government and the varied geographical strength of political parties play prominent roles both in engendering regionalism as a political contest and in curbing the power of regionalist challenges. The federal structure of government creates possibilities for the assertion of regional claims that are less apt to emerge in highly centralized systems. But our political party system generally reins them in.

To appreciate the role of the state in shaping American regionalism, it is necessary to reflect briefly on the origins of its federated form. The original eastern seaboard colonies, highly distinct entities in both their economies and their cultural practices, were yet united by their common enmity for both Native Americans and for their motherland, England. In shaping their new nation, they chose a very different and highly decentralized form of government with strong powers reserved for the states, a model that Benjamin Franklin is said to have borrowed from the Iroquois federation. Thus, a colonial regionalism begot a federal state, which in turn served as a forum within which subsequent regional political battles were to be waged.

In order to win possession of the national legislature and the presidency, however, politically minded people had to organize political parties across state and regional boundaries. These parties remained strongest at the state and local level, and, formally, were almost nonexistent at the national level. But from the outset, successful cross-regional party coalitions produced the governance for the new nation.

Within a century, however, regional conflict between the North and South grew so virulent and unresolvable that it led to this nation's second internal war. Federal structure played a catalytic role. The constitution had guaranteed states' rights to govern on a great number of matters. As different juridical and economic systems evolved on either side of the Mason-Dixon Line, tensions began to mount over how national policy should be designed on a number of key issues: the disposal of the land in the West, infrastructure programs, tariffs, currency regulation, and of course, abolition.

Yet from the time that the two economies began clearly to diverge in the 1830s, it took another thirty years for open warfare to erupt. Political par-

ties had to be completely reshaped, and ultimately thoroughly regional-
ized, for political separation to occur. The Whig party, which tried val-
iantly to maintain its cross-regional coalition of mercantilist elites, died
unsuccessful in its mission. The Democratic party became increasingly
dominated by southern planters and their indigenous mercantilist partners.
And an entirely new party, the Republicans, emerged as a strictly northern
party.

Again, to stress how one moment of regionalism conditions possibilities
for the next, a powerful legacy of this period was the subsequent inertia of
political parties until well into the twentieth century. Long after ideologies
would suggest that certain groups in certain regions might be better off
switching affinities, old enmities and loyalties held them to the party of
their region. One reason that Populist organizers eventually failed in their
effort to create a third party based on the support of southern and western
farmers and urban workers is that elites in both regions "waved the bloody
shirt" and invoked the "Lost Cause,"[9] Not until the New Deal did the Democratic party find a new regionwide constituency in the North, and not until
the post–World War II period did the Republican party succeed in garnering
a respectable share of the vote in the South.

Ironically, although American federalism permits the expression of
strong regional political differences because of its decentralized structure,
it has produced only very weak regional policies. Territorial representation
builds mechanisms for attending to regional interests directly into the political system. For instance, the ability of southern congressmen to dominate the congressional committee system for long stretches in the twentieth
century enabled them to garner a disproportionate share of the nation's
military bases. Similarly, the domination of "interior" committees by western representatives ensured that national policies toward infrastructure, especially dams and water policy, were favorable to the business of elites of
their region. In other words, logrolling and pork-barreling permitted the
satisfaction of certain distinctive regional demand without an explicit regional policy.[10]

The role of federal structure and political parties in shaping regionalism
can be demonstrated in the 1970s conflicts between the Sunbelt and the
"frostbelt." In that decade, three important new regional initiatives were
launched, amid a great deal of rhetoric about "regional robbery." Each was
based on a rather complex set of economic problems that heightened the
disparities among the regions and pitted them against each other. The three
regions were the Northeast (including the Great Lakes states), the Old
South, and the intermountain West. In each case, strong commonalities
among neighboring states induced the formation of three new regional coalitions: the Northeast-Midwest Congressional Caucus, with its research

arm, the Northeast-Midwest Institute; the Southern Growth Policies Board; and the Western Governors' Policy Office.

The issues in the Northeast grew out of a dramatic downturn in the region's economy. Its mature industrial sectors were hard pressed by both import competition and high cost–induced migration of capital toward the Sunbelt. Costs were higher in part because of the maturity of class conflict in the region, although much of the problem was simply that the sectoral structure of the region was heavily skewed toward older, profit-squeezed industries.[11]

With fiscal crises and heavy outmigration drawing down on internal resources, the political leaders of the region turned to Washington to petition for extra help, a move that the federal system encouraged. However, this external orientation on the part of the new coalition was also due to the region's strong two-party system, which prevented the governors, who spanned both parties, from forming a workable organization. The task devolved upon the congressional caucus, and the region's new official presence was to be found in Washington, not within the region itself.

Meanwhile, both the South and the intermountain West were booming, the former with delayed industrialization and the latter with the energy boom. Each confronted new internal conflicts over land use, infrastructure, and environment, producing new tensions.[12] In each case, the governors involved chose to form a new organization to address their newfound problems. Both organizations were headquartered within the region, rather than in Washington, devoted as they were to resolving internal conflicts rather than pressing their claims against those of other regions.

But the political party structure in each region also facilitated the formation of new regional organizations. In the South, the fact that all of the governors were Democrats removed a potential barrier to cooperation. And in the West, where a weak two-party system allowed individual personalities, rather than party machines or ideologies, to dominate politics, governors from rival parties found few difficulties in banding together to confront their developmental issues.[13]

Implicit in the notion of regionalism is the fact that the people of one region self-consciously sense their distinctiveness from people in other regions. In other words, part of the character of regionalism lies in its invidious comparisons. The regionalism of the 1970s demonstrates this forcefully.

Indeed, if during this era one region can be characterized as the aggressor, it was the Northeast. Almost all of the rhetoric of what *Business Week* pretentiously dubbed the "second war between the states" emanated from the Northeast, which claimed that other regions were prospering at its expense. A senator from New York contended that "the redistributional mode of government, with its bias against New York, is now firmly established in Washington. It is sustained by the rewards it provides to others." Neil Peirce, a nationally renowned political columnist, argued that "there's going to be a terrific political issue when the Northeast wakes up to the fact that it's being milked to death for tax money going outside the region." The Northeast-Midwest Institute published an attack on western states' energy taxes that was entitled provocatively "The United American Emirates," a note so subtle comparison with OPEC.[14] The region's congressional caucus proposed a slew of bills that would alter federal funding formulas to channel greater shares to the Northeast.

In response, the Southern Growth Policies Board turned its face outward, moving its major operations to Washington for the last four years of the 1980s. The policies board questioned the facts behind the claim that the Northeast was being "ripped off," demonstrating that poverty was still much worse in the South and incomes much lower. It claimed that the problem was that the Northeast was living beyond its means. As Governor Busbee of Georgia retorted, "This is not a divorce proceeding. You can't expect enough alimony to sustain the manner of line you've been accustomed to."[15] As noted above, the Southern Growth Policies Board was successful in blocking almost all of the important formula changes. Similarly, the western states managed to preserve their newly instituted taxes and siting regulations, designed to ensure lasting and well-managed economic development.

In the end, both the east-west and north-south controversies of the 1970s diminished. For one thing, the underlying economic disparities began to slacken, as the northeastern economy began to recover and the South and West faced their own versions of plant and mine closings. But the nation's political structure was also influential in blunting the newly revived regionalism. Unable to win on a regional basis, especially after the 1980s redistricting, the more aggressive northeastern coalition flagged and its members went back to working for constituents' goals via more traditional logrolling and party platforms.

In this economically induced and politically shaped regionalism, ideologies were not unimportant. Old enmities and prejudices fed these 1970s struggles, as the rhetoric revealed. A bumper sticker seen in Texas reportedly read "Drive fast and freeze a Yankee." Common cultures and long memories made it easier for neighboring states to cooperate—for instance, the membership in the Southern Growth Policies Board was almost identical to that of the Confederacy a century earlier. The point is simply that this regionalism was based upon economic events that found regions' economic fortunes diverging and that when one region complained of troubles that were somehow "the fault" of other regions, regionalism was quickly reignited among the others, especially within the context of the federal political system.

Curiously little dialogue has taken place between scholars working on an economic and political analysis of regionalism and those probing its cultural aspects. This has led, in my view, to an impoverishment of our collective work. I must readily admit to my own bafflement about the cultural content of regionalism, at least from an analytical point of view. For if cultural characterizations of regionalism often omit entirely the underlying economic and political tensions that exacerbate or neutralize cultural factors, political economists suspect that cultural regionalism is highly volatile and malleable. While it is clear on the one hand that cultural habits and legacies are critical to the formation and perpetuation of regional political and economic institutions, it is difficult on the other hand to merge such habits and legacies with traditions of politics and the economy. They often receive only an embarrassed acknowledgment, when they should be woven into the fabric of our explanations.

Notes

1. For a comprehensive account of Native American "regions" in the precolonial period, see Alfred Kroeber, *Cultural and Natural Areas of North America* (Berkeley: University of California Press, 1963).
2. David Horowitz, *The First Frontier: The Indian Wars and America's Origins: 1607–1776* (New York: Simon and Schuster, 1978). Horowitz marshals the evidence that mercantile interests engendered small mountain settlements both as a lucrative market for speculatively held land and as a buffer zone to protect settlements to the east from Indian attack.
3. A fuller account of Native American/colonial struggles and their regional contributions can be found in Ann Markusen, *Regions: The Economics and Politics of Territory* (Totowa, N.J.: Rowman and Littlefield, 1987), ch. 4.
4. For interpretations of economic resources in the war, see George Frederickson, ed., *A Nation Divided: Problems and Issues of the Civil War and Reconstruction* (Minneapolis, Minn.: Burgess, 1975); and Eric Hobsbawm, *The Age of Capital: 1848–1875* (London: Weidenfeld and Nicholson, 1975).
5. For an interpretation of post–Civil War economic restructuring in

the South, see Roger Ransom and Richard Sutch, *One Kind of Freedom: The Economic Consequences of Emancipation* (Cambridge, England: Cambridge University Press, 1977).

6. A summing up of the thinking on southern culture can be found in Raymond Gastil, *Cultural Regions of the United States* (Seattle: University of Washington Press, 1975); and in John Shelton Reed, *The Enduring South: Subcultural Persistence in Mass Society* (Lexington, Mass.: D. C. Heath, 1972).

7. Efforts to correlate regionalism with class structure are common in the care-periphery literature. See C. J. Cuneo, "A Class Perspective on Regionalism," in *Modernization and the Canadian State*, ed. D. Blenday, H. Guindon, and A. Turoweitz (Toronto, Canada: MacMillan, 1978), pp. 132–56; and Trevor Buck, "Regional Class Differences: An International Study of Capitalism," *International Journal of Urban and Regional Research* 3, no. 4 (1979) 516–26. See also Philip Cooke, "Class Practices as Regional Markers: A Contribution to Labour Geography," *Social Relations and Spatial Structures*, ed. Derek Gregory and John Urry (New York: St. Martin's Press, 1985), pp. 213–41; and Richard Walker, "Class, Division of Labour and Employment in Space," in *Social Relations and Spatial Structures*, ed. Gregory and Urry, pp. 164–89.

8. Rick Simon, "The Labor Process and Uneven Development: The Appalachian Coalfields," *International Journal of Urban and Regional Research* 4, no. 1 (1980): 46–71. Simon details this aberrant labor process and shows how it contributed to Appalachian underdevelopment.

9. See the accounts in John Hicks, *The Populist Revolt: A History of the Farmer's Alliance and the People's Party* (Minneapolis: University of Minnesota Press, 1931); and Lawrence Goodwyn, *Democratic Promise: The Populist Movement in America* (London: Oxford University Press, 1976).

10. The Appalachian program, begun in the 1960s, is an exception, although its existence was due more to external factors like Kennedy's political ambitions than to internal demands for aid and relief.

11. Barry Bluestone and Bennett Harrison, *The Deindustrialization of America* (New York: Basic Books, 1982). Bluestone and Harrison analyze the disparate causes of this deindustrialization.

12. The economic evolution of the New South is addressed in Thomas Naylor and James Clotfelter, *Strategies for Change in the South* (Chapel Hill: University of North Carolina Press,

1975); and in Clarence Danhoff, "Four Decades of Thought on the South's Economic Problems," in *Essays in Southern Economic Development,* ed. Melvin Greenhut and W. Tate Whitman (Chapel Hill: University of North Carolina Press, 1964). There is no comparable work on the 1970s boom economy of the intermountain West, although excellent sources on energy-based politics are Lynton Hayes, *Energy, Economic Growth and Regionalism in the West* (Albuquerque: University of New Mexico Press, 1980); and Bob Gottlieb and Peter Wiley, *Empires in the Sun: The Rise of the New American West,* 2nd ed. (Tucson: University of Arizona Press, 1985).

13.   On regional party structure, see Martin Wattenberg and Arthur Miller, "Decay in Regional Party Coalitions: 1952–1980," in *Party Coalition in the 1980s,* ed. Seymour Martin Lipset (San Francisco, Calif.: Institute for Contemporary Studies, 1981); Everett Carl Ladd, Jr. and Charles Hadley, *Transformations of the American Party System: Political Coalitions from the New Deal to the 1970s,* 2nd ed. (New York: Norton, 1978); Frank Jonas, *Politics in the American West* (Salt Lake City: University of Utah Press, 1969); and Neal Peirce, *The Mountain State of America* (New York: Norton, 1972).

14.   *Business Week,* May 17, 1976; *New York Times,* Feb. 8, 1976 and Aug. 4, 1977; Northeast-Midwest Institute, *United Arab Emirates* (Washington, D.C.: Northeast-Midwest Institute, 1981).

15.   The White House Conference on Balanced Growth and Economic Development. "Beyond Sunbelt-Frostbelt: Regional Policy for a Changing Economy," *Final Report* 1: 118–66 (Washington, D.C.: Government Printing Office, 1978).

5   The Media, Politics, and Regionalism
Charles Hamm

In the field of music, the contemporary mass media are often thought to be enemies of regionalism. Radio, television, phonograph records, movies, cassettes, VCRs, and now compact discs blanket the entire country with Top Forty pop and rock, "golden oldies," country pop, and bland "easy-listening" music, dulling us with incessant repetition of the same repertories and making us insensitive to the rich variety of regional and ethnic musics that had vitalized earlier periods of our musical history. Global dissemination of these same repertories is helping to devastate national styles around the world; even the most remote Third World village has its radios and casette players, spewing out Michael Jackson and Dolly Parton while its own music withers on the vine.

Certainly recent decades have brought increasing homogeneity to music in the United States and the world. But I cannot accept the notion that the mass media themselves are responsible for the deterioration of regional, ethnic, and national styles.

FM radio, with its line-of-sight transmission, can broadcast only within a severely limited area. Until the advent of relays, communication satellites, and cable systems, television had a transmission radius no larger than that of FM radio. AM radio has a longer reach, but only if a station has a transmitter capable of sending a signal of ten kilowatts or more. Historically, both radio and television functioned first as local and regional media. It was only in a second stage, after further technological advances, that they were able to reach across regional boundaries.

The phonograph has also functioned within a regional context. In the 1920s, local performers of "old-timey" or "hillbilly" music were recorded in such places as Atlanta, Georgia, or Galax, Virginia; these discs were advertised and marketed only in the region in which this music flourished. Afro-American music was also recorded and marketed regionally, as was the music of Cajuns, Polish-Americans, and many other ethnic groups. More recently, cassette technology has proved to be ideally suited to regional music: recordings of acceptable quality may be made with little capital expenditure, copies are duplicated cheaply, and the product can be marketed at an affordable price even in economically depressed regions and countries. My own collection of commercially released cassettes includes *Sida Di Ore Ao* (Plastik ZPKL 8036), sung by the Brand Choir of Windhoek, Namibia, in the ancient "click" language of the Nama people, which is spoken today by no more than forty thousand persons; and *Coro d'Orgosolo* (Tirsu TRC 167), choral singing by the people of the tiny Sardinian mountain village of Orgosolo, marketed only in the Barbagia province of that island.

Thus, the technological nature of the modern mass media makes them eminently suitable for regional dissemination, and they have in fact functioned historically in this context. If it is true that these media pose a threat to regional musical cultures, the cause lies not in the nature of the media themselves, but in the way in which they have been used. In this case the medium is not the message, and one must look beyond the media to discover this message.

I will begin with some excruciatingly sweeping generalizations. The nineteenth and twentieth centuries have seen a steady increase in the number, size, and power of large national states. Germany, Italy, and of course the Soviet Union come readily to mind as examples of modern countries shaped out of smaller, previously autonomous areas. The history of our own country reflects this trend: we moved from a collection of sovereign states in the late eighteenth century to a union of these states; the events of the 1860s put an end to the notion that one section of the United States could take actions contrary to federal law or the will of the majority of the population; and the twentieth century has brought the further geographical expansion of our country and also increasing centralized control of matters that were once the province of individual states, regions, or communities.

The political boundaries of most large modern nations encompass areas of former political autonomy and populations with a strong sense of ethnic identity. The past century has also witnessed massive shifts of population, with thousands and even millions of persons from one region or country relocating elsewhere. As a result, virtually every country must deal with some degree of antagonism between the central government and its various ethnic and regional populations, which feel that their identity and will have been subverted by the central state. My chief thesis is that the relationship between the government of any central state and its regional and ethnic populations is shaped by political realities, and that the mass media, particularly radio, are employed by most modern nation-states to shape and stabilize situations and attitudes. Radio is only incidentally a medium of entertainment; in most parts of the world it functions most importantly as a political tool, and it is no accident that a first objective of every coup or revolution is to seize control of the central radio station.

I shall begin with a single country as a case history. The Republic of South Africa, occupying the extreme southern tip of the continent, is the

only African country remaining under the political control of a white minority government. In terrain and vegetation it has been divided into four
regions: a Mediterranean strip along the southwest coast; a dry steppe, to
the north of this; a low, wet, fertile, semitropical east coast; and a central
highveld, shading from savannah in the south to semiarid bushland further
north. Politically, there are four provinces, coinciding only incidentally
with geographical features: the Cape and Natal, historically dominated by
English speakers; and the Orange Free State and the Transvaal, settled by
Afrikaners trekking inland to escape English domination in the 1830s and
1840s. These provinces have only token autonomy; virtually all political
power is centralized in the National party, in power since the elections of
1948.

Simply put, the major political problem facing the South African government today is the maintenance of control by a white population number-
ing no more than five million over more than twenty-five million blacks.
The strategy devised to stabilize this situation emphasizes and strengthens
white unity, by downplaying white ethnic (i.e., Afrikaner, English, Portuguese) and regional diversity, while at the same time splitting the majority
black population into as many fragments as possible to inhabit black unity.
Under the policy of "Separate Development," in place since 1960, the
white government has identified and labeled ten so-called "tribal" black
groups. This number is arbitrary: the government's "tribal" classification
sometimes brings together peoples with no common history and even different languages; sometimes it separates groups with historical alliances.
In fact, the whole concept of "tribe" is recognized by contemporary scholarship as a fabrication of European colonialism, having little or no basis in
the realities of African social and political structures. Nevertheless, each
South African "tribe" must live within a prescribed area, sometimes corresponding approximately to the region occupied by this group before European colonization, sometimes not. In any event, the boundaries of these
so-called "homelands" (or National States) are drawn so as to leave the
most fertile farmland and all valuable mineral deposits within the area reserved for whites. We Americans can best understand the situation as being
equivalent to our Indian reservations.

The medium of radio is a servant to the political ideology. Five separate
radio services aimed at the white population, all under the supervision of
the government-controlled South African Broadcasting Corporation
(SABC) in Johannesburg, are beamed to all parts of the country by numerous strategically placed FM transmitters. In addition, there are three regional programs with some degree of autonomy, although much of their
programming is relayed directly from Johannesburg and the remainder is
overseen by the SABC. Thus, white persons all over the country hear the

same news, the same political commentary, the same music—European classical and semiclassical pieces, religious songs, "easy-listening" selections, international pop and soft-rock hits, and sometimes white South African popular music.

The situation is quite different for the nonwhite population. Each of the ten "homelands" has a separate radio service, with the broadcasts in its own language; all ten are under the control of the government through the agency of the SABC. FM transmitters beam these "vernacular services" throughout the appropriate "homelands" and also to urban areas where people of ethnic groups have found temporary labor. Radio Zulu, for instance, is transmitted to the "homeland" of KwaZulu, to Durban and other "white" cities in Natal where large numbers of Zulu speakers are employed, and to the Johannesburg area, where many of these people also live and work. Because of the nature of FM transmission, Radio Zulu cannot be received in other parts of the country. Thus, blacks hear only a regional service, in their own language, as a constant reminder that they are not black South Africans but rather Zulus, Vendas, Sothos, or Swazis. They hear traditional, popular, and religious music mostly in their own language, and quite a bit of American popular music by black performers. This repertory is selected and mediated by whites: Radio Zulu, like each of the "black" services, has a committee responsible for monitoring the text and musical style of each piece before it can be broadcast. Blacks cannot hear, at least on their radios, the "freedom songs" sung at rallies and funerals, or workers' choruses singing at union gatherings, or for that matter specific songs banned by the government or the SABC: "We Shall Overcome"; "Sun City"; Peter Gabriel's "Biko"; or Pink Floyd's "Another Brick in the Wall," which was taken over as an anthem by black students boycotting the state system of Bantu Education. They can, of course, tune their radios to one of the "white" services, but they can hear nothing relevant to their own culture there, and the news and political commentary is no different from what they hear on "their" programs. (table 5.1 lays out the complete organization of SABC programming, as of 1986.)

South Africa is not devoid of regional character and consciousness. Cape Town and its environs—with a Mediterranean climate and vegetation, vineyards and ostrich farms, a unique ethnic mix including the mixed-race "colored" population, and a long tradition of relatively tolerant racial and religious attitudes—has a strong sense of itself as a region. The province of Natal, bounded on the south and east by the lush subtropical Indian Ocean coast and on the north and west by the towering Drackensburg Mountains, has a complex recent history revolving around the powerful Zulu kingdoms of Shaka and his successors; British colonization; political and military conflict pitting Zulu against Zulu, Zulu against Afri-

Table 5.1

Programs of the South African Broadcasting Corporation (as of 1985)

Program	Language	Dissemination
NATIONAL SERVICES ("WHITE")		
Afrikaans Service	Afrikaans	entire republic
English Service	English	entire republic
NATIONAL COMMERCIAL SERVICES ("WHITE")		
Springbok	Afrikaans, English	entire republic
Radio 5	Afrikaans, English	entire republic
Radio Orion (night)	Afrikaans, English	entire republic
REGIONAL COMMERCIAL SERVICES ("WHITE")		
Radio Highveld	Afrikaans, English	Transvaal, Orange Free State
Radio Good Hope	English, Afrikaans	Cape Province
Radio Port Natal	English, Afrikaans	Natal
INDIAN SERVICE		
Radio Lotus	English	Natal
"RADIO BANTU"		
Radio Zulu	Zulu, English	*Kwazulu*, Durban, the Rand
Radio Xhosa	Xhosa, English	*Transkei*, *Ciskei*, Eastern Cape
Radio Tswana	SeTswana	*Bophutatswana*, the Rand
Radio SeSotho	Southern Sotho	*Qwaqwa*, the Rand, Free State
Radio Lebowa	Northern Sotho	*Lebowa*, Northern Transvaal
Radio Tsonga	Tsonga	*Gazankulu*, the Rand
Radio Venda	LuVenda	*Venda*
Radio Swazi	SiSwati	*KaNgwane*
Radio Ndebele	Ndebele	*KaNdebele*

kaner, British against Zulu, and British against Afrikaner; and the development of sugar plantations and the importation of large numbers of Indian workers. The Eastern Cape, the Karoo, the lowveld, and many other areas have equally distinctive geographical and cultural identities. In recent years both Cape Town and Natal, citing geographic, ethnic, historical, and ideological differences with the central government, have put forward proposals for new regional governments in which all population groups would be represented. But both plans have been rejected as contrary to the National party's policy of muting and stifling regional consciousness in favor of national white unity. Simply put, regional identity must be subordinated to state policy, which means most importantly that it may not cut across racial lines.

The Soviet Union will serve as another example of my thesis on the relationships among central states, their regional and ethnic populations, and radio. Occupying the largest land mass of any country in the world, more than 8.6 million square miles spread across Europe and Asia and covering eleven time zones, the Soviet Union has a population of approximately 300 million people speaking some two hundred languages or dialects. Despite the size of the country and the diversity of its population, the entire Soviet Union is linked by a state radio network, a miracle of communications technology. Two programs designed for national transmission originate in Moscow: Program 1 carries news, political commentary, and other official communications; Program 2 offers mostly music and sports, with hourly news summaries. Relayed to all parts of Russia, these programs are beamed by FM transmitters in densely populated areas and by AM and shortwave elsewhere. In addition, each of the fifteen Soviet republics has its own regional service broadcasting in the chief language of the area, carrying local news, sports, weather, and music, mixing these with relays of programs from the two national services.

Regional stations include local music in their programming, and the national programs from Moscow often include regional music from one or another of the Soviet republics. But regional music is mediated by agencies of the central government. Since the end of World War II, various Russian folk ensembles have been organized in the Soviet Union, and often perform abroad as well; their repertory consists of songs and dances drawing on traditional models, but usually arranged and produced by professionals—who are often not native to the region from which the material is drawn and often have conservatory training in classical music or dance. It is in this mediated form, equivalent to the "folk revival" movement in the United States, that regional music is most often broadcast and recorded. Students may learn to perform on folk instruments and in folk ensembles at regional conservatories of music, following curricula established by the central

Committee on Education. Thus, the performance of regional music is gradually shifting from its traditional village setting to the concert stage and the mass media, and its transmission is more and more the business of state-controlled agencies rather than the family or the community.

The basic radio programming for the entire Soviet Union, originating in Moscow, is a constant reminder to each citizen of his or her primary allegiance to the central state and its policies. Regional programs acknowledge and celebrate Russia's ethnic diversity, but as secondary to national unity, never as a threat or alternative to it.

In Zimbabwe, today's political reality revolves around the presence in the country of three groups: a Shona-speaking majority, represented politically by the ZANU-PF party, headed by Prime Minister Robert Mugabe; the Ndebele people of the western province of Matabeleland, mostly backing Josiah Nkomo's ZAPU party; and the English-speaking white farmers, who held political control until 1980, led by Ian Smith. A visit to a session of Parliament affords visual confirmation of this threefold division of the population, with elected representatives of each group seated in separate sections of the chambers; and a few hours spent listening to a program of the Zimbabwe Broadcasting Corporation confirms the determination of the government to see that each group is accorded fair representation. There are four services, each beamed to the entire country: Radio 1 broadcasts only in English, and carries drama, variety programs, classical music, and other items chiefly of interest to the white population; Radio 2 is the pop music station, offering a mix of international and local hits, with announcers and disc jockeys alternating among the English, Shona, and Ndebele languages; and Radio 3 and 4 are designed for the black population, broadcasting in Shona and Ndebele and often featuring traditional and neotraditional music in these languages. The nightly newscast on Zimbabwe Television offers the same information three times, once in each of the three languages of the country.

Thus, the central governments of South Africa, the Soviet Union, and Zimbabwe define and manipulate regionalism to fit their particular strategies, and use the mass media and its music to reinforce these.

Turning now to our own country, I will try to deal with the complex issues of government strategies, regionalism, the mass media, and music by first nibbling around the edges, tossing out a few statistics and other facts, before ending with a series of observations.

According to the thirty-ninth edition of *World Radio TV Handbook,* there are 477 million radio sets in the United States, more than two for every American citizen. In 1984, 5,359 FM and 4,927 AM radio stations were on the air or in the process of construction, for a total of 10,286 licensed radio stations in the United States. As mentioned above, all FM stations have a local or narrowly regional signal because of the nature of line-of-sight transmission; and only 364 of the 4,927 AM stations transmit in the power range of ten to fifty kilowatts, allowing them to be heard some distance away. Thus 96.46 percent of all radio stations in America reached only local or regional audiences in 1984.

The United States has no internal national radio service. Governmental control is exerted through the Federal Communications Commission (FCC), which has three chief charges: the issuance of licenses, without which no radio station is allowed to transmit; the regulation of these stations; and the allocation of broadcast frequencies. Regulation rarely takes the form of direct monitoring, but rather of general guidelines: public morality, however defined, must not be violated; AM and FM programming should somehow differ from each other; and a certain amount of time each week must be given to local public service programs. Several incidents will help define the regulatory role of the FCC: in 1971, a warning was issued to all stations against the playing of songs dealing sympathetically with drug use or expressing antiwar sentiments, under threat of nonrenewal of license; more recently, warnings against playing rock songs with supposedly satanic lyrics have gone out at the urging of the Parent's Music Resource Group. Action against "pirate" stations has been more direct and severe: any individual or group broadcasting without an FCC license is tracked down, forcibly taken off the air, and threatened with fines and imprisonment, as happened in 1987 to a "pirate" station broadcasting its own selection of rock and roll from a ship anchored near New York City.

We live in a country in which most discontent is ethnically or economically but not regionally based; there has been no serious threat of regional insurrection or terrorism for a long time. To the contrary, virtually every region and every ethnic group in the United States understands the benefits, real or potential, of being part of a wealthy and powerful country. As a result, the central government feels that it has nothing to fear, politically, from regional identity and sentiment; it has no political agenda concerning regionalism and is perfectly willing to support regional studies and celebrations through grants from its various agencies. Its policies toward the mass media reflect this reality: the FCC makes no attempt to monitor or control regional radio programming, and in fact encourages it.

Despite this benevolent policy, there is a shocking poverty of regional variety in American radio, in general, and most certainly in music. Wherever one goes, one hears the same Top Forty pop music programming, the same mindless "easy-listening" pieces, the same "golden oldies" from the swing era and the 1950s, and now the same "New Age" music.

The global trend toward consolidation of political power into larger and more powerful central nations has been mirrored by corresponding consolidations of economic power. Taking the phonograph industry as an example, forty-two of the fifty best-selling records in the United States in 1955 were brought out by only five companies (Victor, Columbia, Capitol, Decca, and Mercury). More recently, it has been estimated that five multinational record companies (CBS, EMI, Polygram, WEA, and RCA) produce more than 60 percent of the discs and cassettes sold around the world.

Since live music on the radio is mostly a thing of the past—small stations have neither the space nor the money for studio performance, nor do they have proper equipment for remote broadcasts of live music—one now hears virtually nothing but recorded music on the air. Small stations base their play lists chiefly on records supplied, free, by the largest companies, and on the infamous *Billboard* charts, which are subject to manipulation by these same companies. National and global dissemination, not regional, is the goal of all large record companies, for obvious reasons: it makes more economic sense to produce a single record with the potential of being sold all over the country than to produce a number of different records each aimed at a specific regional or ethnic group.

As simplistic as it may sound, it must nevertheless be said that economic factors play the same role in creating conformity of programming in American radio that political factors play in many other countries.

Now for a few observations on these matters:

1) While many regional and ethnic musics have retained idiosyncratic features, mainstream contemporary popular music, under pressure from economic quarters eager to have a product acceptable to the largest possible market, has developed a relatively homogeneous harmonic, structural, vocal, and instrumental style. The careers of Elvis Presley, Stevie Wonder, and Dolly Parton stand as monuments to the process of mediation by the music industry which is necessary to transform regional styles into much more generally acceptable popular music. Ironically, the musical results of such mediation are remarkably similar to what is produced in the Soviet Union and other socialist countries when regional folk styles are modified so as to make them accessible to a wider audience.

2) A significant percentage of live broadcasting today is devoted to religious services, which usually feature regional music. I learned long ago that Sunday morning was the best time to listen to the radio, in whatever part of the country I find myself, in order to get some sense of regionalism.

3) The pattern of conformity in American radio is sometimes broken by programming aimed at specific ethnic, national, or other interest groups, particularly in our larger cities. In New York City, for instance, one can hear Chinese, Arabic, Greek, Caribbean, Indian, and Korean music on the

radio, if one knows where to set the dial. But listening to any one of these musics gives little sense of New York as a region, only a taste of one of the many cultures found there. The same might be said of one of the genuinely regional radio stations in America, KPFA, a listener-supported station broadcasting from Berkeley, California. In a sense this is a true Bay Area station: its unique mixture of classical, folk, avant-garde, ethnic, and non-Western musics is ideally suited to one distinctive population of the area, which is well-educated, tolerant, mostly white, politically progressive, usually not native to the area, and more accepting of other cultures than is the case in other parts of America. But KPFA has few Hispanic and black subscribers, nor does one hear many radios tuned to KPFA in working-class areas of Oakland and elsewhere.

4) Some regions of the United States—defined by one scholar or another—are populated largely or exclusively by persons of smiliar ethnic or national heritage. In such situations, regionalism and ethnicity coincide. But ethnicity and regionalism are two different things, often intertwined but easily separable, and it seems problematic to identify aspects of a single ethnic group, to the exclusion of others, as regional. The most typically American form of regionalism results from the occupation of the same geographical space by several groups of different ethnic origin, interacting with one another and in the process producing a culture unique to that region. Bill Ferris has already insisted that southern identity was compounded in roughly equal parts from Anglo-American and Afro-American heritages; surely no musician would argue with this. A similar argument might be advanced for New York City in the late nineteenth and early twentieth centuries. Evolving patterns of immigration and internal migration brought about an ethnic mix unique to that time and place: Irish, Italian, Jewish, Afro-America, German. Tin Pan Alley popular music grew out of that mix and was at first a regional musical style, as can be seen in the early songs of Irving Berlin, for instance; by the 1920s the style had become generalized enough to be popular throughout the country, and the Western world.

My suggestion, then, is that the real threat to regional music and culture in the United States comes not from properties inherent in the mass media themselves, nor from governmental utilization of these media to carry out some political agenda, but from economic factors encouraging cultural and musical homogeneity in our country. Properly used, the mass media—particularly FM and AM radio, cassettes, and television—could actually encourage and reinforce regional consciousness and culture. But this would require some redirection of our thinking about the media.

Having been trained in the discipline of historical musicology, which has an unshakable fascination with long-dead musicians, I had developed no code of ethnics useful in working with live musicians when I began my study of contemporary black popular music of southern Africa. Anthropology and ethnomusicology afforded some guidance, and I eventually realized that the most important thing was to give something back in exchange for what I took. Taping live music or interviews, or photographing someone, involves taking. Money is the simplest thing to give back, but not always the most satisfying, for either party. Copies of tapes, or of photographs, are usually much more welcome, and often more productive for both parties. (I recommend to anyone wishing to do photography in a Third World country the practice of carrying two cameras, one for the desired slides or prints, the other a Polaroid camera enabling one to give the subject his or her own photograph on the spot.)

Why could not centers for regional and ethnic studies use the mass media to establish a give-and-take relationship with the musicians whose products are of interest to them? Rather than collecting music only for their own use, and that of other scholars and students, these centers could use inexpensive cassettes, local radio, and even television to disseminate this music back to the population that created and preserved it in the first place. In this way, the often maligned mass media could play a constructive role in regional music.

6   Region and Religion
Samuel S. Hill

Bearings

Let us begin with the scenario of a subject for debate. Religiously, the South is an identifiable region, documentably distinctive in that it is dominantly Anglo-Saxon Protestant (not Catholic and not Lutheran, for example); is consistently Evangelical (not liberal, not Catholic, not directly in the Protestant Reformation tradition); is made up of a high percentage of "born-again" Christians (as the national media and popular opinion regularly claim); is correctly characterized as Fundamentalist (as Americans outside the South usually describe it); is both the headquarters and heartland of the New Christian Right and the Electronic Church; exhibits a notable continuity in affiliation and theological orientation from Maryland to Texas; and is a culture with a center of gravity, namely, the Baptists and Baptistlike bodies. Obviously, an affirmative response to these propositions would suggest that the South is quite unlike any other religious region in the country, is very Protestant, and, beyond that, is the source of many untraditional, even "off-center," religious movements.

One has to wonder how much difference a national survey on these propositions would reveal by contrast with a regional survey. A reasonable guess is that the South is perceived as a comparatively coherent region where conservative Protestant causes are prominent and even culturally dominant. Careful attention to the actual data, however, produces a variety of responses to leading questions. They turn out to be, variously: true; false; true but misleading (which is a real category); in need of more explanation than assertion; more aptly assessed as significant than as true.

Exhilarating and revealing debate aside, we proceed to analysis. This essay must be seen for what it is intended to be, a report and an agenda, not a program. This is a series of observations, a few of which may attain the status of incipient insight, and one or two of which just might be grist for a social scientist's operational mill. The approach emphasizes the interaction of religion and ideas. The ideas that inform religious movements—teachings, doctrines, theology—are basic to those movements and will be noted seriously. But the ideas, theories, typologies, and constructs that underlie cultural analysis are also significant for this particular inquiry, making its approaches akin to those of the sociology of knowledge.

Anyone attempting to understand the reciprocity between a region and its religion must reflect on regional studies as a field of work. Geography would appear to be the queen of these sciences, or at least the terrain over which all students of regionalism roam. Who does regional studies? Why do those who carry it on devote their energies to such a field? Some personal and autobiographical factors always figure in vocational choices, including the field of scholarship an academician enters. Perhaps such factors are especially important in the selection of regional studies as a line of work. Travel is a predictably significant factor, as is reading. Interaction with people who stand outside a person's own tribal networks often stimulates comparative reflection. In my own case, a year of study at Cambridge University proved to be a turning point. There I took special notice of the variety of American answers given to questions raised by Englishmen of Americans whom they (and to some degree this one American) supposed would speak with a kind of unanimity, if not uniformity. The answers did vary greatly in accordance with regional factors, and the liveliness of discussion was as great among the foreigners as between them and their hosts.

It is clear that the study of regionalism faces many problems, but it is a focus of interest and inquiry that will not go away. Perhaps its popularity and prominence operate on a cyclical pattern. Our time is surely a high point in the process. Quite simply, I aver that regional studies are worth doing. One sees each more clearly by looking at both or all. We students of society do not have before us an undifferentiated mass. Whenever we are inclined to think that we do, we had best look again and formulate analytical devices to help us do justice to reality. Regional studies is one such construction.

Regional studies probably has fewer methodological conventions or points of agreement than most areas of study. No discipline, replete with its traditions and methods, is present for us to fall back on. We use each other's work, of course, and may even be loyal subjects of masters, but we are an uncommonly self-determining lot.

Regional studies is an exercise in precision, up to a point, and certainly we must always envision precision as a goal and an object of admiration. We live with a constant desire to avoid a flagrant subjectivism and to transcend impressionistic descriptions and conclusions. In religion, and doubtless in other fields, regionalism collapses under the weight of too much specificity and floats off into thin air when too much generality attends it.

This aim to be precise is not at variance with the employment of imagination, however. Doing regional studies is a task that reveals us at our imaginative best. The essays here by Terry Jordan and Wilbur Zelinsky, two distinguished geographers, exemplify that fact. In no other field does one see more graphic displays of the imagination at work. In other words, regional studies are as much an art as a science.

What we are doing is an exercise in differentiation, identification, and particularization. With respect to my own work, this paper draws together several projects already underway. In this summarizing form, it stresses synthesis more than direct methodological attention. Beneath the conclusions here is a recognition that one modifies one's methods during successive stages of work. This is due in part, of course, to the fact that the data change, are corrected or enlarged, but it also reflects development in insight and analytic capacity as one penetrates the data more deeply.

My own interest is as much in the history of a region as in the contemporary understanding of its culture. Longitudinal analysis is a central part of the effort. I regard historical consideration as virtually essential. Perhaps some features of the culture of a region can be examined with minimal historical reference, but to overlook history when one is treating the religious life of a region is impossible and certainly subversive.

Notations and Cautions

The process of examining the religion of a region requires some general treatment of regionalism and some attention to religion-specific issues. Concerning the former, we need to note that the boundaries used to demarcate a region may be quite artificial. In that connection for our topic here two basic questions beckon: What *is* the South? What are the subregions within it? In an attempt to wrestle with these issues, the possibility arises of imposing or assigning boundaries that are appealing but not solidly defensible. I have tried to address this concern elsewhere:

> To be sure, the people in adjoining counties of northwest Alabama, northeast Mississippi, and west south-central Tennessee are apt to prepare the same foods, speak with the same accent, and be affiliated with the same denominations. Just the same, the political organization of these culture-kin, even blood-kin, people into three separate states makes for concrete differences in the ways their lives are ordered. State borders are somewhat more than political constructions. This may even be true in religious patterns, especially when an area was settled after state lines were drawn and the denomination within a state planted mission work inside its boundaries. Also, the plain truth of the matter is that the career of religion has been different in every state—less specifically so than for political history perhaps, yet discernibly different. The point at which boundaries come closest to being artificial is where they cut through centrally

homogeneous zones, as for example in mountain areas, the District of Columbia suburbs, or the "black belt" territory of Southern Mississippi and Alabama.[1]

"Time lag" is a category of analysis that may be quite inviting but has no pertinence and indeed may be quite misleading. Two examples may serve to highlight the point. First, Know-Nothingism appeared on the national ("northern") scene in the 1840s and 1850s as a political and cultural response to the influx of strange and foreign peoples, Germans and Irish, Catholics and Jews, who threatened to destroy the cultural equilibrium of a stable society. If the kind of response that Know-Nothingism bespoke were going to occur, that was the time for it. Thousands of new peoples were indeed flooding northeastern and midwestern cities and towns, and their presence registered real impact.

The South was also having its problems with people, a particular ethnic/racial community, during those decades. They were, of course, Americans who were anything but newcomers and aliens to the society, the African slave population having been substantial since late in the seventeenth century. The threat of the overhauling of the system of slavery was an almost insane preoccupation of southern society in that era. However, the number of immigrants who came to the South was small, if by immigrant is meant those who volunteered to come from such places as Germany, Ireland, Latin America, Scandinavia, and Greece, which sent many of their people to other parts of the United States. In fact, this kind of immigration has never been marked the southern scene. "Immigrants" did begin to move into the South in sizable numbers after World War II, but they were long-time Americans transferring from one region to another.

What is curious and highly significant about the South is that it experienced its equivalent of the Know-Nothing, nativist spirit during a period when hardly any newcomers from anywhere were settling in the region. The upsurge of these feelings, the phenomenon of xenophobia, played a part in the political life of several Deep South states at a time when there was hardly any demographic provocation.[2]

Focusing on the Know-Nothing issue helps to illuminate what is going on at two different times in two different places. The point concerning "time lag" is that the history of the southern region of the United States has been really quite different from the history of the rest of the country. Its dealing with—in actuality, fabricating—an immigration condition that challenged a homogeneous culture fifty to seventy years later than in the North says nothing at all about superiority or inferiority as implied by "lag." It only says that the South faced conditions when they appeared. We falsify historic reality whenever we presume to judge a development in one place because it has already occurred in another place. The South faced up to immigration when and only when conditions were conducive. No occasion for responding to immigration presented itself to the South in the 1850s. But between 1900 and 1920, various conditions, more sociopsychological than demographic, pressed in on the Deep South consciousness and generated a response to what the arrival of new peoples means to a society.

A second example of the "time lag" factor that highlights the distinctiveness of the South is the religious technique called revivalism. A mechanism that took identifiable form by 1800, revivalism was hit upon as a means to the end of conversion. It was a typical part of the religious scene in the North until 1850 or so, after which it was a planned event only sometimes and, more and more often, a transcongregational (citywide) occasion. The latter plan, that of conducting large-scale crusades, became fairly common in the South by about 1900. But the revival or "revival meeting" had attained regularized status in the more evangelistic churches by the 1880s.[3] By then and to this day, hardly a Baptist or Pentecostal or Holiness or rural Methodist church gets through a year without scheduling a revival or two.

"Time lag" as such serves our understanding poorly in connection with the phenomenon of the revival. It proves nothing that revivals became supra-local in the North before the southern churches integrated revivals into congregational life. But by knowing this we learn a great deal about the particular track on which southern religion has traveled in the nineteenth and twentieth centuries.

In the study of southern religion, the penchant has been to concentrate on earlier periods of historical development. One obvious reason for this practice is the fact that recent history is difficult to assess and chronicle. More pertinent in the southern instance, however, is the standard preoccupation with the nineteenth century, especially the Old South, the antebellum decades. The Civil War, Reconstruction, and New South rank second. The colonial period in the seaboard states from South Carolina northward also claims a disproportional share of a narrative dominated by certain periods which vary somewhat from one set of states to another. But it will be observed by most readers, and should be emphasized in any case, that rhythms differ. What was early for Arkansas is late for Virginia. Anglo-American history had hardly gotten going in the southwestern states before the Civil War.[4]

It is very suggestive to note concurrency—and its absence as well. Perhaps the principal lesson to be learned from doing regional history this way is the fact that rhythms differ greatly. One is instructed—and the imagination enlivened—by asking what was happening in two places during the same period, within the southern region as well as between the South and the North.

An intriguing dimension of regional studies is the correlation of the aspects—Raymond Gastil's word is *subjects*—of which it is composed.[5] Those of us with a major interest in the aspect of religion must be alert to its interaction with other aspects, among them literature, politics, economics, urban life, patterns of agricultural societies, folk culture (including food and music), and many others. But in addition to keeping a watchful eye on the integrated nature of a culture, resisting all temptations to isolate one's own primary object of attention and exalting it as the most determinative, the student of regional studies must keep before him the question: If there is a southern region in religion, must there also be one in literature—or politics or style of urban life?

The answer, of course, shows us that there is a general regionalism and aspect (or "subject") regionalism. Quite a fine tradition has developed of studying American religious (and political and botanical) regions, an enterprise that pays little attention to any single dimension's organic ingrediency within a general complex of dimensions (the study of which would be a worthy task). At the same time, the study of general regions beckons—the study of general regions requires that *aspect* inquiry be undertaken, as in the study of southern religion. For one thing, the boundaries of the southern region must be established with sensitivity to factors other than religion. For another, one must note how religion makes an impact on literature, racial relations, and other aspects. Deterioration into frivolity is always a possibility when one is tackling so complex a subject. More profoundly, the student has sedulously to avoid confusing the two meanings of regionalism: general study and aspect study.

Because each aspect of regionalism is tied in with numerous other aspects, we regional scholars must and do practice inter- and multidisciplinary methods and techniques. At the least, we do so as a lot, extending respect and a curious eye and ear toward our colleagues who take different approaches. But we also, most of us fairly frequently, make use of methods associated more directly with other disciplines than our own. Throughout the process, we are taking for granted the interactive power of the various aspects or subjects, politics, folklore, architecture, religion, and so on.

As if all this were not enough for us to juggle and manage, we students of religion-by-region also learn while doing this work how difficult it is even to define what religion is. We are presented with quite a challenge when we bring together the complex enterprise of regional studies with a reflection on the nature of religion. Sometimes scholars treat religion "stat-

ically," as little more than a belief system. Placing it in the setting of regional studies exposes the fallacy of such thinking. In a defined setting, the
term *religion* refers to several quite distinct configurations. One of those is
by whole regions: within a region, all of the named bodies are examined
and numerical rankings are noted. A second is *by whole denominations:*
tracing the development, pattern, and size of, say, Methodists in the South
and in the Midwest is an essential and fruitful undertaking.

A third application of the term *religion* when it is applied to regional
study is *by social and cultural influence:* one looks at the contribution a
religious group makes to shaping the values of an area. Some specific
issues that bear investigation are: interracial attitudes and practices; state
lotteries; the pattern of local options regarding the sale of alcoholic bev-
erages; and convictions about governmental isolation or intervention in
international affairs. Also, what is the extent of the hold of a world view
or a notion of the ideal American society as perpetrated by the dominant
religious groups? Is there an organized resistance to the encroachments
of secularism, as in the case of the "Fundamental-conservative" party in
the 1980s within the Southern Baptist Convention? Is there a public
sense that "our world has been taken away from us," that some harmful
force has wrested dominion from the godly people and values once in
charge?[6]

Turning to more theological categories, we note two other significations
of *religion*. The fourth is *"sacrament words":* that is, what are the central
concepts, the keynotes, that animate church life, and a regional society's
outlook? The fifth is *by the configurations of supernaturalism and intensity:* does a region see supernatural reality in straightforward or ironic
terms? Is a person's religious dedication arranged in a compartmentalized
or an integrated manner? Are doctrines taught by the churches deployed in
hierarchical fashion or related organically and dialectically? Concerning
the intensity of religious expression, is what is encouraged and practiced
high and constant? or high, occasionally? or casual but earnest? or smol-
dering? or something else? The geographer J. R. Shortridge has touched
on the intensity issue in his innovative formulation of religious regions in
America. He lists four regions as: Catholic; super-Catholic; intense, conservative Protestantism; and diverse, liberal Protestantism. (His fifth is
"transitional" or "none of the above," by which he points to the absence of
the intensity issue.)[7]

Other "notes" and "cautions" might be added to this list. *Region* is
hardly a univocal term, and certainly *religion* is not. When the two are
correlated and then applied to a specific place, the complexity enlarges
further. The listing provided here reveals one examiner's concerns and may
serve for others working in the field of religion-by-region.

Comparative Reflections

The southern religious region extends, geographically, from Virginia (or Maryland) to South Texas and, turning the other way, from the Missouri River in Missouri to Interstate Highway 4 in Florida.[8] There are, of course, a few notable exceptions, to which Zelinsky points with his five national subregions, and of which four are in the South: Hispanic Texas, French Louisiana, peninsular Florida, and the German-influenced piedmont of Virginia–North Carolina–South Carolina. To this vast area, taking note of the exceptions, must be added southern Illinois and southern Indiana. Because they belong culturally to the South, they are rightly included in the southern religious region.

As distinctive as the South is in religious and general cultural terms, we must never overstate the facts. Historian Carl Degler makes the point well in describing the South's as a "limited distinctiveness." Elsewhere I have argued the same position through a "near/far" device for empirical assessment and a "close/distant" device to address the regional differences in attitudes. Quoting from that effort, the case runs as follows. The "near-far" pair treats the question of interaction between South and North. In the three epochs surveyed—1795–1810, 1835–50, and 1885–1900—what was the state and degree of actual relations between the two regions? Were people in touch; corresponding; involved in common enterprises; traveling back and forth in business, pleasure, education, and the like? Was commerce active between the two regions? The second device is the "close-distant" device, and it involves the cultural similarity and harmony, or their opposites, between the two regions. Does each take for granted the other's membership in the same national society? Is there respect by each for the other? To what degree do they see eye to eye and cooperate on significant issues? Is there a fundamental agreement on what is valuable and on what is the desired nature of American society? Are they traveling in the same direction on parallel tracks, or not? The "near-far" and "close-distant" devices are used to help ascertain the relations between South and North along empirical and attitudinal lines, respectively.[9]

Such analytic devices as these are intended to highlight the very real identifiability of the southern region while dramatizing its vital coexistence with the North. Both items in the pair are true and both are significant. The South is American and it is also a unique area and culture.

In describing the southern religious region, we are aided by acknowledging the reality of both proper nouns and common nouns. Obviously the list of proper nouns includes Protestant, Catholic, Jewish, Methodist, Baptist, Pentecostal, Church of God (for which great specificity is required), Southern Baptist, National Baptist, and African Methodist Episcopal, among many others. But common nouns must be marshaled as well to treat their respective and collective strength, influence, distribution, pervasiveness, historical origins and career, and the like.

One more word is insistently important: *Evangelical.* The South is regularly described as the region where Evangelical denominations prevail. That is a correct characterization—and far more accurate than the term *Fundamentalist.*

But we should note quickly that the heartland of classical Evangelicalism is a stretch from Grand Rapids to Chicago to the Twin Cities—with Chicago, particularly its western suburbs, as the capital city. *Classical* as used here refers to older forms of Evangelicalism, those directly descended from Dutch, British, and Scandinavian forebears, and confessional more than conversionist. Classical Evangelicalism is informed by a comprehensive world view elaborated in systematic theology and not in doctrines serially ordered, ranked by priority, and left explicitly unrelated. The Evangelical family of Christianity is the major form of religion in the South, but the conversionist type is far more popular than the confessional. That is to say that its more representative forms accentuate the decisive personal experience and do not develop a systematic formulation of Christian truth to which assent is required. That confessional way of defining Evangelicalism is the mainstream northern way of doing it and not the South's, which is derived largely from the cultural heritage of the American frontier.

In the South, Evangelicalism pervades the "secular" aspects of society as well as institutional religious life. While Evangelicalism sets the pace for the religious life of others who are not Evangelical, its teachings are taken for granted as the essence of religion. On the theological side, it creates the checklist by which all individuals and all other groups are evaluated.

Two popular denominations, the Baptist and Methodist, enjoy strength and influence virtually everywhere. Their popularity has to do with their ubiquity and their familiarity for almost everyone. A key factor in their prominence and their social and cultural significance is their strength within both black and white societies. To do any real justice to the profoundly biracial society that the South is, serious attention must be given to the religious life of black southerners. These four features are especially significant:

1) The denominational names are the same (in most cases) for black and white Christians. But the "first" names differ dramatically, so much so that one can often be certain that a local congregation named on a billboard or in a newspaper is a black church or a white church.

2) Historically, white Christians of specifiable affiliation converted black people to membership within that affiliation. Earlier, in the colonial

period, whites had not been very effective at Christianizing their black fellow southerners.

3) In turn, black Christians had an impact on whites: their slave status forced into being particular forms of church architecture, whether galleries or specially marked-off seating sections. During the services, blacks were present—to sing, to respond audibly to prayers and sermons, and to dictate the inclusion of special points in sermons that had to do with slaves acknowledging their rightful places before their masters, heavenly and earthly.

4) Both black and white Christians have been evangelical: expressive, "up front" about their identity and commitment, and demonstrative in their religious faith. Thus, black Christians have shared, and helped perpetuate, the dominant form of religion in the region.

At the same time, there are major differences between the religious ways of blacks and whites. One is that the teaching about hell, the consignment of an unsaved person to eternal punishment and separation from God, is quite recessive in the black church. More importantly, the threat of hell is not a motivation for blacks to straighten out their lives and to seek salvation. A second is the status of doctrine and the place of authority. In the black church, doctrines are accorded poetic, dramatic, and evocative power, but are not regarded as definitions or substantive propositions calling for assent. The Bible, thus, is less an authority to be defended and appealed to than the source of narratives that elicit meaningful responses.

Returning now to the earlier mention of "sacrament words," we find another configuration that distinguishes religion by region. Six phrases have notable prominence within American Christianity: "body and blood of Christ," "word of God," "born-again" "love your neighbor," "body of Christ," and "New Testament Christianity." Let us recall that "sacrament word" is a concept that points to the animation of the metaphors, the keynote themes, around which a group of Christians rallies. In the South, the "body" metaphors fare poorly. "Love your neighbor," while everywhere taught and often admirably practiced, is regularly regarded as a derivative and ineffectual teaching; when made central, it issues in true "liberalism," a stance to be avoided. The South's religious people are schooled in the "word of God," the "born-again" experience, and "New Testament Christianity," in one rank ordering and configuration or another.[10]

The "sacrament word" concept is similar to the kind of construct that Roger Stump treats in his discussion of the "macro" variable. He states: "Unfortunately, 'macro' variables like the cultural importance of religion are difficult to operationalize and measure at the individual level. They often express vague concepts, and their effects may be unnoticed by the individual adherent because they take so much for granted. I suspect, however, that such variables account for much of the unexplained variance in religious participation."[11]

Stump readily acknowledges that most studies in the geography of American religion have served well to show the "spatial distributions of denominational membership." But he regrets that they have emphasized "abstract theological distinctions *at the expense of experiential, social, and behavioral variations among regional groups.*" Perhaps the "sacrament words" construct stands as a bridge metaphor between "abstract theological distinctions" and "experiential, social, and behavioral variations." It also may have the merit of being a "macro" variable of a kind Stump regards as an ingredient in the religion of a culture.[12]

Any treatment of religion in the South in our era is expected to address at least a few salient features of regional religion's connection with the New Christian Right and the Electronic Church. First, the principal support for the two causes is in the border states, not exclusively the southern states and not heavily in the Deep South states. Second, Jerry Falwell's Fundamentalism and Pat Robertson's charismaticism are not historically at home in the South, and are well outside its mainstream. While tending to be identified by the general public as southern styles of religion, these conservative religious-political movements are only marginally so.[13]

Any study of the South as a religious region must be alert to its history with regard to continuity and discontinuity. Is the line from the colonial period to today relatively straight, unbroken by major disruptions? It is tempting to see the South as homogeneous and as having followed a rather true and predictable course from 1750 to the present. But there have been at least four periods of genuine change. Within the southern regional setting, these approximate revolutionary shifts took place:

1) Between 1740 and 1790, the Church of England and aristocratic and genteel religion were replaced by "people's churches" and democratic religious ways.[14]

2) In the second quarter of the nineteenth century, those same "people's churches" attained an informal establishment. The earlier legal standing of the Church of England was, if anything, surpassed by the cultural dominance the Evangelical churches came to enjoy.

3) In the days, months, and years following the Civil War, separate black denominations and congregations were formed with astonishing speed. Their creation altered the face of the white denominations that had included many biracial congregations and provided the black population with a widely influential organizational life.

4) During the period around 1900, the Pentecostal and Holiness movements erupted within Baptist and Methodist ranks or among isolated and economically deprived people who were thought of by these two largest

denominations as their potential recruits. As with the blacks earlier, the Baptist and Methodist bodies were deprived of membership and the flavoring impact of groups that withdrew to create bodies that were at first small and composed of the dispossessed classes but that have grown to considerable size and social significance.[15]

Continuity characterized the South if the comparison is made with developments in the North where novel conditions became a constant. Similarly, we may conclude that *continuity* prevailed if the point of reference is disruption from the outside, as a result of external forces that produced alien peoples and folkways. The South knew little of major immigrant invasion or the importation of revolutionary ideologies. But what happened is accurately portrayed as *discontinuity* with respect to disruption from the inside, since stable and even normative patterns were challenged and upset by changes in the religious orientations of millions of white and black people.

The continuity of southern religious life over the past three centuries, as modified by the internal changes that have given it a somewhat different face, have resulted in a gravitational pull to the left on the spectrum of historic Christianity. That is to say, the flow has been toward more conservative—Evangelical—forms of Protestantism and away from the traditional expressions represented by Roman Catholicism and the national churches of the sixteenth-century Reformation. Marking the South off from the rest of the nation is the placement of its span, from center to left on that spectrum, that is, from Presbyterian to Baptist, Pentecostal, and Fundamentalist forms. The North's span has ranged from center to right, owing to Catholicism's pervasive presence.

So much for one person's interpretation of the religion of a particular region. The task is worth tackling, but the route is strewn with problems and issues that demand imagination and rigorous reflection. As one who does it with great relish, I hope that readers find this effort stimulating and informative.

Notes

1. Samuel S. Hill, *Religion in the Southern States* (Macon, Ga.: Mercer University Press, 1983), p. 4.
2. Rowland T. Berthoff, "Southern Attitudes Toward Immigration," *Journal of Southern History* 12 (1951): 328–60; J. Wayne Flynt, *Cracker Messiah* (Baton Rouge: Louisiana State University Press, 1977), ch. 4.
3. William G. McLoughlin, *Revivals, Awakenings, and Reform* (Chicago, Ill.: University of Chicago Press, 1978), ch. 5.

4.   Hill, *Religion in the Southern States.* A comparative reading of
          state histories is quite revealing.
5.   Raymond Gastil, *Cultural Regions in the United States* (Seattle:
          University of Washington Press, 1975), ch. 1.
6.   Nancy T. Ammerman, "The New South and the New Baptists,"
          The Christian Century 103 (May 14, 1986), pp. 486–88.
7.   James R. Shortridge, "A New Regionalization of American Reli-
          gion," *Journal for the Scientific Study of Religion* 16 (1977):
          143–53.
8.   Wilbur Zelinsky, "An Approach to the Religious Geography of
          the United States: Patterns of Church Membership in 1952," *An-
          nals of the Association of American Geographers* 51 (1961):
          139–93.
9.   Samuel S. Hill, *The South and the North in American Religion*
          (Athens: University of Georgia Press, 1980), p. 9.
10.   Samuel S. Hill, "Region and Religion in America," *Annals of
          the American Academy of Political and Social Science* 480
          (1985): 132–141.
11.   Roger W. Stump, "Regional Variations in the Determinants of
          Religious Participation," *Review of Religious Research* 27, no. 3
          (1986): 222.
12.   Ibid.
13.   Samuel S. Hill, "Religion and Politics in the South," in *Religion
          in the South,* ed. Charles Reagan Wilson (Jackson: University
          Press of Mississippi, 1985), pp. 139–154.
14.   Rhys Isaac, *The Transformation of Virginia, 1740–1790* (Chapel
          Hill: University of North Carolina Press, 1982).
15.   David E. Harrell, Jr. has analyzed these events of the period
          around 1900 in three essays, "Religious Pluralism: Catholics,
          Jews, and Sectarians," in *Religion in the South,* ed. Charles Rea-
          gan Wilson (Jackson: University Press of Mississippi, 1985), pp.
          59–82. See also his "The Evolution of Plain-Folk Religion in the
          South, 1835–1920," in *Varieties of Southern Religious Experi-
          ence,* ed. Samuel S. Hill (Baton Rouge: Louisiana State Univer-
          sity Press, 1988), and his "The South: Seedbed of Sectarianism,"
          in *Varieties of Southern Evangelicalism,* ed. David E. Harrell
          (Macon, Ga.: Mercer University Press, 1981).

7   Gender and Regionalism
Susan H. Armitage

Regionalism as a category of historical analysis has been with us for a long time; gender is a much more recent historical concept. On one level, the notions of regionalism and gender are flatly contradictory. Regionalism assumes that some aspects of a particular place shapes the experience of all of the people, of both sexes, that live there. In contrast, the feminist hypothesis is that "shared concerns of gender transcend national, cultural, racial and geographical boundaries."[1] My task in this paper is to work with both ideas and to see in what ways the two concepts—one old, one new—can become complementary, rather than remain contradictory. I will direct my thoughts above gender and regionalism to the region I know best, the American West.

We historians owe our particular usage of the term *regionalism* to Frederick Jackson Turner, and like Turner's more famous theory, the frontier thesis, the legacy is ambiguous. Turner's own interest in regional topics prompted prodigious amounts of research from his students and from their students in turn. Most of these historians used the concept of region both confidently and sloppily, certain "in their bones" that the notion had a widely accepted meaning, but not being quite able to agree on precisely what it was; and assuming that some thing or things in the region bound people together in ways that superseded cultural and racial boundaries, but unable to reach agreement on exactly what those things were. Moreover, the assumption of general regional commonalities, while recognizing conflicts *between* regions, ignored conflicts and differences *within* regions. In effect then, regional historians wrote only the history of the dominant cultural group and not that of subordinate ones, ignoring class and race conflict and difference. When, in the 1930s, the use of these categories of analysis became general within the historical profession, regional histories inevitably went into decline, eclipsed by a national perspective which usually ignored the West.[2]

Today's resurgence, however, of regional studies within the historical profession differs from the Turnerian heritage. Thanks to historians' growing awareness of the work of historical geographers and the very rapid growth of environmental history, our definitions of regionalism are getting much more precise. Drawing on those perspectives, Donald Worster recently offered this succinct definition: "The history of the region is first and foremost one of an *evolving human ecology*. A region emerges as people try to make a living from a particular part of the earth, as they adapt themselves to its limits and possibilities. What the regional historian should first want to know is how a people or peoples acquired a place and, then, how they perceived and tried to make use of it."[3] Similarly, Patricia Limerick in *Legacy of Conquest* put a somewhat less environmental and slightly more cultural twist on the same basic notion: "Western history has been an ongoing competition for legitimacy—for the right to claim for oneself and sometimes for one's group the status of legitimate beneficiary of Western resources. *This intersection of ethnic diversity with property allocation unifies Western history.*"[4]

Both Worcester and Limerick propose a formulation of regionalism that is firmly rooted in social history, that is, in the history of ordinary people, not the elite. Worster, for example, proposes that the regional historian will look at the peoples of a given region and "identify the survival techniques they adopted, their patterns of work and economy, and their social relationships,"[5] that is, at the ordinary details of their daily lives. And Limerick, in contrast to Turner, assumes that the basic regional event is conflict, not commonality.

One problem with the Worster-Limerick definition is the perennial problem of boundaries: where does one region stop and another begin? The classic western American answer, to define the West by rainfall, or more precisely by the lack of rainfall, founders in my home ground, the Pacific Northwest. Yet residents of Seattle are no less "westerners" simply because they are a little damper!

A second problem with the Worster-Limerick definition is one that haunts western U.S. history as a whole. Frederick Jackson Turner, disputed and discarded endless times, refuses to die: although historians no longer accept his theories of frontier and region, the general public does. The frontier flourishes in the popular mind, and so does the notion of a generalized but distinctive regional identity. The concept of region as an arbitrarily bounded place in which to explore the conflict and adaptation of diverse groups *before* reaching conclusions about commonality is still a new idea. As historians begin to practice this concept, it will doubtless gain general currency, even though the ghost of Turner will linger.

I came to terms with Turner and his progeny when, as I began my research on western women, I confronted a version of western history, at both the popular and academic levels, where women had no claim on the great and stirring events of western history. After all, as T. J. Larson once said, women "did not lead expeditions, command troops, build railroads, drive cattle, ride Pony Express, find gold, amass great wealth, get elected

to high public office, rob stages, or lead lynch mobs."[6] If I had accepted
Turner's and Larson's versions of western history, my efforts to understand
the role of women in western history would have been short-lived! Using
the concept of gender as a critical tool, stressing diversity rather than
homogeneity, I and other women's historians began to criticize this Turnerian West. And in the process we contributed to the newer, social history
definition of regionalism that is emerging today as an important aspect of
western history.

Women's historians began by underscoring the male bias in Turner's organizing notion of struggle with the environment. Despite the obvious ab-
surdity inherent in the image of men struggling while women demurely
kept house for them,[7] the masculinist bias engendered two important concepts: the figure of the heroic man, and the emphasis on all-male work
groups.

Western historians frequently wrote about heroes, larger-than-life men
whose exploits symbolized the stages of frontier development. Sometimes
these men—like Mike Fink, Pecos Bill, and Paul Bunyan—were truly leg-
endary, that is, fictional. Sometimes, as in the case of Jedediah Smith or
Jesse James, they were real-life men who acted in an exciting episode in
western history. Folklorists have shown us that the counterparts of these
larger-than-life men are a set of female figures—the lady, the helpmate,
and the bad woman—who have come to symbolize all women in the West.
The lady, who might be a schoolteacher, a missionary, or merely a woman
with some civilized tastes, was defined as too genteel for the rough-and-
ready West. She was either uncomfortable, unhappy, or literally driven
crazy by the frontier—proving her gentility by becoming a victim. On the
other hand, the strong and uncomplaining helpmate adapted to the West,
and stood by her husband and children in all circumstances, her individu-
ality subsumed in the sentimental image of the work-worn superwoman.
The bad woman briefly had what the other two stereotypes lacked, glamour
and power, but she lost them along with her life as she came rapidly to her
appointed end—a bad one.[8]

The first concern of western women's historians was to disprove these
stereotypes. We needed both to analyze the function of these images and to
show that real western women were more complex than the stereotypes
allowed. We disproved the stereotypes by appealing to the actual experience of western women themselves. In the past fifteen years, a number of
firsthand accounts—memoirs, reminiscences, and diaries—have been discovered and published by local, regional, and national presses. Although
accounts by white women make up the majority, increasing efforts are
being made to find accounts by American Indian, Hispanic, and other

women of color.[9] We are on our way, then, to replacing the popular stereotypes with the genuine multicultural diversity of western women's experience.

This multicultural perspective means that women's history has much to
contribute to the study of race relations in the West. The Indian Wars and
removals have long been among the set pieces of western history. The history of white-Indian cultural contact has been violent one. As told mostly
by white males, there was also a history of sexual contact between white
men and American Indian and Hispanic women in the exploration and fur
trade eras; we are beginning to be able to assess that contact from the wom-
en's perspective.[10] With the arrival of numbers of white settlers, the topic
of race relations, as experienced by women of all races, became more complex. Glenda Riley has shown that, in white-Indian relations, both on the
Overland Trail and in later settlements, white women were more placating,
more peaceful than white men. Women offered food, made some friend-
ships with Indian women, and were less likely to resort to threats and violence than were white men.[11]

As we move into the twentieth century, women's historians are looking
at women who were part of in-migrating groups—Mexican, Japanese,
German-Russian, and black, among others—and their roles in family and
group adaptation. Research is just beginning to be published in quantity,
but it is already clear that multicultural twentieth-century western women's
history has much to contribute to the fields of labor and immigration history, as well as to western history itself.[12]

Women's historians have also criticized western historians' preoccupation with male groups. (Once, in desperation, I coined the term *Hisland* to
express my protest at the pervasiveness of the unconscious masculinist
bias.)[13] While it is true that certain groups, for example cowboys and miners, were indeed all-male work groups, most—trappers, soldiers, and miners—did not live in completely masculine societies. Women's historians
looked first at how the work of the groups was actually accomplished. Sylvia Van Kirk and others have shown that Indian women played a vital part
in the Canadian fur trade both as work partners and as liaisons with their
own tribes. Whether this was true in the much smaller American fur trade
is still to be seen, but recent research shows much more of a family orientation than the mythic figure of the solitary trapper would have led us to
believe.[14] In the case of soldiers, a number of accounts by military wives
have recently been published, but they are not yet integrated into earlier
all-male accounts of military life. Nor are accounts by women who lived in
western mining towns yet integrated into the older view. The first serious
studies of prostitution, a significant female occupation in most large min-

ing towns, have only recently been published,[15] and have only begun to replace older, more sexist interpretations.

The inclusion of women's experience in events heretofore viewed solely through men's eyes does more than add a few new facts: it changes history at a basic level. Earlier historians, in making decisions about interpretation, basically believed that the *work* men did was important and that their domestic lives were merely incidental. Women's history challenges that assumption and insists that all parts of one's life are important for historical study and understanding.

For too long, much western history has been told as the adventure story of solitary men. In contrast, women's historians argue that the individual should be examined in the context of larger groups.

When we look at mixed groups—families, for example—we need to look at what women do and say. This seems quite obvious, but it has not, in fact, been the way in which most historians have approached the family. They have written, consciously or not, with the assumption that the patriarchal idea of the family—the man as head, spokesman, and decision maker for the entire family—was still an historical reality. This has had strange consequences, particularly in a field like agricultural history, where the notion of the family farm is sacrosanct but the only farmers we find in historical accounts are men. Even in the history of the American West, where another Turnerian legacy was an emphasis on the agricultural frontier, most information about women until very recently came in the form of children's books. The Laura Ingalls Wilder *Little House* books, for example, are a rich source of information about family life, sex roles, and power dynamics within the family. The Ingallses moved west, constantly and restlessly, until the moment when "Ma" Ingalls refused to follow any longer, because, she said, the children were of an age when they needed to go to school.

This fictional, although autobiographical, glimpse into family life underlines the point that if we are to understand regionalism we must understand families and what women do within them. I say this for two reasons. First, if Worster is right and the key to regionalism is the understanding of adaptation to the environment, then it is *family* adaptation, not just that of men, and especially not that of solitary men, we should be looking at. The settlement of the West was a family affair, but until recently we have not asked, in Gerda Lerner's wonderful phrase, "what the women were doing while the men were doing what *they* thought was important."[16] Until we know what women were doing and feeling, we only have half of the story, if that much.

As these examples show, women's historians have used the concept of gender as a way to explore difference *within* the region of the West and to challenge an exclusively male version of western history. To look at the West through women's eyes is to look at earlier, accepted theories and explanations in a new way and to thereby gain new insights. By stressing diversity, women's historians have given us a richer sense of the western past. There is a second and more controversial way in which gender has been used by western women's historians. When "gender" is used inclusively, it asserts that the common experience of womanhood transcends regional differences. The major experience shared by nineteenth-century American women, in all parts of the country, was domesticity.

One of the earliest and most influential books in western women's history, Julie Roy Jeffrey's *Frontier Women,* exemplified this inclusive perspective. Employing the theoretical tools of women's history, Jeffrey laid heavy stress on the ways in which eastern American sex role expectations determined the attitudes of pioneer women. Jeffrey found western women who took the Victorian cult of true womanhood—the injunction to be pious, pure, domestic, and submissive—as central to their personal identities. They brought eastern sex role patterns west with them and were reluctant to discard them even when they were obviously a hindrance.[17] In a widely quoted prefatory statement, Jeffrey remarked: "My original perspective was feminist: I hoped to find that pioneer women used the frontier as a means of liberating themselves from stereotypes and behaviors which I found constricting and sexist. I discovered that they did not." At first, many historians were disconcerted and upset by the finding that many women did not view the West as liberating—in other words, as Turner had portrayed it. We were so accustomed to viewing the West as a land of freedom and opportunity that this new argument was unwelcome. Yet there was substantial evidence to support it.

The different experiences of men and women within the family have been most carefully studied in Overland Trail families. John Faragher analyzed the different patterns of work roles within the family: adult men and women had different tasks, rhythms of activity, and attitudes. In contrast to home roles, men's activities on the trail were constant (driving and herding) and women's activities sporadic (cooking at night for the next day, washing only on infrequent and layover days). Attitudinally, for adult men, the journey west was a test and a challenge; for women, it was primarily housekeeping under much more difficult circumstances than at home. Men were challenged constantly by change: choices about route, equipment, careful of animals, and speed of travel were directly affected by the changing environment. On the other hand, women had the job of holding the fabric of daily life together, of providing continuity, a job that got harder and harder as the trip lengthened and exhaustion deepened. Given these task differences, it would have been genuinely extraordinary if male and female perspectives on the experience had been identical.[19]

Lillian Schlissel's *Women's Diaries of the Westward Journey,* the first study based exclusively on women's diaries and reminiscences, argued that the women's experiences of the westward journey were those of worry, privation, and loss. Schlissel placed primary emphasis on the ways in which childbearing and child tending shaped women's attitudes. In one of her most striking observations, Schlissel pointed to the way in which women never lost their personal awareness of death: they counted graves. Men tended to aggregate and abstract the figures; women kept precise daily counts and lived with their impact.[20]

The evidence that men and women experienced the Overland Trail differently is fully in accord with recent research in eastern nineteenth-century women's and family history. The two sexes inhabited separate spheres: men's was the public sphere, women's was the home. What women did was dramatically different from what men did, and their perceptions were shaped accordingly.

The diary of one particular pioneer woman illustrates this gender difference in more detail. Amelia Buss, who moved to Fort Collins, Colorado, in 1866, moved west unwillingly, leaving friends and family behind, because she believed it was a wife's duty to follow her husband. She filled her diary with details of daily housekeeping in a primitive cabin and with complaints about hard work, isolation, and loneliness. She wrote: "George went to the mountains yesterday morning to be gon all week . . . after he had gon gave vent to my feelings in a flood of tears. it may seem foolish to those that have neighbors and friends around them. I get a long very well through the day but the long evenings and nights are *horrible.*"

Amelia developed rituals to sustain herself in her new surroundings. On Sunday, she held Bible readings with her young daughter, evoking warm memories of companionable Sabbaths in the East. She lived for letters from home. And she used her diary, which was given to her by her sisters as a parting gift, as a place to acknowledge her fears: "I have not had a letter in over two weeks till today I got one from A. and one from L. there was good news from home but some how I have felt very low spirited ever since and that old homesick feeling comes back to me an other week is gone and O how cold the wind sounds tonight. G. and V. are a sleep and I am a lone." Amelia's diary ended with a retrospective entry, dated exactly one year from her arrival in Colorado. She had become resigned: "Now I have settled down with the belief that here I shall end my days and the sooner I make it home the better."[21]

At first reading, Amelia Buss appears to be a perfect example of the western stereotype of the lady, pitiful and frail, too gentle for the harshness of the West. But her experience is an example of female role definition. Women in the eastern United States, confined to domestic life, built strong female support networks within their sphere. Carroll Smith-Rosenberg and Nancy Cott have demonstrated that while men were experiencing the risks and rewards of the new competitive individualism, many women derived primary emotional sustenance from a traditional female subculture composed of mothers, sisters, and female friends.[22] The female subculture did not usually survive the move to the pioneer West. In agricultural areas women were too far apart, and in mining camps the diversity of the population and extreme mobility seemed to have created something like modern suburban privatization. Women were no longer embedded in a tight community with all of the customary attendant female supports. Frontier individualism was forced upon these women: they had to be more self-reliant and less communal than they had been before.

Most women keenly felt their isolation from other women and from a shared female value system. As soon as they could, once the hard early years of settlement were past, they joined together with other women to help to build community institutions such as churches and schools. This role is celebrated in frontier literature in the image of woman as a "gentle tamer," as the culture bearer who brings civilization to the West. What has not been so noticed is the criticism of male values that this "civilizing" activity represents. The first stage of pioneering required that both men and women adopt the individualism and self-reliance that we have been taught to view as the result of the frontier process. However, what becomes clear from a close look at female sources is how much most women disliked that very process. They did not accept individualism willingly; they missed the shared support of the female subculture; and they recreated that network when they could. In the meantime, they worked side by side with their men.[23]

Mostly, women worked at home, or in paid domestic employment in another home or in restaurants, laundries, or the like. The West certainly did not offer opportunity for women, if by opportunity we mean new possibilities in careers and paid work. An ambitious woman had more opportunity in a large industrialized eastern city than she did even in western cities (not to mention agricultural areas). This discrepancy between the rhetoric of opportunity and the female reality was first pointed out by David Potter in the early 1960s. In his pathbreaking article, "American Women and the American Character," Potter used this disparity as a particularly telling example of the neglect of gender in history.[24]

As these brief examples show, the feminist perspective poses a strong challenge to older regional interpretations. The reaction of western historians has been mixed. Some historians have welcomed the feminist approach regarding the persistence of eastern sex roles as a significant illustration of Earl Pomeroy's argument that continuity, rather than Turnerian adaptation, characterized the American frontier.[25]

But other historians have reacted negatively. One of the strongest critics, Sandra Myres, claimed that feminist historians had simply added a new female stereotype, that of the downtrodden drudge, to the existing list of inadequate portraits. In her own book, *Westering Women,* Myres sought to present a sympathetic but more regional portrait of western women. Myres found herself in the curious position of writing a book with an exclusive focus on women while at the same time maintaining that reactions to the West were individual rather than gender specific. Myres did indeed acknowledge that the pace of female adaptation to the frontier was often slow, a process to be measured in generations, not in individual lifetimes.[26] This important insight was more fully elaborated by Paula Petrick, whose *No Step Backward,* a study of women in Helena, Montana, is the first to show us clearly the ways in which the daughters of pioneer women—that is, the second generation—were the women who first felt at home in the West.[27]

Other criticisms of the inclusive feminist perspective have come from within the ranks of historians of western women themselves, and raise issues that are more than regional. We have begun to wonder whether the key organizing notion, the cult of domesticity, adequately explains the lives of most western women. Four case studies concerning women in Colorado can illustrate the concerns. Two studies show that nineteenth-century Colorado farm women found ways to make sex role stereotyping compatible with lives that contained a high degree of mutuality and sharing, while miner's wives in Cripple Creek shared a female subculture that was more authentic than the cult of domesticity allowed.[28] Another study shows that women's reform activities in Denver were conducted by separate, class-based groups, rather than by comprehensive organizations.[29] And yet a fourth study shows how Hispanic women who played a central domestic role in the villages of northern New Mexico became marginalized when they moved to join their husbands who worked in the Anglo farm economy in Colorado.[30]

In the most general sense, these studies, which pay careful attention to matters of race and class in women's lives, raise the question of how generally applicable a concept derived from the historical records of white, upper-class eastern women is to other women of different classes, races, and locations. We may be asking a question about class rather than about region—this is not yet clear. What is certain is that what we know about western women will no longer fit into one single and simple notion of domesticity. Future studies must pay careful attention to variation; and some of those variations may be regional.[31]

The key question in U.S. western history has always been how to adequately describe and analyze the process of adaptation—what Donald
Worster means when he writes that "a region emerges as people try to make
a living from a particular part of the earth, as they adapt themselves to its
limits and possibilities."[32] Two current topics in women's history, women's
work and their perceptions of the landscape, bear directly on this question
of adaptation, while also illustrating the complex relationships between the
notions of gender and region.

Because there was relatively little opportunity for paid work in the
West, western women's historians have paid more attention to unpaid, domestic work than have women's historians in other regions. They have
shown that although opportunities for paid work were limited, women's
work within their own households was important in the pioneer West. In
the early stages of settlement, women's household activities often made a
crucial contribution to the family economy. For example, Abigail Scott
Duniway produced thousands of pounds of butter every year of her early
married life; so did many other farm women throughout the country. Mollie
Dorsey Sanford cooked for an entire Colorado mining camp of which her
husband was a member; other women of other races and later historical
periods cooked in other settings. The wives of young professional men in
Nevada City and other western mining towns took in boarders to augment
the family income; Jewish immigrant women took in boarders in New York
in 1900 as well.[33] Obviously, the domestic work of pioneer women made
an economic contribution to the household income. Just as obviously, these
forms of women's work were taken for granted and women derived little
public respect for their work. Was the pioneer West different? Was traditional women's work valued and did it lead to an appreciation of women's
activities and a rough notion of equality? Or rather, was it true, as Abigail
Scott Duniway charged, that Oregon farmers ignored the fact that their
wives were exhausted by overwork and too-frequent childbearing?

The questions about the public value accorded to women's domestic activities is more than a matter of giving "credit where credit is (over)due": it
directly affects our assessment of women's suffrage in the West. In every
western state except New Mexico, women secured the vote before ratifi-
cation of the Nineteenth Amendment in 1920. In Wyoming, women had
voted since 1869! The reasons for this pattern are still in dispute, and early
western suffrage has been largely ignored by eastern women's historians.
Popular sentiment in the West tends heavily toward the equality argument
and a widespread sentimental reverence for brave pioneer women. Historians are more skeptical: T. A. Larsen's influential articles explain western
women's suffrage solely in terms of practical local politics (between men,
of course, as women could not yet vote.)[34] Recent work by women's his-

torians is beginning to uncover a hidden story of widespread, well-organized activity by women on their own behalf, but this of course was true in other parts of the country, without positive result. At the moment, women's suffrage in the West must be regarded as a "curious case of regionalism" (as one historian has put it) for which there is as yet no agreed-upon answer.[35] The answer, as Elizabeth Jameson has suggested, will make a connection between the privacy of the household and public affairs that ought to be of significance for women's history in other regions as well.[36]

For most people, the American West summons visions of grand landscapes. "Coming to terms with the land" is not an idle concept in a Montana winter or an Arizona summer. How did women view the western land? Women's historians have had very little to say on this subject. Nationally, feminist literary critic Annette Kolodny has set herself the task of unraveling gender difference in responses to the American landscape. In two books (one his, one hers), *The Lay of the Land* and *The Land Before Her,* Kolodny discerns startling differences in male and female attitudes: men harbor fantasies of rape and conquest, while women dream of domestic gardens.[37] Kolodny argues this provocative thesis brilliantly, and there is much that historians can learn from her writings, but we must wait for her forthcoming book on women's attitudes toward the trans-Mississippi West to learn her perspective on how female perceptions were influenced by the region that concerns us in this paper.

In the meantime, western women's historians, aware of the Kolodny thesis, are exploring subregional variations. The compelling landscape of the multicultural Southwest has produced the most comprehensive regional study of women's attitudes toward the land. In their fine study *The Desert Is No Lady,* Vera Norwood and Janice Monk have produced a volume that discusses women's writings, art, and crafts from three cultures (Anglo, Hispanic, and American Indian). Amid this cultural diversity they do not find domestic gardens—there are few of them in the desert—but they do discern a common antiheroic female approach which values survival within the limitations the landscape imposes. Artistic images, while not necessarily domestic, tend to focus on the patterns and routines of daily life.[38]

Elizabeth Hampsten, writing in the very different western climate of North Dakota, remains persistently skeptical about the very notion of women and "landscape." The ordinary farm women she studies apparently never had the time or the inclination to think about themselves in relation to the land: they simply lived it: "This other view of land is highly experiential in particular and set in time rather than in space; it is expressed in particular and concrete writing. These authors do not take in distances at a glance. They describe, instead, activities that we know have taken place out of doors, in what painters and photographers would term 'Nature,' but they take these surroundings for granted, as though they were indifferent to them."[39] Thus we find, in different subregions of the region we call the West, the same sorts of diversity of viewpoints about landscape that we saw earlier in historical studies of women's work and the concept of domesticity.

Western women's historians are today in a situation remarkably akin to that of the traditional regionalists I described at the beginning of this paper: certain "in our bones" that the shared concerns of gender transcend other boundaries, but not quite able to agree on what the common bonds are. The way out of this dilemma is the very course the new regionalists have chosen: many small and specific case studies, and then overarching theories appropriate to western American women of all races, classes, and historical circumstances. Our most pressing need is to develop a methodology that is equal to the diversity we hope to explain. As Glenda Riley, writing about the Great Plains, has suggested:

> The study of women on the Great Plains requires a systematic methodology that can encompass diversity. The contributions of American Indian and European women to the development of the plains are of the utmost importance. American female settlers on the Great Plains cannot be slighted in favor of men or bypassed with the assumption that they were just like women in other frontier regions. Contemporary plainswomen of all types must also be studied and interviewed in order to establish a continuum of women's experiences from the earliest era to the present. An approach committed to diversity would also involve a wide variety of sources, research questions, guiding perspectives, techniques, eras, and regions.[40]

This feminist methodology—cooperative and not competitive, based on a model of long-range sharing and learning—is as appropriate to the study of regionalism as it is to the study of gender, for it is abundantly apparent that gender and regionalism cannot be studied in isolation from each other. A study of women that overlooks regional differences is inadequate; a regional study that ignores women is obviously incomplete.

Surely the challenge of coming to terms with the new western American environment was experienced by everyone, not just by men. A study of family strategies of adaptation gives us a way to reevaluate or rephrase Turner's basic question about adaptation—which is also Worster's question—with today's tools and insights.

I suggest that we need to look at women to answer the most basic question of how one develops a sense of regional identity. Western historians have mainly written about the development of regional identity in political terms, forgetting that most western women were barred from direct participation until they achieved suffrage in the 1890s or later. Clearly we need to look at other, nonpolitical kinds of activity for answers. We need to look within the family, at the work and authority patterns of all family members, the children as well as the women. Surely the development of regional identity must have been a multigenerational experience, and parental transmission of ideology an important aspect of that development. How did western women develop a sense of regional identity and transmit it to their children? Or perhaps I have the question backward: perhaps, like eastern immigrant families facing the new American culture, the children adapted first, and then turned to help their elders understand their new circumstances. At the moment we simply don't know. In the future, through careful study of gender *and* region, we can understand how regional identity forms, how it is maintained, and why it persists.

Notes

Portions of this paper have appeared in other articles by Susan Armitage on the subject of western women's history.

1. Carol Rupprecht, "The Second International Interdisciplinary Congress on Women," *Women Studies Quarterly* 14 (3–4) (Fall/Winter, 1986): 30.

2. Richard Jensen, "On Modernizing Frederick Jackson Turner: The Historiography of Regionalism," *Western Historical Quarterly* 11, no. 3 (July, 1980): 307–22.

3. Donald Worster, "New West, True West: Interpreting the Region's History," *Western Historical Quarterly* 18, no. 2 (Apr., 1987): 149 (italics added).

4. Patricia Limerick, *The Legacy of Conquest: The Unbroken History of the American West* (New York: Norton, 1987), p. 27 (italics added).

5. Worster, "New West, True West," p. 49.

6. T. J. Larson, "Women's Role in the American West," *Montana: The Magazine of Western History* 24 (Summer, 1974): 4.

7. Turner ignored women completely in his writing; Walter Prescott Webb, his most ardent follower, while attributing great spiritual power to women, still consigned them to the sod hut.

8. Beverly Stoeltje, "A Helpmate for Man Indeed: The Image of the Frontier Woman," *Journal of American Folklore* 88, no. 347 (Jan.–Mar., 1975): 25–41.

9. The University of Nebraska Press has taken the lead in reprinting women's memoirs.

10. See, in particular, Patricia Albers and Beatrice Medicine, *The

Hidden Half: Studies in Plains Indian Women (Washington,
D.C.: University Press of America, 1983).
11.   Glenda Riley, *Women and Indians on the Frontier, 1825–1915*
(Albuquerque: University of New Mexico Press, 1984).
12.   Elizabeth Jameson, "Toward a Multicultural History of Women
in the Western United States," *Signs* 13, no. 4, 761–91.
13.   Susan Armitage, "Through Women's Eyes: A New View of the
West," in *The Women's West,* ed. Susan Armitage and Elizabeth
Jameson (Norman: University of Oklahoma Press, 1987).
14.   Sylvia Van Kirk, *Many Tender Ties: Women in Fur-Trade Society, 1670–1870* (Norman: University of Oklahoma Press, 1983);
and W. R. Swagerty, "Marriage and Settlement Patterns of
Rocky Mountain Trappers and Traders," *Western Historical
Quarterly* 11 (Apr., 1980): 159–80.
15.   Marion Goldman, *Gold Diggers and Silver Miners: Prostitution
and Social Life on the Comstock Lode* (Ann Arbor: University of
Michigan Press, 1981); Ann Butler, *Daughters of Joy, Sisters of
Misery: Prostitutes in the American West* (Urbana: University of
Illinois Press, 1985); and Paula Petrick, *No Step Backward:
Women and Family on the Rocky Mountain Frontier, Helena,
Montana, 1865–1900* (Helena: Montana Historical Society,
1987).
16.   Gerda Lerner posed this direct question in her 1981 American
Historical Association pamphlet, *Teaching Women's History.*
17.   Julie Roy Jeffrey, *Frontier Women* (New York: Hill and Wang,
1979).
18.   Ibid.
19.   John Faragher, *Women and Men on the Overland Trail* (New Haven, Conn.: Yale University Press, 1979).
20.   Lillian Schlissel, *Women's Diaries of the Westward Journey*
(New York: Schocken Books, 1982).
21.   Diary of Amelia Buss, 1966–67, Special Collections, Colorado
State University Libraries, Fort Collins, Colo.
22.   Carroll Smith-Rosenberg, "The Female World of Love and Rit-
ual," *Signs* 1, no. 1 (Autumn, 1975); and Nancy Cott, *The Bonds
of Womanhood* (New Haven, Conn.: Yale University Press,
1977).
23.   For further exploration of these themes, see Susan Armitage,
"Reluctant Pioneers," in *Women and Western American Literature,* ed. Helen Stauffer and Suzanne Rosowski (Troy, N.Y.:
Whitston Press, 1982).

24. David M. Potter, "American Women and the American Character," in *History and American Society: Essays of David M. Potter,* ed. Don E. Fehrenbacher (New York: Oxford University
Press, 1973), pp. 277–303; for a detailed case study, see Janice
Reiff Webster, "Domestication and Americanization: Scandinavian Women in Seattle, 1888 to 1900," *Journal of Urban History*
4, no. 3 (May, 1976): 275–90.

25. Richard W. Etulain, "Shifting Interpretations of Western Cultural
History," *Historians and the American West,* ed. Michael Malone (Lincoln: University of Nebraska Press, 1983).

26. Sandra Myres, *Westering Women and the Frontier Experience
1800–1915* (Albuquerque: University of New Mexico Press,
1982).

27. Petrick, *No Step Backward.*

28. Katherine Harris, "Homesteading in Northeastern Colorado,
1873–1920: Sex Roles and Women's Experience," and Elizabeth
Jameson, "Women as Workers, Women as Civilizers," both in
The Women's West, ed. Armitage and Jameson.

29. Carol Stefanco, "Networking on the Frontier: the Colorado
Women's Suffrage Movement, 1876–1893," in *The Women's
West,* ed. Armitage and Jameson.

30. Sarah Deutsch, *No Separate Refuge: Culture, Class and Gender
on an Anglo-Hispanic Frontier in the American Southwest,
1880–1940* (New York: Oxford University Press, 1987).

31. An interesting discussion of these issues vis-à-vis national wom-
en's history is Joan Hoff-Wilson, "Righting Patriarchal History,"
The Women's Review of Books 3, no. 2 (Nov., 1985): 17–19. In
that article, Hoff-Wilson, herself a westerner, lamented the lack
of regionalism and described western women as "the orphans of
women's history."

32. Worster, "New West, True West," p. 149.

33. Donald F. Danker, ed., *Mollie: The Journal of Mollie Dorsey
Sanford in Nebraska and Colorado Territories, 1857–1866* (Lin-
coln: University of Nebraska Press, 1959); Ruth Moynihan, *Abi-
gail Scott Duniway: Rebel for Rights* (New Haven, Conn.: Yale
University Press, 1983); and Ralph Mann, *After the Gold Rush:
Society in Grass Valley and Nevada City, California 1849–1870*
(Stanford, Calif.: Stanford University Press, 1982).

34. T. A. Larsen's extensive case studies are summed up in his
"Dolls, Vassals, and Drudges: Pioneer Women in the West,"
Western Historical Quarterly 3 (Jan., 1972).

35.   Petrick, *No Step Backward,* p. xv.
36.   For specific and general perspectives on suffrage, see the Stefanco and Jameson articles in Armitage and Jameson, eds., *The Women's West.*
37.   Annette Kolodny, *The Lay of the Land: Metaphor as Experience and History in America* (Chapel Hill: University of North Carolina Press, 1975); and Annette Kolodny, *The Land Before Her: Fantasy and Experience of the American Frontiers 1630–1860* (Chapel Hill: University of North Carolina Press, 1984).
38.   Vera Norwood and Janice Monk, eds., *The Desert Is No Lady: Southwestern Landscapes in Women's Writing and Art* (New Haven, Conn.: Yale University Press, 1987).
39.   Elizabeth Hampsten, "Land in Time and Space," in *Reclaiming Paradise: American Women Photograph the Land,* ed. Gretchen Garner (Duluth, Minn.: Tweed Museum of Art, 1987).
40.   Glenda Riley, "Women on the Great Plains: Recent Developments in Research," *Great Plains Quarterly* 5, no. 2 (Spring, 1985): 88.

8   The Language of Regionalism
Frederic G. Cassidy

Our national motto, *E Pluribus Unum,* is not a contradiction in terms, not merely a nationalistic slogan, but the description of a reality in which we all participate. I do not like the metaphor of a simple melting pot. As Americans we have developed a character of our own; yet it is not like some smooth cream soup. It is more like a rich stew, with various components still distinguishable, the carrots, onions, potatoes, meat. Our soups and stews themselves differ geographically. There's the New England clam chowder, the Kentucky burgoo, the Wisconsin and Minnesota booya, the Louisiana gumbo, Mulligan stew, Brunswick stew, and more—from different sources but all American. Pizza became naturalized as a much larger production than the original Neapolitan delicacy. Tacos and guacamole and gazpacho are now all over the northern states. The simple croissant of France has been transformed within a very few years to a crescent big enough to serve as a sandwich with all kinds of fillings. The process of Americanization is in full swing with foods—less obviously with language, although in this country we have taken in many, many foreign words and phrases, some in one part of the country, making slow headway, others sweeping across the land, achieving general usage almost overnight. The most recent seems to be *glasnost,* a welcome immigrant, which, in time, may become naturalized, though it is not yet an everyday word, and certainly not a regional one.

What, then, regarding language, is a "regionalism"? It is a word, a phrase, a grammatical structure, or a feature of pronunciation used in one part of the country but not everywhere. For more than two centuries, American English has been recognized to have at least three distinct regional varieties: northern, southern, and western. Although these terms have reality, they are far too broad and general to be very meaningful. Linguistic geographers have therefore spent the past fifty years trying to map the country more accurately, to find out where the lines of regional difference run and to distinguish the valid features that set the regions apart.

The first such American linguistic atlas covered the six New England states and was completed in 1943 under Hans Kurath. It revealed so much about the speech of New Englanders, unrecorded or known only sketchily before, that its basic research method has since been followed in other parts of the country. The entire area east of the Mississippi River has now been surveyed and atlases are approaching completion for the Middle and South Atlantic states and the north-central states, in both of which Raven Mc-David was the leader, and for the Gulf states (including Texas) under Lee Pederson. West of the Mississippi, Harold Allen has completed and published the *Linguistic Atlas of the Upper Midwest,* and some field collecting has been done in most other western areas. So the detailed picture of language variation in the United States is gradually emerging.

But presentation of the data in atlas form is not the only possible presentation. Almost a hundred years ago, the American Dialect Society was founded (in 1889) with the goal of collecting American regional and folk language and presenting it in the form of a dictionary, and this is what the *Dictionary of American Regional English* is now trying to do. We rather like our acronym, *DARE.* The first volume was published in 1985, the second in 1991, and four more volumes will follow.

Volume 1 (A–C) contains an introduction explaining the history of the project, the principles and methods followed, what is and what is not in the dictionary, and why, and how it differs from the general run of dictionaries. First, *DARE* does not treat the common or "standard" words or meanings, nor literary, scientific, or technical terms. It does not treat slang or occupational jargon or criminal or underworld terms except those few that have escaped into more general use. *DARE does* treat two kinds of words and phrases, what we call "regional" and what we call "folk" words. *Regional* is a cover term for any form or meaning of limited geographical extent. It may be the generally northern *backlog* used in a fireplace as against the central-southern *backstick;* it may be the eastern New England *dropped eggs* as against the general *poached eggs,* or it may be the Texas *bar ditch* rather than the northwestern *barrow pit.*

These are all found in fairly broad areas. But some words are used in very narrow areas, perhaps only one small section of a state or a single city. For example, a distinctively Baltimorean word is *arab,* for a street vendor; a Cincinnatian word is *pony keg* for a store where you buy supplies for a beer party. The strip of grass and trees between the sidewalk and the curb is called the *devil strip* in Akron, Ohio, and hardly anywhere else. One of our most interesting examples is the small vehicle in which you push a baby around: *baby carriage* or *baby buggy.* It turns out that although both terms are known throughout the country, *baby carriage* is heavily concentrated in the Atlantic coast states, both north and south, whereas *baby buggy* is heavily concentrated in the middle and western states. There is also a small area in southeastern Pennsylvania and adjoining New Jersey where *baby coach* is the common term. Now these are only a few examples, but when they run into the thousands, and when they tend to cluster together on our maps, it becomes clear that regionality of language is a reality, and we look for reasons to explain this regionality—we ask what other factors correlate with language to make these patterns.

Our second criterion: what does *DARE* mean by "folk" language? Perhaps folk music or folk dance will get us closer, suggesting that these are not in origin highly cultivated or elaborated forms. They are the creation of nonprofessionals. So with folk language. It is what we learn first at home, in the family, in the hometown, at everyday work and play—not the language of education, not book language. We say that a clumsy person is *all thumbs;* we go fishing and use *angle-dogs* or *talpin worms* for bait; we see wild chicory plants in flowers along roadsides and call them *blue sailors;* we suspect that an employee is malingering and, in the language of marble playing, tell him he'd better *knuckle down.*

It must be admitted that there are borderline cases between folk expressions and slang. Slang is found at every social level. But it always has a degree of extravagance, it calls attention to itself, it is show-off language, and it has little staying power. On the other hand, folk speech usually is in a tradition, and in stable communities it has continuity. At present, folk language is under special pressure by the schools, by radio and television, and by the decay of the three-generation family home. Quite small children learn nonlocal language from the media, grandparents live apart from grandchildren, school playgrounds organize the sports. I have not seen kids playing marbles or hide-and-seek for twenty years or more. So, folk language hangs on less and less firmly, except, perhaps, as regards pronunciation. That, at least, is still regionally quite distinctive.

Words and phrases accepted for inclusion in *DARE* as regional or folk expressions are presented alphabetically, with their part of speech given as well as their variant pronunciations and the various ways we have found them spelled when they have gotten into print. For many words, the regional differences are not in the meaning but in the pronunciation. The phrase *nice white rice* or *ten cents,* pronounced *nahs waht rahs* and *tin cints,* are well-known shibboleths of southeastern speech.

DARE does not give etymologies when they are obvious or well known, but we have tracked down some fine ones that other dictionaries do not treat adequately or at all. My favorite is *bobbasheely,* meaning a very close friend. We have found it used in Arkansas, Mississippi, and Texas near the Louisiana border. This comes from Choctaw Indian, *itibapishili,* "my brother," often said as a greeting. Interestingly, William Faulkner used it, in *The Reivers,* as a verb, meaning to saunter or move along in friendly fashion. A young man escorting his girl friend is told, "You and Sweet Thing bobbasheely on back to the hotel now."

Another unusual word is *astamagootis,* a restless person, a "worry wart." We found it in Connecticut, Michigan, and Iowa, in settlements of

Dutch-speaking background, and indeed it is derived from the Dutch phrase *als het maar goed is!*—an exclamation meaning, roughly, *If all goes well,* or *May it all turn out well.* A person who keeps repeating this nervously may be told, "Don't be an astamagootis!" Other etymologies to which we have been able to contribute inclue *Borinki,* a Hawaiian nickname for a Puerto Rican; *astorperious,* a blend of *Astor* and *imperious* meaning haughty; *broadus,* the same as lagniappe; and *coonass,* clearly a folk etymology of the French *conasse,* used as an insult.

These are all regional, and most of them have currency only in an area where a language other than English was spoken. It is obvious that the demographic or settlement pattern of the United States must correlate in a number of ways with language. Well-known early contributors of loan words to American English were the Germans of southern Pennsylvania. The more isolated ones, religious separatists such as the Amish who keep up their German, are bilingual, but inevitably they adopt and Germanize some English words, and of course some of their words become current in otherwise English contexts. When they do that and are used on a par with English words, they are naturalized loanwords. One of the best known is *all,* in the sense *all gone, finished:* "The potatoes are all"—there are no more potatoes. This is clearly from the German *alle.* In the 1942 play by Patterson Greene, *Papa Is All, all* meant *dead.* This usage is strongest in Pennsylvania but has either spread or been reintroduced in later German settlements in the north-central states. The loaning process can continue as long as the foreign language survives or as long as immigration continues. A very few years ago a Pittsburgh-area newspaper reported that the police were having trouble with *hoofties,* who are apparently young people committing acts of vandalism. I could find the word nowhere else, but suddenly it occurred to me that *Hufd* is the German word for *hip.* This is no more than a guess—perhaps a bad one—but it might be that for those troubled coppers *hippies* are *hoofties.* (Any further evidence of the use of this word would be welcomed.)

There is hardly a state in the Union where some non-English language has not contributed to local usage. The French origins of Louisiana Creole words such as *batture* and *banquette* are well known; and Cajun words are now beginning to get around—*boudin,* the sausage; *fais-do-do,* the dancing party; *zydeco,* the musical style; and *coonass,* already mentioned, now in the process of amelioration. The tide of Spanish words from the Mexican border into Texas English is too familiar to need more than passing mention, with physiographic terms such as *arroyo* and *canyon* adopted long ago and now spreading out; food terms such as *cabrito* and *chayote;* cattle-herding terms such as *chaps, cabezon, caballada;* and more current ones such as *bracero* and *mariachi*. Some of these remain fairly local; others have spread or are spreading, enlarging their area. A few have become virtually national or "standard." But this has been an ongoing process: the Spaniards were often the first to adopt native Indian words, to Hispanicize them in various ways, and to pass them on to the French, English, and others. Such words as *avocado* pear, the Florida *Keys,* and *bronco* have long been standard.

But let me say something about the process of collecting the evidence for such a regional study as *DARE*. The point I would make is that any serious study, one that will add to our knowledge and have results of permanent value, must be systematic. Evidence cannot be merely picked up here and there, wherever it happens to come to attention. There must be a plan of collecting within the chosen area. The chosen area for *DARE* was the entire United States. Dictionaries in general get their information from printed sources, yet a great part of the language that most people use every day does not get into print and is simply not known, or is known inaccurately. For a dictionary of regionalisms it was essential to go directly to those who actually speak the language. *DARE* therefore undertook the necessary field collecting, which means that, in the fifty states, we chose one thousand communities for investigation and sent out eighty trained fieldworkers with a carefully constructed questionnaire that they used with local informants in the chosen communities.

Why one thousand communities? Because we had funding for only five years from the U.S. Office of Education, and knew, on the basis of linguistic atlas experience, that it took, on the average, one week to complete one questionnaire. So we had to complete two hundred questionnaires each year—or four every week to reach that goal. It was a close thing, but we managed it; from 1965 to 1970 1,002 questionnaires, to be exact, were completed.

How were the communities chosen? Obviously, there could not be the same number in each state, since population differs so much. The number of communities was therefore proportioned to population, not to square miles: our survey was not geographic but populational. The *DARE* maps, computer made and set directly into the columns of the dictionary, are "distorted" or adjusted to the facts of population. This moves the Mississippi River two-thirds of the way west, instead of the actual one-third, and it shrinks the underpopulated states such as Wyoming and Alaska and expands the heavily populated states such as New York and California. But by in effect spreading the population evenly throughout the country, it shows more clearly the distribution of local and regional features. The choice of communities also took into account the general nature of each state. Communities are of five types: urban, large city, small city, village, and rural; and these, again, were chosen to constitute a representative cross-section of each state's population and activities.

How were the informants chosen, and by what criteria? Again, the attempt was made systematically to balance the main social factors by which language usage is known to vary. First, of course, was the age of informants, at three levels: *old,* sixty or more; *middle,* forty to fifty-nine; and *young,* eighteen to thirty-nine. The numbers were deliberately proportioned in favor of the older generation. Since our study is historical, we had to gather as much of past usage as of present, and older informants would know both. It is a standard complaint of dialectologists that the older expressions are constantly dying out with their speakers, and if not gathered they will be lost. We found that our older informants knew the younger people's usages more often than the younger ones knew the older people's usages.

After age, the next important social factor affecting language was the level of education. *DARE* records four levels: less than fifth grade, at least fifth grade, at least two years of high school, and at least two years of college or vocational schooling. The other two social factors that correlate to some extent with language usage are sex and race. *DARE* informants are almost exactly balanced as to sex; of the four races recognized, American Indian and Oriental are numerically very small; blacks are the only minority of significant size, and their usages have been carefully studied. In volume 1 of *DARE* there is a full list of informants, with the essential facts about each. The reader who wants to trace a particular usage back to the individual who used it can thus find out that person's age, level of education, sex, race, occupation, the date of the interview, and the type of community represented. Furthermore, each of the five main social factors is computer coded so that these facts are put into the editor's hands when he or she is writing up an entry. This makes it possible for the editor to evaluate the usage objectively and to assign usage labels more accurately than most dictionaries are able to do.

Another systematic feature of the *DARE* field collecting was the structure of the questionnaire. In general it followed the method of the linguistic atlases, with the questions in a natural sequence of topics, beginning with such neutral ones as time, weather, topography, and moving to others such as honesty and dishonesty, emotional states and attitudes. Thus the informant could get used to the process and see that the fieldworker had no surreptitious purpose—had *no beans up his nose,* as they say in Wisconsin—and was not selling anything. Each question is carefully phrased in nonacademic, everyday language. Fieldworkers were instructed not to alter the questions but ask them exactly as they were phrased, thus ensuring comparability of results throughout the country. This method is not perfect; fieldworkers occasionally did vary the questions, and informants sometimes misunderstood them and answered at cross-purposes. But on the whole the method worked: the questionnaire elicited close to two and a half million responses. It is printed in full in volume 1 of *DARE,* and the responses it produced will be digested in the final volume.

The data gathered directly from local speakers of known age, sex, race, and education, in communities of known types, is the unique part of the *DARE* corpus. But it is only about half of the total data base. While the fieldwork was in progress, a large file was made from appropriate publications: *Dialect Notes, Publication of the American Dialect Society, American Speech,* and others. Several large private collections were donated to the project. Unpublished data from the *Linguistic Atlas of New England* was put at our disposal. A program of reading was carried out, especially of American diaries from the seventeenth century forward, and of "regional literature"—novels, plays, poetry, biographies, and autobiographies of people associated with particular parts of the country. Although some of these sources are not as valid evidence as that derived in oral interviews with local speakers, they cannot be ignored. They have furnished us with a great deal of valuable evidence and are quoted plentifully.

Our fieldwork proved beyond question that there is a lot of American English "out there" that is definitely regional, that people in one part of the country regularly use but people in other parts of the country do not. There proved to be a great deal more variation than anybody realized. Over and over again we would find that we, the editors, knew a few variants, the common ones, but that there were dozens more. Let me give you just one example.

One question (F46) is, "What do you call the kind of matches you can strike anywhere?" We got ninety-eight different responses! I will not go through them all, only the most frequent (the name, and the number of informants who used it):

kitchen matches	333	strike-anywhere matches	5
farmer matches	59	friction matches	5
sulfur matches	53	gopher matches	4
barn burners	33	birdseye matches	3
stick matches	22	country matches	3
household matches	11	cowboy matches	2
diamond matches	8	married-man's matches	2
brimstone matches	6	rat burners	1
lucifers	6	insurance matches	1
house matches	5		

And seventy-eight more.

Are any of these names regional? *Kitchen matches* is all over the country and may be considered the "standard" term. *Barn burner* is concentrated in Pennsylvania, with some usage in adjoining states. *Brimstone matches* is limited to the Northeast. *Lucifers,* introduced from Britain, is mostly in the East and California. *Friction matches* is mostly northern: New York, Michigan, Missouri, Washington State. We have had no explanation of *married-man's matches,* used in Iowa and Wisconsin, but I suspect that some local joke underlies it. *Cowboy matches,* the Hawaiian term, refers to the way cowboys in the movies strike matches on the seat of their pants. Very macho! *Insurance matches,* recalling the much commoner *barn burners,* are the kind you use if you want to collect on your insurance.

As I say, this is only one set of variants out of hundreds, and many of these terms would have remained unknown outside of their special regions or localities if we had not systematically dug them out. The world of spoken language, which is real language—some people insist that it is *the* real language—has needed to be collected, recorded, and studied. At *DARE* we feel that, in this long-awaited dictionary, we are making a gift to the nation.

Let me conclude these remarks with some more general ones. First, language is a specifically human invention and activity. Even if it began in the Garden of Eden, the language of Adam differed somewhat from that of Eve. Clearly, Cain and Abel had their differences; some of them were surely linguistic. The Tower of Babel symbolizes the variations that are inevitable in language change and development. The early tribes of central Europe may at one time have talked enough alike to communicate, but they split up, migrated, lost touch, and found themselves talking Germanic, Hellenic, Slavic, and Romanic variants of Indo-European, having long since forgotten the mother tongue. No need to detail the subsequent splits, as of Latin into French, Spanish, Portuguese, and Romanian. The point is that, for many reasons, language is never standing still. A condition of living is that there will be change. The Roman soldiers in Gallia Omnia had language contacts with Celts and Germans. Caesar's legionnaires in any case did not speak the same language as Caesar—and certainly not that of Cicero. We tend to speak of languages as if they were single, unified things. They are not. Variation, internal variation, is a basic fact of language. It cannot be avoided. It *is* possible to set up, temporarily at least, a certain type or variety of language, to give it social approval, to use it in education, in printed forms, in official and formal situations, in creative literature, to designate it as the "standard" form. But it is not the whole language.

The English language, now used worldwide, has as many types as its speakers, for no two people speak it exactly alike. But just because it has broken up somewhat, as Indo-European did long centuries ago, English is not merely a collection of idiolects. There are national types, and American English, for a variety of reasons, chiefly nonlinguistic, is now a major one. Returning to our national motto, though we should never forget *Unum,* let us not fail to remember *Pluribus.* Before we can claim to know our language well, or know it truly, we must know what its components are, the tradition of its sources and growth, the factors that characterize it, the ways in which it differs from other types of English. It is a fascinating story over which I have had time for no more than a hop, skip, and jump. For the present that will have to do. The first two volumes of *DARE* make a beginning in recording all the riches of our folk speech and its regional variations. There is much more to come, we hope, in the not too distant future.

Part III Directions

These chapters point toward important considerations for interdisciplinary research on the interplay of land and people. The integration of these concepts should further scholarship and institutionalize generative approaches to understanding how and why regions form and reform.

9 The Changing Character of North American Culture Areas

Wilbur Zelinsky

Setting forth the identity, territorial attributes, and dynamics of the culture areas that make North America such a special place, and doing so in an intellectually respectable fashion within the pages available here, is no mean assignment. Indeed the task of arriving at a rigorous definition of *culture area* has been a daunting experience for geographers, anthropologists, and other scholars, and one that could readily claim a hefty tome. And beyond that intimidating chore lies the much greater challenge of arriving at a consensus concerning the meaning of *culture*.

But suppose, for the purpose of minimizing verbiage and anguish, we agree on a skeletal definition. My subject thus becomes a set of places, each of intermediate magnitude and inhabited by a substantial number of persons, occupying a fairly extensive patch of real estate, each characterized by a real or imagined cluster of cultural traits specific to the community that set it apart from other such areas near or far. Thus we can avoid such technically absorbing questions as whether the entities in question are formal, or homogeneous, regions or of the nodal, or functional, type. But I would add one crucial stipulation: that there be an actual, or at least latent, awareness on the part of the inhabitants of their peculiar identity, of the fact that they share some unique traditions and memories, along with their own special combination of social and cultural practices. The depth of such regional self-consciousness can vary all the way from the raging sense of thwarted autonomy that has brought about bloodshed in the South and Quebec to the muted vagueness about their collective personality that pervades the Pennsylvania culture area.

You will note that, for the purposes of this discussion, I am ignoring the macro-region entirely—such enormities as the Islamic World, Latin America, or Polynesia, not to mention the vast Western, or pan-European, culture realm to which North America most emphatically belongs. I am also bypassing the cultural micro-region, for which much the same set of claims could be made. In such countries as India or Mexico, for example, we encounter many thousands of villages, each so distinctive in landscape and mode of existence as to constitute a genuine, if miniature, culture area. But that is another essay for another day.

The central thrust, the organizing theme, of this essay is simple enough to articulate, although, as far as I am aware, it has not yet been treated

Table 9.1
A Typology of Culture Areas

Type	Dates	Location and Extent	Mode of Origin
Older Traditional Region	Prehistory to present	Nearly all of premodern world; much of Old World today, plus scattered portions of Latin America	Interaction with local habitat and accessible aliens over extended periods; local inventions and cultural drift
Latter-day Traditional Region	Seventeenth century a.d. to present	Most of neo-European lands, i.e., eastern North America, Siberia, Brazil, Argentina, Chile, Mexico, South Africa, Israel, Australia, New Zealand, inter alia	Scrambling of European, African, and other immigrants from varied source areas; interaction with new habitat and aboriginal populations
Voluntary Region	Late nineteenth century to present	Selected areas of varied magnitude in U.S. and other advanced countries	Spontaneous, selective migration of like-minded persons to places with desired qualities
Synthetic Culture Area	Late twentieth century	Scattered localities, many quite small, in U.S. and, possibly, other postindustrial lands	Deliberate, self-conscious revival of traditional region or creation of make-believe places; may be ephemeral

explicitly in the scholarly literature. *During modern times, culture areas throughout the world have been experiencing profound change, so that we can detect a sequence of distinct types or stages in their evolution* (see table 9.1). Nowhere are the dynamics of this process so rapid and obvious as in the United States. Furthermore, it is likely that nowhere else have these developments advanced as far as they have in this country, for reasons to be offered presently. The theoretical and practical implications of these notions are, I believe, rather considerable.

Let us begin with the earliest phase of the development of culture areas, one that we can call the *older traditional* type: a form of cultural geography that stretches back many centuries, even millennia, past history into prehistory within areas inhabited over extended periods by sedentary folk or those following routinized nomadic circuits. Under such circumstances, there is an intimate blending of physical habitat, livelihood pattern, modes of social interaction, and cultural practice that generates within each locality a unique personality of place. It was a slowly changing, cellular pattern of life for nearly everyone, with permanent out-migration occurring infrequently—a mosaic of distinctive cultural territories, generally coalescing, in broader perspective, to form larger regions of relative homogeneity. But, however intense one's awareness of the immediate neighborhood may have been, there were few observers, or none, to watch and comment on the larger picture, and probably almost no local consciousness of extended regional or ethnic affiliations. So ancient and deeply rooted in vanished circumstances are most of these venerable culture areas that origins are difficult or impossible to track down.

This was the shape of things in premodern Europe and, indeed, throughout the greater part of the world until virtually yesterday; and, as a matter of fact, it still prevails over much of the Third and Fourth worlds, in spite of accelerating disintegration. Even today, vestiges of the older arrangements are still plainly visible in much of rural England, France, Germany, Switzerland, Italy, Spain, Yugoslavia, and other relatively advanced societies despite the heavy onslaughts of modernization.

When the great outward swarming of Europeans began in the 1600s, they automatically carried with them their traditional languages, religions, music and art, dress, diet, technologies, and the remainder of their portable cultural baggage, and were able to keep much of this patrimony intact. But, for obvious reasons, the highly variegated patchwork of culture areas in the homeland was not so easily exportable. Thus the advent of European settlers in South Africa, Canada, Brazil, Argentina, Australia, and Siberia created a new, generally much less emphatically differentiated order of regions in the colonized territories. This came about because either the colonists were nonrandomly preselected or their regional cultures had been scrambled and simplified in the course of transplantation. (Such was definitely the case, of course, for the African slaves introduced into North America.)

The outcome in the future United States was somewhat different. In contrast to other neo-European lands—Canada partially excepted—several different ethnic strains from within the British Isles and the European continent, some of them further differentiated into distinctive religious communities, immigrated and managed to retain much of their social identity and even a certain degree of territorial separateness.[1] Moreover, the place-to-place differences in physical geography and early economic patterns along the Atlantic Seaboard were sharp enough to nurture divergent modes of sociocultural development. Less well recognized but undoubtedly also contributing to the speciation of the embryonic colonial culture areas were

interactions with various aboriginal groups, who were by no means all cut
from the same cultural cloth, as well as contacts with Africans who were
much more numerous in certain areas than in others. Historical geographers have confirmed the establishment of at least four distinctive nodes
of early settlement (in the Chesapeake Bay area, the lower Delaware and
Susquehanna valleys, southern New England, and the lower St. Lawrence
valley) which subsequently blossomed into substantial culture areas that
were to exert decisive impacts upon the genesis of the continenal interior
and its sociocultural complexion.[2] In the course of events, the expansive
European presence almost totally obliterated the antecedent set of aboriginal cultural domains.

What we are witnessing in this instance (and in other neo-European settings as well) is the genesis of a fresh generation of culture areas, but of a
form rather different from their Old World ancestors: the *latter-day traditional* type. The American variety came into being rapidly—in the case of
the Mormon culture area, virtually overnight[3]—and, in most early cases,
the origins and scenario of development can be documented, although
sometimes only by dint of intensive research. The formation of these latter-
day traditional entities is still going on by means of the time-honored processes of alien immigration and mutual acculturation, or so Joel Garreau
has convincingly argued for what he calls "Mex-America" and "The Islands."[4] The former embraces a broad swath of the American Southwest,
along with the northern states of Mexico, while the latter is an archipelago
including the West Indies and the Venezuelan coast but dominated by the
recently Hispanicized Miami metropolitan area. Because of the conditions
of North American settlement history and demography, members of this
newer generation of traditional culture areas have tended to be larger than
the ancestral Old World types and generally less divergent among themselves in terms of cultural and social characteristics. Their rate of change
has also been markedly swifter, especially in recent decades, in part because of unusually high, persistent levels of mobility among the native
born, heavy influxes of immigrants from sources other than the originating
homelands, and the pervasive effects of modern modes of communication
and transportation.

The accompanying map (see map 9.1 and table 9.2) published in 1973,
is, I believe, a reasonable approximation of the recent situation in the
United States and a portion of Canada. Unfortunately, we do not have a
similar drawing for all of Canada, but in that country we can assume that
the interprovincial boundaries, except those for the three prairie provinces,
serve, at least roughly, to separate cultural as well as political entities.

Over the past few decades, cultural geographers and other scholars en-
amored of regional themes have devoted much effort to exploring the iden-

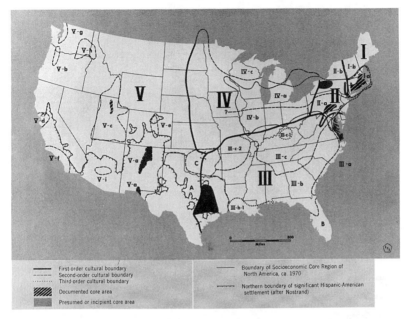

Map 9.1. Culture areas of the United States

tity, personalities, structure, and other attributes of the various European-ized culture areas that have flourished in America from colonial times to the present. In doing so, they have pursued varied lines of evidence which, it is gratifying to note, tend to yield generally compatible results. Much of the evidence is displayed in graphic form in an anthology of maps dealing with the societies and cultures of the United States and Canada.[5]

Geographers, folklorists, and other devotees of American studies have demonstrated commendable zeal in tracking down the clues to regional identity and history to be found in the built landscape, with special empha-sis on the older, rural elements. Thus, we now have a clear perception of the regional patterns of farmhouses and farmsteads and their historical ge-ography;[6] and, indeed, questions associated with log buildings are being pursued to the point of diminishing returns.[7] Barns and fences have also excited a fair amount of scholarly curiosity, and with useful, mappable results. But there are still many other aspects of the visible, man-made landscape for which information and analysis are still relatively sparse and rudimentary.

Thus we are only beginning to focus on townscapes and the morphology of agglomerated settlements ranging from the hamlet up through the me-

Table 9.2

Culture Areas of the United States

Region	Approximate Dates of Settlement and Formation	Major Sources of Culture (listed in order of importance)
I. New England	1620–1830	England
I-a. Nuclear New England	1620–1750	England
I-b. Northern New England	1750–1830	Nuclear New England; England
II. The Midland		
II-a. Pennsylvanian Region	1682–1850	England and Wales; Rhineland; Ulster; 19th Century Europe
II-b. New York Region, or New England Extended	1624–1830	Great Britain; New England; 19th Century Europe; Netherlands
III. The South		
III-a. Early British Colonial South	1607–1750	England; Africa; British West Indies
III-b. Lowland, or Deep South	1700–1850	Great Britain; Africa; Midland; Early British Colonial South; aborigines
III-b-1. French Louisiana	1700–60	France; Deep South; Africa; French West Indies
III-c. Upland South	1700–1850	Midland; Lowland South; Great Britain
III-c-1. The Bluegrass	1770–1800	Upland South; Lowland South
III-c-2. The Ozarks	1820–60	Upland South; Lowland South; Lower Middle West
IV. The Middle West	1790–1880	
IV-a. Upper Middle West	1800–80	New England Extended; New England; 19th Century Europe; British Canada
IV-b. Lower Middle West	1790–1870	Midland; Upland South; New England Extended; 19th Century Europe
IV-c. Cutover Area	1850–1900	Upper Middle West; 19th Century Europe

V. The West

V-a. Upper Rio Grande Valley	1590–	Mexico; Anglo-America; aborigines
V-b. Willamette Valley	1830–1900	Northeast U.S.
V-c. Mormon Region	1847–90	Northeast U.S.; 19th Century Europe
V-d. Central California	(1775–1848)	(Mexico)
	1840–	Eastern U.S.; 19th Century Europe; Mexico; East Asia
V-e. Colorado Piedmont	1860–	Eastern U.S.; Mexico
V-f. Southern California	(1760–1848)	(Mexico)
	1880–	Eastern U.S.; 19th and 20th Century Europe; Mormon Region; Mexico; East Asia
V-g. Puget Sound	1870–	Eastern U.S.; 19th and 20th Century Europe; East Asia
V-h. Inland Empire	1880–	Eastern U.S.; 19th and 20th Century Europe
V-i. Central Arizona	1900–	Eastern U.S.; Southern California; Mexico

Regions of Uncertain Status or Affiliation

A. Texas	(1690–1836)	(Mexico)
	1821–	Lowland South; Upland South; Mexico; 19th Century Central Europe
B. Peninsular Florida	1880–	Northeast U.S.; the South; 20th Century Europe; Antilles
C. Oklahoma	1890–	Upland South; Lowland South; aborigines; Middle West

---

tropolis. We are still in the pioneering stage of work on the regional implications of vernacular church buildings or the tens of thousands of cemeteries that are such splendid repositories of cultural data. Even within the countryside, we have made only the most limited progress in charting such landscape items as bridges, field patterns, modes of stacking grain and hay, the historical geography of draft animals and farming gear, lumbering camps, or other phases of the rural economy. Within the towns, we have scarcely begun to look at commercial structures, factories, schools, mon-

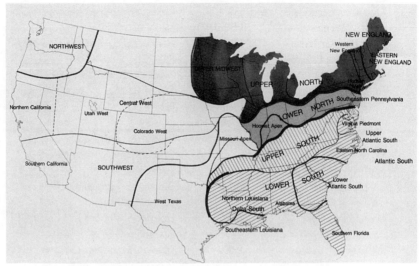

Map 9.2. Major dialect regions summarized. *Source:* Craig M.
Carver, *American Regional Dialects* (Ann Arbor: University of
Michigan Press, 1987), p. 248.

uments, or public buildings. And, in either town or country, who has been
looking systematically at folk gardens?

As fruitful as landscape study for the mapping of our traditional culture
areas have been the labors of those linguists who have been plotting the
local peculiarities of American English speech, the latest version of which
is depicted in map 9.2.[8] In this context, I must pay special homage to the
herculean feats of the editors of the ongoing *Dictionary of American Regional English,*[9] as well as the earlier *Linguistic Atlas of the United States*
project, aided and abetted, I am glad to say, by geographers intrigued by
place-names.[10] But even within this quite active linguistic realm, there is
still room for new initiatives since we know so little about the regional
implications of personal names or the terms applied to all manner of enterprises and other objects not classified as regular place-names.

Flawed though they may be, the available statistics on religion fall into
spatial patterns that tend, in reassuring fashion, to reinforce other experi-
ments in regionalization.[11] Political behavior also offers rich potentialities
for the delineator of regional patterns, although, here again, the tasks remaining greatly exceed whatever knowledge has been garnered to date.
Maps from Kenneth Martis's ongoing—and truly heroic—multi-volume

atlas of congressional membership and voting patterns from 1789 through the 1980s illustrate the substantial rewards of exploiting such data.[12]

I wish that it were possible to say something sensible about the regional configurations of one of the most central complexes within any cultural system: what we might call the "food ways" of North Americans. Although we all realize the distinctiveness of certain regional practices and preferences within North America as to food, drink, meal patterns, and other elements in that long list of items that have to do with the sociology of ingestion, systematic data gathering and observation have barely begun. Almost as sketchy is our understanding of the geography of folk music, although a few intrepid geographers and folklorists have begun to investigate both the down-home origins of the phenomenon and its commercialized manifestations.[13] The geography of American dance is still terra incognita.

The serious study of the geography of organized sport has only just left the starting gate, and we know even less about the territorial dimensions of other leisure time activities, such as hobbies, adults' and children's games, hunting and fishing, or partying, but the opportunities are certainly there. This likelihood is illustrated by a single foray thus far into the geography of voluntary associations and special interest magazines.[14] American scholars have lagged behind their European colleagues when it comes to mapping costume and that broad spectrum of phenomena falling under the heading of social customs and practices, e.g., those associated with holidays, weddings, funerals, and other rites of passage, or with the usages of ordinary etiquette, not to mention folklore, folk tales, jokes, riddles, rhymes, and bodily gestures and postures.

One of the simpler, more obvious ways to discover the what and where of culture areas is to interrogate the people in question; and that is exactly what a number of investigators have attempted lately, and with useful results. The strategy was apparently initiated by Joseph Brownell,[15] who sent questionnaires to a wide array of postmasters throughout the central portions of the country inquiring whether or not they considered themselves to be located in the Middle West. This example has been emulated by a number of academics who have plied college students with similar questionnaires.[16]

In another indirect approach invented by sociologist John Shelton Reed,[17] which I later plagiarized,[18] the researcher can plot the incidence of certain terms with regional connotations that appear in telephone directories, with results as shown in map 9.3. The entities so generated, whether through direct quizzing or via surrogate measures, are called "vernacular regions," i.e., regional concepts that exist in the minds of the general pub-

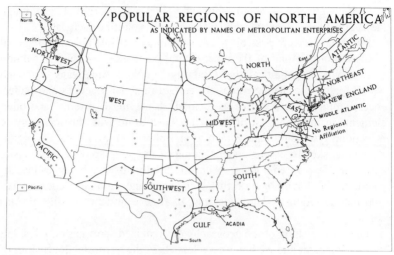

Map 9.3. Regional terms used in enterprises

lic. They must be accepted with caution. Although this category of territories does include genuine cultural areas, it also embraces simple locational perceptions, e.g., the Eastern Shore, the Panhandle, or the Gulf Coast, along with a number of coinages created by journalists or chambers of commerce, such as the "Heart of Texas" or South Carolina's "Grand Strand."

Despite the shortcomings of the evidence collected and sifted to date, we have learned enough about the territorial array of certain items, most particularly those having to do with settlement landscape, language, religion, and politics, to draft the boundaries of most American culture areas with a fair degree of confidence. We have also learned something about the internal structure of our major areas and some of their subregions. The scheme that has earned widest acceptance is that devised by Donald Meinig for initial application in his classic account of the Mormon culture area.[19] In its original form, the model postulates three concentric zones of diminishing concentration and centralized influence. In the author's own words:

> A *core* area . . . is taken to mean a centralized zone of concentration, displaying the greatest density of occupance, intensity of organization, strength and homogeneity of the particular features characteristic of the culture under study. It is the most vital center, the seat of power, the focus of circulation. . . .

The *domain* refers to those areas in which the particular culture under study is *dominant*, but with markedly less intensity and complexity of development than in the core, where the bonds of connection are fewer and more tenuous and where regional peculiarities are clearly evident. . . .

The *sphere* of a culture may be defined as the zone of outer influence and, often, peripheral acculturation, wherein the culture is represented only by certain of its elements or where its peoples reside as minorities among those of a different culture.[20]

With some modification, including the addition of a fourth outer zone of marginal affiliation, Meinig has applied the same basic approach to Texas[21] and the American Southwest.[22] It also fits comfortably into the evidence for New England and the Pennsylvania culture area, although there is much uncertainty in the latter case as to the identity of the core. However, I should not mislead the reader into believing that the Meinig model has universal applicability. For reasons having to do largely with their origins, we can detect no such geometric disposition of cultural attributes in the invertebrate Middle West of the American South.[23]

One important point I cannot overstress in discussing American cultural regions of the conventional variety, whatever their internal anatomy may be, is the difficulty, and usually impossibility, of plotting definitive outer limits. The problem is not limited to the North American scene. Almost everywhere we find the same fuzzy, indeterminate edges of adjoining culture areas, the fraying, mingling, or interdigitation of diagnostic traits except, of course, in the case of such islands as Madagascar, Iceland, or Malta, or, within a North American context, such possible examples as Newfoundland, Prince Edward Island, or the quasi-insular Mormon culture area.

The technical complications are well documented in Craig Carver's recent volume on the regional dialects of the United States in which, instead of using more primitive measures, he introduces the concept of multiple overlapping "dialect layers" in establishing the areal extent and intensity of the principal dialect regions.[24] A specific dialect layer can ooze over a considerable fraction of the country, and when one assembles all of the relevant dialect layers to ascertain the bounds of a major dialect such as, for example, New England's (see map 9.4) or that most significant of all such interregional seams, that between northern and southern speech (see map 9.5), the result is a broad band of transition rather than any sort of abrupt line.

So far so good, or so bad, depending on one's point of view. If this paper

124 **Wilbur Zelinsky**

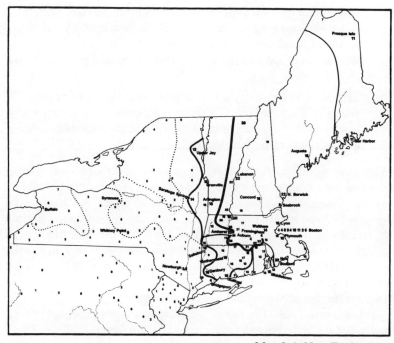

Map 9.4. New England dialect layer. *Source:* Craig M. Carver, *American Regional Dialects* (Ann Arbor: University of Michigan Press, 1987), p. 29.

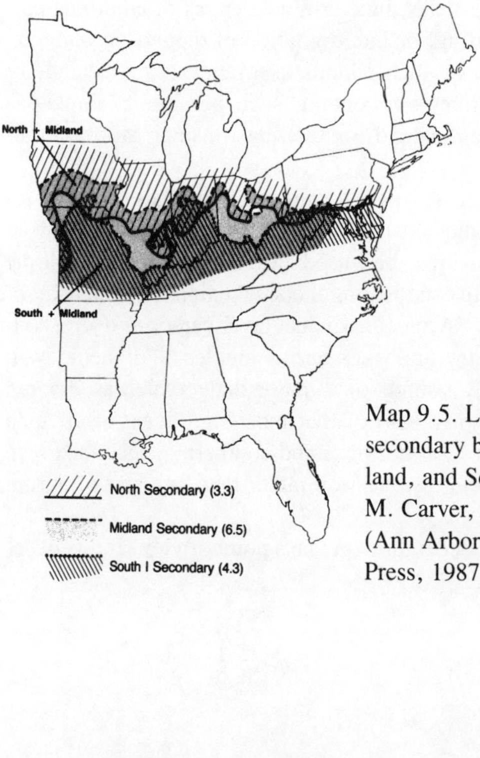

///// North Secondary (3.3)

------ Midland Secondary (6.5)

〰〰 South I Secondary (4.3)

Map 9.5. Linguistic divide in terms of secondary boundaries of the North, Midland, and South I layers. *Source:* Craig M. Carver, *American Regional Dialects* (Ann Arbor: University of Michigan Press, 1987), p. 196.

were being written not too many years ago, I might well be winding up at this point after relieving myself of a few more platitudes. But I have become aware of some new developments that are revising the contours of our cultural landscape in an unprecedented and theoretically provocative fashion. These developments are recent enough to have escaped methodical scholarly scrutiny so far. What follows, then, is largely impressionistic.

As already suggested, the older American culture areas, those dating from colonial times or from the mid-nineteenth century at the latest, have lingered on in spite of much blurring and dilution brought on by the forces of modernization and cultural convergence. The South may be something of an exception, for it seems to be retaining its integrity and even intensifying it, most notably in the realm of religion but probably in politics and the regionalization of organized sport as well. In any event, the older generation of culture areas has been joined by a new breed of region, one that I call the *voluntary region,* which is very much the offspring of the present century and by no means limited to the United States.

While the older species of culture area was the product of traditional social and economic forces (i.e., migrants seeking out places with perceived economic advantages and/or those that kinfolk, friends, and coreligionists had previously settled in, and then the subsequent interactions among communities and physical habitat), the voluntary region crystallizes with the coming together of individuals driven not by economic calculation or the craving for old-fashioned social coziness but rather by the individualistic quest for the good life, for the best physical environment, for particular cultural and social amenities, for the company of other footloose persons with the same sorts of predilections. Personal choice rather than accident of birth or job history is the key factor.

In some cases, the birth of voluntary regions meant a massive reordering of the personalities of extensive patches of territory, for example, virtually all of southern Florida and southern California, a revivified northern New England, the entirety of urban Nevada, northern Virginia's Hunt Country, the Kentucky Bluegrass, and James Vance's "Arcadia."[25] At the other extreme, the process may transform only a single city or neighborhood such as, for instance, San Francisco's Castro and other gay enclaves, the yuppifying districts of such metropolises as Chicago, Cincinnati, Philadelphia, or Columbus, any number of college and R&D communities, including my very own State College, Pennsylvania, havens for the retired military, such as La Jolla or San Diego, or those many localities in Arizona, the Ozarks, and elsewhere that are dominated by retired persons and are neither urban nor rural. Basic to the genesis of such voluntary regions, whatever their size, is the fact of their spontaneity. Such places were not plotted or engineered by any cabal of master planners; they simply materialized through the shared perceptions and yearnings of significant numbers of free agents. I must also note that this new family of culture areas is archipelagic in form, a galaxy of scattered islands that fall far short of blanketing the entire country.

I turn next to the emergence of still another mode of organizing cultural space, the most recent, least recognized, and most embryonic: the *synthetic culture area*. These are self-conscious artifacts. The majority of them represent efforts to resuscitate or reinvigorate real or imagined regions or communities of the past, but a minority are totally original in concept; and they are the handiwork of local enthusiasts, business interests, and governmental agencies.

In a sense, such synthesizing has been going on in the United States and elsewhere for some two hundred years in that grandest and most totally consummated of artificial culture areas: the modern nation-state. Insofar as the United States, France, Italy, Israel, Mexico, or East or West Germany, for that matter, have become distinctive and relatively homogeneous places in a cultural sense, and they most certainly have done so, it is mainly because of the workings of a powerful, determined central state apparatus with leverage over so many phases of our social and economic activities and attitudes.

The United States is an ideal example of the synthetic region at the macro scale, a community that began as a rather novel sort of nation but later became a full-fledged nation-state because it was created essentially *de novo* without the venerable roots, the real or imagined age-old traditions, that the budding European nation-states were able to capitalize on so effectively.[26] At the micro scale, however, this country is unique or nearly so in its profusion of short-lived utopian colonies that have come and gone from colonial days to the present. These are indeed miniature, self-conscious spatial and social entities of the synthetic variety, and, in a sense, they anticipated both the voluntary and the synthetic culture areas by quite a few decades. It is not until the late twentieth century that we begin to see a widespread emergence of synthetic culture areas in the United States, localities that are indubitably synthetic and probably less ephemeral than their utopian antecedents.[27] But, before confronting this latest generation of culture areas head on, we must take an apparent detour and examine the ethnic factor in the historical geography of American culture areas.

Indeed, one cannot escape discussing ethnicity when dealing with the shape of American regionalism, past, present, or emerging. To take the grandest case of all, there is considerable force to the argument that the American South, the most populous and emphatic of the nation's culture areas, is the domain of a special ethnic group, that once-upon-a-time, would-be independent nation of southerners, who represent the blending of English, Celtic and African ingredients within a particular ecological and economic setting during a particular formative period. Similarly, the Pennsylvania culture area inherits much of its distinctiveness from a mingling of English, Celtic, Teutonic, and Scandinavian elements not to be found elsewhere in early America. The case for the equivalence of region and ethnicity in southern Louisiana, or Acadiana, and in the American Southwest is open and shut, as it is for any number of micro-regions of ethnic concentration within larger cities.

We cannot evaluate the role of ethnicity in American life and the making of regions without considering the fact of immigration. The United States, as we all realize, has been the world's greatest reception area for international migrants and, indeed, remains so today, at least in absolute terms. But both the volume and makeup of this mass movement have shifted sharply over the years. It is useful to segment American immigration history into four active periods, each separated from others by lulls of military turmoil or economic depression. The earliest, and the most decisive in molding the character of the eventual Republic, occupied the entire colonial era from 1607 to 1775, and witnessed the introduction of persons mainly from the British Isles, the Rhineland, and Africa, with minor contributions from several other Old World areas. A second period lasting from about 1820 to 1860 was dominated by a heavy influx of Germans, the Irish, and additional arrivals from the British Isles. Largest of all of the tidal waves of newcomers was the one starting in the 1870s and ending in 1914 when immense swarms of eastern and southern Europeans reached our shores, along with significant trickles from other parts of the world, and selecting rather different sorts of destinations than had their predecessors.

After a long hiatus created by two world wars, a major depression, and restrictive legislation, we enter the vigorous immigration episode that started in 1945 and continues without letup to this day. The magnitude of legal immigration is impressive (around half a million each year), while the extent of illegal entries is also substantial, although figures are highly uncertain and subject to much academic as well as official controversy. The composition of the current wave of new Americans is strikingly different from anything experienced in the past. Increasingly, we are receiving newcomers from eastern and southern Asia and from Latin America, with lesser streams from the Middle East and Canada, and declining numbers from traditional European sources. Although also heavily weighted by Latin Americans from many countries beside Mexico, the illegals include a wide variety of other folks, among them Asians, Canadians, the Irish, and other Europeans.

But it is not just the source regions that have changed, and, to some degree, the places chosen for settling down. Even more germane to this essay is the kind of welcome accorded these newcomers. In place of the hostility and xenophobia confronting earlier non-British immigrants, there has been a rather amazing change in general attitudes. Admittedly, many of the incoming Mexicans, Puerto Ricans, Haitians, Iraquis, and Salvadorans do not enjoy the jolliest of times in their new domiciles; but consider the nearly 180-degree turnabout in our perceptions of the recent Japanese, Korean, and Chinese immigrants, or Hungarian, Czech, Vietnamese, and Cuban political refugees, and their remarkably fast climb up the socioeconomic ladder, along with that of many persons from Thailand, the Philippines, Pakistan, and India.

The fact that their average levels of education and skills are higher than those of earlier generations of their compatriots is only a partial explanation. No longer are we revolted by their weirdness—indeed we relish their fascinating customs, foods, and crafts, and actively seek them out—and, if there is any problem, it is that they are assimilating too rapidly, becoming super-Americans almost overnight. In a way, this new sensibility is transnationalism brought back home, tourism with minimal exertion, and certainly a basic revision of earlier American attitudes toward the exotic. The shrewder entrepreneurs among the newcomers have lost no time in capitalizing on this mass hunger for the strange and different, doing so in ways I shall relate in a moment; but it is essential to remember that such enterprises would have been unthinkable not too long ago.

Not only are many of the newer immigrants to the United States enjoying a degree of cultural hospitality and respect that was previously unknown, we also find the older "hyphenated" Americans bestirring themselves, remembering, restoring, and celebrating the ways of their forebears as they join the ethnic revival, a movement occurring in Canada and various European countries as well as here. The European ethnics—Poles, Czechs, Slovaks, Magyars, Jews, Ukrainians, Croats, Basques, Italians, Germans, Irish, Welsh, Greeks, Portuguese, Lithuanians, and Romanians, among others—are not the only players in the game. In fact, the first great burst of ethnic revivalism was the Black Pride movement of the 1960s, to be followed by the awakening of the Cajuns in Louisiana and adjacent states, the Chicanos in the Southwest, the Native American movement among the scattered remnants of our aboriginal population, and some revitalization of the Polynesians in Hawaii. Closely parallel to, and simultaneous with, all of this neoethnicity was the rediscovery of the fact that there are genuine, interesting regions within this country, and, in fact, as I have already suggested, these two developments have overlapped and intertwined.

There are other factors beside the rediscovery of ethnicity that can help account for the current surge in regional sentiment, in effect the restoration of culture areas as they were or, rather, as they should have been. There are connections, I suspect, with the advent of professional planning, especially at the regional scale. Regional planning is a movement that came into its own during the New Deal period and has persisted since in many venues, but there were interesting stirrings among some visionary thinkers as far back as the 1920s. Concurrent with the acceptance of regional planning during the Great Depression was an unprecedented interest in the folk cultures of the land, which undoubtedly accompanied the popularity, on an unprecedented scale, of regional fiction, drama, and art. This rediscovery and celebration of regional diversity in both folk and sophisticated media has persisted to the present. The 1930s, that decade of such remarkable intellectual and artistic ferment, also witnessed the attainment of a certain degree of academic respectability for students of regionalism, most notably at the University of North Carolina.[28]

Moving into the contemporary scene, we find a major boom in historic preservation in whatever direction one might turn and a general craze for all things nostalgic. I do have some preliminary notions as to why all these trends—the neoethnic, the neoregional (expressed in a wonderful diversity of ways), historic preservation, the bull market for nostalgic objects and experiences—are not only coincident in time but also interlinked in some profoundly meaningful fashion within our collective psyche. Ignorance and the lack of sufficient space prevent me from further pursuit of this truly deep question here and now.

Three characteristics set the current ethnic and regional revivals apart from earlier forms of ethnic and regional existence. First, these are *self-conscious* phenomena among people who have been made aware, by one means or another, that they are rather special and ought to be doing something about it. In the past, members of particular regions or ethnic groups were barely cognizant of their distinctiveness, sometimes only subconsciously so, or were ashamed to be identified with them. Second, these entities are no longer the exclusive, private preserves of their members; they are meant to be touted and shared as widely as possible. In the immortal words of that classic subway ad, "You don't have to be Jewish to enjoy Levy's Rye Bread." Now we have transnationalism, or rather transregionalism and transethnicity, at the intimate scale. Third, and consequently, the commercial exploitation of ethnic and regional attractions has become rampant.

These essential features bear repetition: self-consciousness; a sharing of identities and cultural heirlooms with the world at large; and vigorous commercialization. However, I do not wish to oversimplify the situation. If there is all that touristic hype and schlock in portions of Lancaster County,

I can show you picturesque pockets of Teutonic culture in central Pennsylvania still unmolested by outsiders. And not all of New England or New Mexico has been gussied up to ensnare the wallet of the passerby.

Let us look at some of the specific ways in which our revivals have made themselves felt in contemporary America. As striking as anything has been a boom in new journalistic efforts catering to regional and ethnic appetites. The year 1987 witnessed the launching of *Midwest Living,* with a press run, I understand, in the hundreds of thousands, and it joins the prosperous ranks of *Yankee, Southern Living, Sunset,* and *Arizona Highways* magazines. Over the past couple of decades, every self-respecting metropolitan area has spawned its very own monthly periodical, sometimes two. Quite recently, State College, Pennsylvania became a member of this company, even though, in terms of population, it ranks somewhere around 260th among the standard metropolitan statistical areas (SMSAs) of the United States. A number of university presses have become explicitly regional in their publishing strategies, and regional institutes have been sprouting of late in various localities around the country. Although the old foreign-language press has been languishing for some time, the new immigration has produced a fresh generation of such periodicals; but more to the point has been the initiation of Afro-American, Jewish-American, Italian-American, and other English-language magazines aimed at third- or nth-generation foreign stock.

Language maintenance or revival has not been as burning an issue in the United States as in Canada, Wales, Ireland, or portions of Spain, France, or Belgium, although some 200 percent Americans are flustered by the vitality of the unofficial Spanish language. But some groups have mounted formal efforts in and out of the schools to foster their ancestral tongues. An increasing number of radio stations devote all or part of their broadcast time to programs directed to the so-called minorities, using the foreign language or English, or some combination thereof. The Hispanic and black stations are only the most numerous in this category, while at the other extreme are single weekly programs in Cajun French and Navaho. But all such broadcasting, along with similar television programming in some of the larger markets, not only helps maintain the language, it also reinforces cultural identity and pride.

While dwelling on the topic of language and ethnic journalism, I cannot resist mentioning the veritable explosion, within the last few years, of bumper stickers and T-shirts bearing ethnic messages. Also noteworthy are the elaborate outdoor murals celebrating ethnic themes to be seen in many American metropolises. Although compositions by Mexican, Puerto Rican, and other Hispanic artists (both amateur and professional) are the most numerous, the black and Chinese communities are also well represented within this genre. The artistic quality of the better examples is truly out-standing.

I am also intrigued by the popularity of traditional regional building motifs in recent upscale suburban architecture. Admittedly, this is not something that began just yesterday. Some time ago, the formerly highly localized Cape Cod house migrated from New England to become one of the more conspicuous elements on the American landscape coast to coast. And in southeast Pennsylvania, there has been no break over time in the ways homes and barns are designed, just a gentle evolution. But if we look at various spots in Quebec, Acadiana, California, the suburbs of almost every Deep South city, just about any of the burgeoning towns of the South-west, and many another locality, we find deliberate efforts to mimic and update the old indigenous buildings, to use the home or commercial struc-ture as a badge of regional belongingness. This recycling of venerable building types is not entirely in character, since we seem to be experiencing a nationwide vogue for neo-Victorian residences; but, at the other extreme, this archaeological approach to domestic building can be quite place spe-cific, as in the suburban homes in Austin, Texas that are modeled after the distinctive German-American structures of nearby Fredericksburg.

Turning to the vigorous recent upsurge in regional and ethnic festivals, we confront an impressive picture and a business that, in aggregate, is ap-proaching the megabuck level. Such celebrations are not entirely new, of course. The Mardi Gras has been observed in traditional style in small-town Louisiana, as well as New Orleans, for many years, and so too the St. Patrick's Day parade in many major cities; Fourth of July and Memorial Day observances, now quietly fading from the scene, frequently had local or regional overtones; and county and state fairs have been with us for some time, retaining all their old robustness. No one has yet properly stud-ied the centennial, bicentennial, and other commemorations of the found-ing of towns, states, or nation, but they are certainly rich in both general cultural meaning and as expressions of localized loyalties.

But, quite apart from these rather timeworn practices, we are now ex-periencing a new breed of festival, one with many subcategories, but all involving the hawking of merchandise amid a wide range of activities. Thus we have events featuring the arts, music, sports, crafts, flowers, ag-riculture, and a bewildering array of esoterica, but certainly one of the leading varieties is the ethnic festival. Although statistical documentation is meager, there is little doubt that such annual occasions have been multi-plying vigorously in recent times. One of my students, Catherine Harding, has been able to map these festivals for most of the United States at the state level as of the mid-1980s. It is apparent that they are now widespread and diverse in character. In some large cities, such as Detroit, these are multi-ethnic spectaculars, with one group following another each succeeding week. Less numerous, but still worthy of note, are the regional museums, frequently historical in tone, that have been popping up hither and yon, as well as the occasional ethnic museum and library. Finally, at the micro level, amid all the carefully engineered, synthetic environments that are coming to dominate the North American scene, one can observe shopping malls, theme parks, restaurants, retirement villages, gentrifying urban neighborhoods, and trailer camps that exploit regional themes in the most calculated of fashions.

Trying to anticipate future trends in North American regionalism and ethnicity would be a foolhardy exercise. Much depends on developments we cannot foresee or control, such as immigration policy, the changing shape and health of the economy, the extent and impact of intermarriage among different groups, and the more general long-term, structural results of the homogenizing forces of modernization, especially as they operate via mass communications and high-speed transportation.

It is all too possible that, amid the welter of details and asides, the essential message of this essay may have gone astray. Let me close, then, by reiterating the three central ideas I have been trying to advance.

1) The nature of human society is such that cultural regions of many shapes, sizes, and descriptions have always been part of the scene. The oldest variety of such region, the traditional culture area, is spontaneous in origin and essentially premodern in character; but it still lingers on in North America in its latter-day incarnation, even though often rather battered, bent out of shape, and bleached out by recent social and technological processes.

2) There is another species of spontaneous culture to be seen in the more socioeconomically advanced parts of the world: the voluntary region. It materializes from the coming together in an appropriate locality of like-minded people sharing certain proclivities and interests or those in search of particular sorts of social or physical environments.

3) Finally, we have today an apparent contradiction, a sort of dialectical situation: on the one hand, there are all those pulverizing forces of modernization, via mass communications and modern methods for mass-producing goods, services, and attitudes and transporting people, mechanisms that tend to flatten out differences among places; but, at the same time, we observe the deliberate, self-conscious fabrication of new local pockets of social and cultural peculiarity, what might be termed space warps or time warps. Thus another kind of culture area has begun to hatch, one that, in lieu of a better term, we can label the "synthetic region." Although it is not always sharply defined territorially, we cannot afford to

ignore it, especially since it is obviously akin to the ethnic revival and the entire historic preservation and nostalgia phenomenon. What makes this development distinctive is the fact that it is *not* spontaneous in origin. Instead these are calculated, artificial, self-conscious creations, whether the motivations be mercenary or high-minded.

The uneasy conclusion, then, is that there are no pat answers to the question that troubles so many of us, that of whether the whole world is shrinking into one uniform cultural blob—only evasive yeses and nos. My own belief is that we will never outgrow regional peculiarities, whether within North America or at the world scale. The bottom line is that the nature of all manner of regions has forever been changing and will keep on changing, and that, if we are at all clever, we shall keep a sharp lookout for these changes and what they mean not only in livelihood terms but, even more importantly, in terms of our general well-being.

Notes

1. Bernard Bailyn, *Voyagers to the West: A Passage in the Peopling of America on the Eve of the Revolution* (New York: Knopf, 1986); David Hackett Fischer, *Albion's Seed: Four British Folkways in America* (New York: Oxford University Press, 1989).

2. Henry Glassie, *Pattern in the Material Folk Culture of the Eastern United States* (Philadelphia: University of Pennsylvania Press, 1969); Fred Kniffen, "Folk Housing: Key to Diffusion," *Annals of the Association of American Geographers* 55 (1965): 549–77; Robert D. Mitchell and Paul A. Groves, *North America: The Historical Geography of a Changing Continent* (Totowa, N.J.: Rowman and Littlefield, 1987); and Wilbur Zelinsky, *The Cultural Geography of the United States* (Englewood Cliffs, N.J.: Prentice-Hall, 1973), pp. 109–34.

3. Donald W. Meinig, "The Mormon Culture Region: Strategies and Patterns in the Geographies of the American West, 1847–1964," *Annals of the Association of American Geographers* 55 (1965): 191–220.

4. Joel Garreau, *The Nine Nations of North America* (Boston: Houghton Mifflin, 1981).

5. John F. Rooney, Jr., Wilbur Zelinsky, and Dean R. Louder, eds., *This Remarkable Continent: An Atlas of United States and Canadian Society and Cultures* (College Station: Texas A&M University Press, 1982).

6.   Fred Kniffen, "Folk Housing: Key to Diffusion," *Annals of the Association of American Geographers* 55 (1965): 549–77; and John R. Stilgoe, *Common Landscape of America, 1580 to 1845* (New Haven, Conn.: Yale University Press, 1982).

7.   Terry G. Jordan, *American Log Buildings: An Old World Heritage* (Chapel Hill: University of North Carolina Press, 1985).

8.   Craig M. Carver, *American Regional Dialects: A Word Geography* (Ann Arbor: University of Michigan Press, 1987).

9.   Frederic G. Cassidy, ed., "Introduction," *Dictionary of American Regional English,* vol. 1: *A-C* (Cambridge, Mass.: Harvard University Press, 1985).

10.   Wilbur Zelinsky, "Some Problems in the Distribution of Generic Terms in the Place-Names of the Northeastern United States," *Annals of the Association of American Geographers* 45 (1955): 319–49.

11.   Edwin S. Gaustad, *Historical Atlas of Religion in America* (New York: Harper and Row, 1962); James R. Shortridge, "A New Regionalization of American Religion," *Journal for the Scientific Study of Religion* 16 (1977): 143–53; and Wilbur Zelinsky, "An Approach to the Religious Geography of the United States," *Annals of the Association of American Geographers* 51 (1961): 139–93.

12.   Kenneth C. Martis, *The Historical Atlas of Political Parties in the United States Congress, 1789–1989* (New York: Macmillan, 1989).

13.   George O. Carney, *The Sounds of People and Places: Readings in the Geography of American Folk and Popular Music* (Lanham, Md.: University Press of America, 1987).

14.   Wilbur Zelinsky, "Selfward Bound? Personal Preference Patterns and the Changing Map of American Society," *American Geography* 50 (1974): 144–79.

15.   Joseph W. Brownwell, "The Cultural Midwest," *Journal of Geography* 39 (1960): 81–85.

16.   Terry G. Jordan, "Perceptual Regions in Texas," *Geographical Review* (1978): 293–307.

17.   John Shelton Reed, "The Heart of Dixie: An Essay in Folk Geography," *Social Forces* 54 (1976): 925–39.

18.   Wilbur Zelinsky, "North America's Vernacular Regions," *Annals of the Association of American Geographers* 70 (1980): 1–16.

19.   Donald W. Meinig, "The Mormon Culture Region: Strategies and Patterns in the Geographies of the American West, 1847–

1964," *Annals of the Association of American Geographers* 55 (1965): 191–220.

20. Donald W. Meinig, "The Mormon Culture Region: Strategies and Patterns in the Geographies of the American West, 1847–1964," *Annals of the Association of American Geographers* 55 (1965): 213–16.

21. Donald W. Meinig, *Imperial Texas: An Interpretive Essay in Cultural Geography* (Austin: University of Texas Press, 1968).

22. Donald W. Meinig, *Southwest: Three People in Geographical Change, 1600–1970* (New York: Oxford University Press, 1971).

23. John C. Hudson, "North American Origins of Middlewestern Frontier Populations," *Annals of the Association of American Geographers* 78 (1988): 395–413.

24. Craig M. Carver, *American Regional Dialects: A Word Geography* (Ann Arbor: University of Michigan Press, 1987).

25. James E. Vance, Jr., "California and the Search for the Ideal," *Annals of the Association of American Geographers* 62 (1973): 185–210.

26. Wilbur Zelinsky, *Nation Into State: The Shifting Symbolic Foundations of American Nationalism* (Chapel Hill: University of North Carolina Press, 1988).

27. Philip W. Porter and Fred E. Lukermann, "The Geography of Utopia," *Geographies of the Mind,* ed. David Lowenthal and Martyn J. Bowden (New York: Oxford University Press, 1976), pp. 197–223.

28. Howard W. Odum and Harry E. Moore, *American Regionalism: A Cultural-Historical Approach to National Integration* (New York: Holt, 1938).

10   A Binational Region: The Borderlands

Oscar J. Martínez

In the historical literature on the U.S.-Mexican borderlands, Herbert E. Bolton stands out for energetically promoting the study of early Spanish exploration and colonization of the region. Bolton's "Spanish Borderlands" encompassed a huge land mass of New Spain's northern frontier, including territories from Florida and Georgia to California in the present-day United States.[1]

Bolton's prominence in borderlands historiography rests on descriptions of a distinctiveness along the Mexican northern frontier—a distinctiveness that took generations to form. During the Spanish colonial period, territories to the north of central Mexico became the northernmost crust of the Spanish empire in the New World, a remote, arid, and generally uninviting land populated by nomads, ranchers, and miners. To the people of a very different central Mexico, El Norte was simply too isolated, too unattractive, and too dangerous for them to consider relocating there. Only the most adventuresome and reckless dared to venture to the northern frontier.[2]

This image of the region persisted after Mexico became independent in 1821. For decades El Norte presented a major headache for the central government because of the difficulties of governing a remote and relatively autonomous frontier. Even today, Mexicans in the interior see the population in the northern border states as having a life-style that is not synchronized with the rest of the country.[3]

American views of this borderland and the parts of the United States that stretch along it from the Rio Grande to Tijuana are similar in nature, if not in detail.

While there is thus implicit agreement that the Mexican north and the American Southwest constitute a distinct geographic and cultural unit, there is little consensus among scholars regarding the limits of the modern borderlands. Some seem to define the borderlands the way J. Frank Dobie once defined the American Southwest. "The principal areas of the Southwest," he remarked, are "Arizona, New Mexico, most of Texas, some of Oklahoma, and anything else north, south, east, or west that anybody wants to bring in."[4]

Adherents of the Dobie approach formulating definitions might think of the borderlands as the U.S. border states and the Mexican border states, plus a number of corridors into the interiors of each country through which the influence of the border travels. Using the flow of migration from Mexico as prime indicator of border reach, the border would run along certain U.S. interstate highways and air routes into such cities as Denver and Chicago. Going the opposite way and following American forms of influence in Mexico, the border would reach all the way to Mexico City and Acapulco.[5]

My own preference is to visualize the U.S.-Mexican borderlands as a long and pliant subregion defined as much as by what it is not as by what it is. Sandwiched between two different cultures that have been remarkably similar in their treatments—or mistreatments—of this region, this binational borderland consists of all or parts of forty-nine U.S. border counties and thirty-six Mexican *municipios,* plus selected population centers within two hundred to two hundred and fifty miles of the boundary.

More than anything else, the level of transboundary interchange distinguishes the U.S.-Mexican borderlands from most border zones in the world. Nowhere else do so many millions of people from two so dissimilar nations live in such close proximity and interact with each other so intensely. This two-thousand-mile border has produced a vibrant binational economy and a society that thrives on cultural adaptation and experimentation.

The binationality of the area is well established historically, and innumerable transborder relationships continue to this day. The interdependence of the Mexican and American sides of the border is most evident in the economic integration of cities like Ciudad Juárez and El Paso, but such integration extends also into interior centers such as Monterey, Nuevo Leon, and San Antonio, Texas. In the borderlands corridor, industrial exchanges, trade, tourism, migration, and cultural interaction take place daily on a grand scale.

The regionalistic tendencies of the borderlands originated in the early history of New Spain's northern frontier. Beginning in the sixteenth century, Spaniards pushed northward from central Mexico and founded settlements in modern-day Tamaulipas, Nuevo Leon, Coahuila, Chihuahua, Sonora, Texas, New Mexico, Arizona, and California. Isolation and a harsh environment shaped a way of life in the north different from that found in the core of New Spain. A spirit of independence developed throughout El Norte, and eventually political drift contributed to the separation from Mexico of what is now the American Southwest. Mexicans in Texas and California in particular felt neglected by the government in Mexico City, and that discontent played well into the hands of Anglo-American expansionists who wanted the far northern Mexican frontier incorporated into the United States.

With the signing of the Treaty of Guadalupe Hidalgo in 1848, the Mexican north was split in two, approximately half remaining in Mexico and the other half going to the United States. Thereafter, each subregion belonged to a separate political system, but the economic and cultural interaction that had existed before continued to grow despite the presence of an international boundary.

American investors soon discovered numerous business opportunities in the Mexican border region. Chihuahua and Sonora in particular lured foreigners into mining, ranching, and agricultural ventures. In the latter state, the Cananea Consolidated Copper Company and the Sonora Land and Cattle Company had a substantial hold on the local economy and influenced politics as well. American railroad companies such as the Mexican Central Railroad built important lines intended to link the mining and ranching areas of northern Mexico to processing centers and consumer markets in the United States. After 1876, U.S. entrepreneurs were particularly favored in their activities by President Porfirio Díaz, who felt that Mexico's modernization hinged on the country's ability to attract capital from abroad. In 1910, on the eve of Díaz's fall from office, about one-fourth of the U.S. capital invested in Mexico was concentrated in Coahuila, Nuevo Leon, Chihuahua, and Sonora.

The dependence of the Mexican border region on the United States at the turn of the century is well illustrated by the presence of the Zona Libre, or Free-Trade Zone, in the border cities. Free trade had existed in certain communities after 1858, but President Díaz extended this privilege along the entire border in 1885, pleasing *fronterizos* who had lobbied for official recognition of their unique needs. The ability to import foreign goods duty free became a necessity on the Mexican side because of the heavy burden borne by border residents who had to pay high tariffs on many basic U.S. commodities that they needed for daily living, and that the Mexican economy could not supply because of great distances between the nation's production centers and the northern frontier.[6]

While it lasted, the Zona Libre stimulated significant commercial activity in the Mexican border communities, but it also created considerable resentment within Mexico because it was seen as a detriment to the growth of native industries and an unwarranted special favor to one part of the nation. The Mexican government finally eliminated the Zona Libre in 1905, justifying its action on the ground that the railroad system in the country now reached most of the border region. *Fronterizos* protested the action, however, arguing that even with modern transportation their needs could not be supplied by their own nation, and their cost of living would necessarily increase as they continued to consume foreign goods no longer exempted from import duties. American merchants welcomed the elimination of the Zona Libre, for they had long complained, with some justification, that it created unfair competition for them and stimulated smuggling into the United States.

The 1920s accentuated the external orientation of the Mexican border region as Prohibition in the United States drove Americans into Mexico in search of liquor and other vices not readily available north of the boundary. Tourism flourished all along the border, but especially in Ciudad Juárez and Tijuana, where both ordinary and famous *norteamericanos* found bars, casinos, cabarets, racetracks, and other establishments ready to satisfy their needs for recreation and entertainment. The Great Depression and the end of Prohibition in 1933 temporarily terminated the tourist boom along the border, but this activity resurfaced with renewed vigor during the World War II and the Korean War years. Millions of U.S. soldiers regularly patronized the border nocturnal centers, while other Americans visited more traditional tourist attractions. Unsavory entertainments that catered heavily to foreigners tarnished the reputation, within Mexico and in the United States, of the Mexican border cities—giving rise to the epithets "Gomorrah City," "New Sodom," "Sin City," and "Center of Prostitution" to refer, for example, to Ciudad Juárez.[7]

In recent decades the traditional interdependence between the two sides has increased dramatically. The most important cause of that expanded integration has been the U.S. demand for Mexican labor. During World War II, the two nations initiated a labor exchange known as the Bracero Program, allowing millions of Mexican *campesinos* to work in U.S. agriculture under contract with employers. At the same time, millions of undocumented peasants crossed the border to satisfy the tremendous needs for cheap labor that existed in both the rural and urban American economy. The pattern of large-scale Mexican immigration into the Southwest that began in the 1940s has continued into the present. Despite the passage in 1986 of the Simpson-Rodino law to curtail the migration from Mexico, undocumented migrants continue to cross the border in support of an underground labor system in the borderlands that is so institutionalized and profitable that it is questionable whether laws will significantly alter the migration.

Another contemporary manifestation of transborder interdependence is the pronounced trade between both sides. U.S. border cities such as Laredo and El Paso are heavily dependent on Mexican consumers from directly across the border as well as from interior points in Mexico. The special "rapid" train that runs daily from Chihuahua City to Ciudad Juárez (a four-hour ride) is a dramatic example of the magnetism that El Paso has for Chihuahua City residents who like to buy American products. Apparently the Chihuahua City-Ciudad Juárez *rápido* was created especially for Chihuahuense shoppers who could arrive at the border by eleven in the morning, do their shopping in El Paso, and begin their return trip home at six in the evening. The heavy dependence of American border cities on Mexican shoppers has been demonstrated most dramatically by the decline in business following devaluations of Mexican currency, particularly in 1976 and 1982, when the worst declines in Mexican buying power took place.

Just as the American border cities depend on Mexican shoppers and tourists, so do the Mexican cities depend on Americans. The importance of the American trade is illustrated by the establishment in the 1960s of the Programa Nacional Fronterizo (PRONAF), a government initiative that had as a central goal the physical improvement of the Mexican border cities in order to make them more attractive to foreign visitors. Today millions of Americans continue to visit Ciudad Juárez, Tijuana, and other border cities in search of bargains or entertainment, generating employment for large numbers of border workers. In addition to luring more foreign tourists, the PRONAF also sought to make more national goods available to the local clientele, thereby lessening the need for border Mexicans to shop on the American side.

The current economic interdependence at the border is also evidenced by the Border Industrialization Program (BIP), which consists of foreign-owned assembly plants located in the Mexican borderlands, most of them directly on the border. Many factories have tandem operations on the American side, making the program binational in nature. The BIP began in 1965 at a time of great unemployment along the border because of the end of the Bracero Program, which left many former *braceros* stranded in border cities. This presence of abundant and inexpensive labor close to the United Sates attracted countless American multinational companies as well Japanese and other foreign firms to locate in Mexico. By the late 1980s hundreds of assembly plants employed over 250,000 Mexican workers. The program has become so vital for Mexico that it now is the second most important generator of foreign exchange, behind oil and ahead of tourism.[8]

The economic integration found in the binational borderlands has often been a source of tension between the border communities on both sides and their respective central governments. Underlying that tension is the pronounced transboundary regionalism that has frequently caused borderlanders to resist national policies that are deemed detrimental to local needs, which are seen as fundamentally different from the needs of interior zones free of the special effects of international interaction. The consistency of the core-periphery conflict over time springs to a significant degree from the remoteness of the borderlands from the major population centers of each nation. By nature, frontiers far removed from the core develop strong regionalistic tendencies, and border frontiers carry that tradition even further because of the bonds that often develop with foreigners.[9]

The opposition of borderlanders to policies and laws formulated in faraway places by decision makers uninformed about or insensitive to regional needs is long established in the U.S.-Mexican borderlands. Such conflict is a classic manifestation of the friction universally found between border zones and core areas. Borderlanders deeply resent centralized actions that are seen as unfavorable to local growth and progress. Their view of the border, and the function that it is supposed to serve, differs fundamentally from the perceptions of those in the interior. While the core population views the border as a barrier to foreign "intrusion" and "contamination," borderlanders see their destinies as intrinsically joined with the people from "the other side." That "deviation" is a constant irritant to those who bear responsibility for governing the nation as a whole. In the eyes of central governments, borderlanders too often place their regional loyalties above the national interest.

Indeed, many examples can be found of participation by borderlanders in movements for greater political autonomy and less economic interference from the central government. Self-assertive regionalism is a well-known cause in Latin America for the political fragmentation of many nations. Of course, the United Sates has not been immune to problems of sectionalism, having suffered through a civil war in the nineteenth century that seriously threatened the future development of a large and powerful nation. And although U.S. sectional frictions subsided sufficiently to prevent future threats to national unity, regionalism has continued to play a major role in the modern history of the country.

In the case of the Mexican border region, the underdeveloped condition of this part of Mexico and the advanced economy of the region to the north of the boundary has created a particularly strong orientation toward the United States and has weakened the links with the rest of Mexican society. This has caused tremendous concern in Mexico City that "de-Mexicanization" is rampant on the northern frontier.[10]

The "drift" of the Mexican border region toward the exterior is an important consideration in understanding Mexico's loss of half of its national territory to the United States. It also played a significant role in the Mexican Revolution of 1910–17, in the sense that independent-minded *norteños*, with their lower tolerance for dictatorial government, led that revolutionary struggle and subsequently shaped the creation of a new national political and economic sytem. In the 1980s, the *norteños* have once again forcefully expressed their spirit of independence by giving unprecedented support to the Partido Acción Nacional (PAN), the principal political opposition party in the country. Recent PAN victories in Chihuahua in particular prompted the Partido Revolucionario Institucional (PRI), the ruling party for almost six decades, to engage in massive electoral fraud in 1986 to retain shaky gubernatorial seats in the northern states and to recapture congressional, legislative, and municipal offices lost in 1983 and 1985.

The current political controversy south of the border is an extension of the economic crisis that has gripped Mexico since 1982, when the drop in oil prices sent the economy into a tailspin. Many Mexicans are unhappy with an electoral process that makes the PRI virtually invincible, and nowhere is that discontent greater than in the north, where the crisis has severely hurt large sectors of the population linked in a variety of ways to the dollar economy. With the catastrophic devaluation of the peso, many *norteños* have seen their standard of living plummet. In previous years, *norteños* have tolerated government inefficiency, corruption, and even one-party rule, but personal economic devastation has changed all that, and today they seek to bring about fundamental reforms in the country.

Just as the Mexican borderlands have experienced alienation from the interior of the country, the American borderlands likewise have felt estranged from the American mainstream society. Throughout the nineteenth and early twentieth centuries, the U.S. border region functioned as perhaps the most exploited zone in a giant internal colony made up of the southern and western portions of the United States, which found themselves dominated by the northeastern states. With little capital of their own to promote development, the borderlands provided raw materials and cheap labor for the benefit of eastern capitalists and received expensive manufactured goods in return.[11]

Important economic changes, however, began to take place in the American borderlands during the World War II period, when military necessity spurred the U.S. government to invest heavily in defense installations throughout the West. Fortunately for the border region, the government spending extended also to infrastructural projects such as modern highways, stimulating the development of new industries, population growth, and increased urbanization. In the 1960s and 1970s another major trend in the United States helped the American borderlands to grow and progress. Strong international economic competition began to drive U.S. industries from the high-wage parts of the country to the low-wage "Sunbelt," initiating a boom for the Southwest. As the region having the lowest domestic wages and one of the warmest climates in the nation, while furthermore enjoying proximity to Mexico and that country's huge labor pools and rock-bottom wage rates, the U.S. borderlands quickly expanded their economic base.

Thus in the 1980s the U.S. border region, along with the rest of the West and the South, found itself increasingly in the mainstream of U.S. economic life. Yet many of the old "colonial" structures remained in place in a region that was still underindustrialized and still supplying raw materials and cheap labor for other parts of the nation. Old resentments against the dominant Northeast still lingered in the borderlands.

One of the long-standing conflicts between the border region and the U.S. government centers on immigration policy. Historically, Washington has opened the border to Mexican workers when demand for their labor has been high in the United States. But when demand has dropped or political pressures against foreign workers have mounted, policymakers have scrambled to close the border. That fluctuating approach to policy has damaged the border economy and elicited loud and repeated criticism of the Immigration and Naturalization Service (INS). In late 1974 and early 1975, for example, merchants and leaders from El Paso complained bitterly about rigid inspections and "interrogations" conducted by the INS at the international bridges, which interrupted the normally heavy flow of traffic. Politicians and community activists in Ciudad Juárez also protested the INS tactics, pointing out that tourism in *their* city had been harmed and that many Mexicans attempting to cross into El Paso had been subjected to humiliating searches and insults. In 1979 the INS created an international incident at the bridges when it conducted a "crackdown" against Mexican women suspected of unlawfully using local crossing cards to work in El Paso. Mexican protestors, who had the sympathy of many El Pasoans who objected to the INS actions, took over the bridges and shut down traffic for two days.[12]

During the prolonged debate over the Immigration Reform and Control Act, known popularly as the Simpson-Rodino law, U.S. border residents vociferously made known their opposition to any legislation that would bring economic harm to the region or result in discrimination against American Hispanics. Some local leaders, who felt ignored by Washington, pointed out that the federal government did not understand the peculiariates of the border region and therefore could not pass a good immigration law. Employers, in particular, objected to interruptions in the supply of Mexican workers to which they had long been accustomed. After the passage of the landmark Simpson-Rodino law in 1986, those borderlanders opposed to immigration restrictions resigned themselves to playing a waiting game, convinced that employer sanctions and other parts of the law were doomed to failure, and that the federal government would be forced to amend the law in such a way that the traditional system of border labor exchange—both documented and undocumented—would be preserved in the long run.

A related issue that underscores the border dissatisfaction with policies made in Washington is the handling of the drug-smuggling problem. In the early 1980s U.S. borderlanders with close links to Mexicans became upset with the "bashing" of Mexico in the White House, in Congress, and in the media. Tensions that ensue between the two nations as a result of verbal sparring are seen as interfering with the normally amicable relations along the border. Americans who do business in Mexico sometimes find themselves uncomfortably explaining Washington's actions regarding the drug issue or even apologizing for offensive statements made about the Mexican government by U.S. national leaders.

The greatest irritant for border residents pertaining to the drug problem is the periodic imposition by the U.S. Customs Service of rigid inspections at the international crossings. For example, in 1969 the Nixon administration conducted "Operation Intercept" along the border, hoping to stop the drug flow. For a month, inspectors subjected border crossers to painstaking searches that stalled vehicular traffic and halted border trade. Business and tourism eventually recovered from the trauma imposed by Washington, but resentment and bitterness remained alive along the border for many years. In 1985 the U.S. government once again ordered tight inspections at the international crossings following the murder in Mexico of an American drug agent. Predictably, business transactions took a sharp dive, and many borderlanders protested the resulting inconveniences. In Ciudad Juárez, community leaders organized a campaign known as "Operación Respeto" (Operation Respect), which encouraged Mexicans not to go to the United States because of the perceived American insults against their country. It appears that apart from the agent's death and Washington's perception of noncooperation from Mexico in solving the drug problem, the Reagan administration also used the pressure at the border to "encourage" Mexico to change its Central American policy to conform closer to that of the United States.

Another aspect of the core-periphery theme is the inattention often felt by isolated frontiers when public resources are distributed by the nation-state or by provincial representatives of the central government. In the case of the Mexican border region, a constant complaint in communities such as Ciudad Juárez has been that the state and federal governments have not treated the border citizenry fairly with respect to resource allocation. Especially loud complaints have been heard during those periods when the border cities have generated large dollar earnings from their tourist activities, only to have the government take excessive amounts in taxes that seldom return to the border.

In the 1960s, however, the Mexican border communities witnessed a reversal of the traditional policy of neglect when Mexico City made large investments in the region under the Programa Nacional Fronterizo. Public works proliferated as the government sought to make the region more attractive to foreigners. Thus *fronterizos* derived substantial benefits from the construction of roads, highways, buildings, shopping centers, museums, theaters, and other public facilities. Two decades later Mexico City decided once again to make physical improvements along the border as a way of retaining the political support of *fronterizos* who had drifted in large numbers into the opposition camp of the Partido Accion Nacional. The renewed interest in the border on the part of the federal government has benefited Ciudad Juárez in particular, since this is the principal stronghold of the political opposition in the nation.

Pronounced governmental centralization in Mexico complicates the task of obtaining public resources for the Mexican border area, while in the United States greater local control over certain taxes gives American borderlanders more opportunities to raise revenues to improve their communities. Just the same, the U.S. border cities also depend heavily on state and federal expenditures, as well as on state and federal officials whom the borderlanders often consider insufficiently responsive to the needs of the border region. For example, Texas border counties consistently rank at the bottom of economically depressed areas in the United States: unemployment is high; educational achievements are low; health is poor; and the living conditions among the poverty stricken resemble what is found in developing nations. Of course, the government is not solely responsible for the underdevelopment of the border region; other important factors that have caused economic retardation include the remoteness of the area, inherent local disadvantages for attracting high-wage industry, and large numbers of poor migrants from the interior of Mexico. Nevertheless, many Texas borderlanders feel that official disregard for their problems, both at the federal and state levels, is a major cause of underdevelopment.

Border *Tejanos* (Mexican-American Texans) often point to education policy in Texas to support their view that they have not received their fair share of public revenues. In the early 1980s several border school districts brought a joint suit against the state over the distribution of funds, arguing that the formula in use discriminated against poor districts. In 1987, Judge Harley Clark of the state district court in Austin agreed with the plaintiffs, declaring the state's school financing system unconstitutional.[13]

Higher education constitutes another arena in which Texas border residents feel unfairly treated. Frustrated by the seeming impossibility of bringing about reforms through the legislative process, in late 1987 Mexican-American politicians and important community organizations such as the League of United Latin American Citizens and the G.I. Forum joined the Mexican American Legal Defense and Educational Fund in filing a wide-ranging lawsuit against the state, charging that the current public university and college system discriminates against Hispanics.[14]

Under the present arrangement, the universities that serve the border population are funded at much lower levels than universities in other parts of the state, and the number of academic programs offered is also lower. Universities in the border region are allowed to have only the most basic baccalaureate and masters programs. Texas A&I University and the University of Texas at El Paso have a single doctoral program each, but in both cases these programs are highly specialized: the Texas A&I program in bilingual education, the El Paso program in geology. Mainstream doctoral and professional programs—including law and medicine—are found nowhere in the border region. Since the funding formula used by the state heavily favors universities with doctoral and professional programs, the consequence of the border universities is that they are forced to operate on "survival" budgets, even in the best of times. During lean years, the border universities are forced to cut back on basic programs, further reducing already limited opportunities for border students.[15]

In effect, the system of public higher education in Texas resembles Third World structures designed to generously channel resources and services to core areas, while seriously neglecting outlying regions. Public and private resources available to Texas for higher education are heavily concentrated at the University of Texas at Austin and Texas A&M University, the two flagship universities in the state. By constitutional mandate, these institutions have privileged access to the Permanent University Fund, annually drawing millions of dollars denied to other institutions to enrich their academic programs. By virtue of their comprehensive program offerings, the University of Texas at Austin and Texas A&M University attract massive numbers of students, yielding profitable credit-hour production that greatly increases the public funds allocated to each university. At the same time, the underdeveloped status of the border universities causes many local students, often at considerable sacrifice, to go elsewhere; moreover, the limited academic offerings attract few students from out of state to the border universities. The result is that universities like the University of Texas at El Paso, Texas A&I University, and Pan American University constantly struggle to maintain the enrollments necessary for minimally acceptable state funding.

The self-determination that borderlanders demand from the nation-state springs from a deep belief in the right to conduct transborder relationships and to practice cultural traditions particular to the region without impediments from the government or the dominant society. These convictions are so strongly held that borderlanders routinely ignore, circumvent, or otherwise deviate from national laws that erect barriers to the way of life to which they are accustomed.

Smuggling is one of the best examples of an activity that appears to be universally sanctioned in border areas. Products smuggled across the line range from groceries to electronic products and drugs. Most borderlanders occasionally take part in this surreptitious game. Significant numbers make a lifelong habit of it. Many make their living from it. Cognizant that such activity cannot be stopped, governments attempt to regulate smuggling by maintaining a highly visible presence at the ports of entry and by conducting periodic, well-publicized campaigns to "eliminate" smuggling. When authorities succeed in drawing attention to the problem, smuggling does in fact subside for short periods, but eventually the illegal practice returns to normal levels.

Another example of "deviant" behavior among many borderlanders is their hiring of undocumented aliens. In the case of the U.S.-Mexico border, Americans have historically hired illegal Mexican workers in great numbers. In many cases, borderlanders who are otherwise law-abiding citizens even assist undocumented workers in crossing the border or protect them from the Border Patrol during their stay in the United States. How can usually upstanding citizens engage in such illegal activity? The answer is to be found in their understanding of international migration, whether legal or illegal, as historically normal, economically beneficial, and therefore culturally and morally acceptable.

Among the immigrants themselves there is general awareness that they have broken the laws of the United States when they cross the border without proper documentation. Yet immigrants are driven by a higher, desperate need to survive economically. Moreover, they are fully aware that American employers and consumers alike desire Mexican labor, since they derive significant benefits because low wages keep prices low for such products as fruits and vegetables, while also making a host of services affordable. At the same time, the heavy presence of Hispanics in the U.S. borderlands makes the immigrants feel "close" to home. The historical awareness that the American Southwest was once Mexican territory also lessens the perceptions that immigrants might otherwise have of themselves as "intruders" in a foreign land.[16]

What distinguishes borderlanders from the rest of the citizenry is the effect of the boundary on their daily lives. On the one hand, the border is a barrier that limits activity and hinders movement, but, on the other, it offers tremendous opportunities to benefit from proximity to another nation. Vast differences in wealth between the American side and the Mexican side and heavy demand for each other's goods and services offer ideal conditions for the law of comparative advantage to be put to profitable use. For those with entrepreneurial instincts and skills, potential gains from conducting transborder operations range from moderate to extraordinary. When such opportunities to profit exist, local people will find ways to take advantage of them, and officials may frequently also collaborate. Together they will devise a mutually acceptable system that facilitates relatively unobstructed exchange across the boundary. That understanding between the authorities and the citizenry is a part of the human psychology of the border.

The preceding paragraphs underscore the desirability of using an interdisciplinary approach for conducting border research. Yet relatively few scholars possess the necessary tools to examine border phenomena from perspectives other than those inherent in their own disciplines. Historians and social scientists would do well to consider using techniques and sources common to such fields as literature, folklore, and music. With creativity such themes as interdependency, conflict, and unconventional behavior can be richly illustrated with perspectives from novels, short stories, poetry, and ballads—resulting in engaging, vivid, and interesting portrayals of border life.

In addition to interdisciplinarity, border research often requires knowledge of different languages, cultures, and national traditions, not to mention an ability to work effectively in different bureaucratic systems. The discussion that follows draws upon experiences encountered in the U.S.-Mexican borderlands to illustrate common challenges faced by border researchers.

At the initial stage of any project pertaining to the U.S.-Mexican borderlands, the researcher finds few published background studies that treat both sides of the boundary as an integrated geographical entity. This is explained by the practice followed by most scholars of stopping their investigations at the border, either because the "other side" is outside—sometimes artificially outside—the geographic limits placed on the studies, or because they cannot conduct research in another language, or because they know little about the neighboring country. Consequentially, many published works are incomplete, parochial, and ethnocentric.

A related problem is the difficulty in finding source materials on the Mexican side of the border. Research is much easier on the U.S. side because the published literature and collections of archival materials are more abundant than on the Mexican side and the libraries better. The Mexican side lacks resources to maintain and make available basic research materials, although in recent years Mexican institutions have started to rectify this problem. On topics pertaining to the Mexican borderlands the researcher is, however, well advised to spend some time in Mexico City, where national libraries, private research centers, and government agencies may have as much information as is to be found in the border region itself.

Researchers who use statistics are seriously thwarted by the lack of uniformity and comparability in the data that are available. There is little coordination by the two sides in the conceptualization or the collection process and in the presentation of the data. Census data, for example, yield few opportunities for making direct comparisons between one side of the border and the other. Consequently, researchers can only present part of the reality of the border. Little possibility exists that the two nations will coordinate their data-gathering activities along the border because each government collects information for its own purposes; cooperation is also impeded by strong nationalistic feelings on both sides.

Obtaining access to data is always a problem if the researcher is investigating a sensitive topic—and there are many of those along the border. And even if sensitivity is not at issue, on the Mexican side the absence of research facilities and the presence of bureaucratic obstacles frustrate scholars. The difficulty of research south of the Rio Grande can be overcome to some extent by working cooperatively with Mexican scholars who are closer to the data sources and who know their own country's bureaucracy much better. This consideration as well as other advantages springing from transborder cooperation have led a number of U.S. and Mexican institutions to undertake joint border projects.

Another area of concern is that it is very rare to find studies of the U.S.-Mexican borderlands that take into account how the research findings on this region relate to work done in other border areas of the world. Little attempt has been made to compare our borderlands with borderlands elsewhere. If this approach were followed by even a handful of scholars, perhaps we would be in a better position to generalize about the functioning of borders in the modern world. In the relative absence of such comparative research, we in the United States and Mexico will continue to examine our borderlands through a parochial lens, in isolation from other parts of the world.

The following examples can be cited to illustrate the shortcomings in the way border research is conducted, and the consequent incomplete understanding of the region.

The lack of binational research makes it difficult for scholars to describe in precise terms the distinctiveness of the borderlands as an entity. Economic and cultural interpenetration in both directions is easily observed, but empirical measures of cross-border influences are lacking. Many examples given in this paper are drawn from the historical record and from the author's observation of border behavior. It would be preferable to have a body of literature and/or a large collection of raw data to draw from to construct a more complete picture of what borderlands "binationality" really means. How deep into the interior of each nation does that binationality extend? Why? To what extent is it shaped by the geography of oceans, rivers, mountains, and desert?

An example of a topic where a binational approach would be very fruitful is the condition of the Mexican-origin population in the borderlands. Existing studies of Chicanos, or Mexican Americans, incorporate little information about the impact of the Mexican side on their lives. Similarly, studies of the Mexican border population have failed to establish links with conditions on the U.S. side. It is widely assumed that the relationship between these two groups is significant, but the nature of those ties remains largely unexplored, even in individual disciplines.

A related question that begs for more research is the extent of the cultural and economic differences between the two border regions and their corresponding heartlands. Specifically, what is it that sets apart these border zones from their core areas? How far inward to the unique features of the border areas extend? What are these features?

As indicated earlier, the interests of the border population often clash with those of the central governments on both sides. While the essence of this phenomenon can be demonstrated without much difficulty, we do not know the degree of that conflict, or precisely what characteristics it assumes. To better understand intrinsic core-periphery tension, questions such as the following need to be addressed: Precisely how do the interests of interior populations differ from those of borderlanders? Does each government have a clear and consistent policy toward its own border area? What is the process by which decisions are made concerning issues that directly affect the border population? What exactly is the role that borderlands play in the formulation of those decisions?

By examining a few selected topics related to the U.S.-Mexican borderlands, this paper has sought to illustrate that binational border zones possess special qualities not found in interior regions of nation-states. The uniqueness of a binational region lies in the international processes and relationships that link populations on both sides of the dividing line. Thus the research strategies and methodologies are necessarily different for binational border researchers than for scholars who do not have to contend with the variable of internationality.

The universality of border phenomena offers opportunities for versatile researchers to pursue comparative studies that would further our understanding of border functions and impacts on local populations as well as on nation-states. For example, the migration experience between Mexico and the United Sates might be compared to that of Colombia and Venezuela, where undocumented migration has also been a source of contention for many years. American economic and cultural influences on the Mexican border region might be compared to what the Canadian border zone has experienced. Both Mexicans and Canadians have expressed alarm over the

American presence in their countries, and it would be instructive indeed to examine how each nation has sought to counteract such foreign influences.

In short, much can be learned about the phenomenon of regionalism through the study of areas that abut international boundaries. Such research is especially significant in an age in which the world economy has become increasingly integrated, and in which spectacular breakthroughs in transportation and communication have brought even distant nations ever closer together.

Notes

1. See Herbert E. Bolton, *The Spanish Borderlands: A Chronicle of Old Florida and the Southwest* (New Haven, Conn.: Yale University Press, 1921). A more recent overview of early borderlands history is John Francis Bannon, *The Spanish Borderlands Frontier, 1513–1821* (Albuquerque: University of New Mexico Press, 1974). The most comprehensive guide to borderlands issues and scholarly literature is Ellwyn R. Stoddard, Richard L. Nostrand, and Jonathan P. West, eds., *Borderlands Sourcebook: A Guide to the Literature on Northern Mexico and the American Southwest* (Norman: University of Oklahoma Press, 1983).

2. The uniqueness of the northern frontier in early Mexican history is discussed in Miguel Leon-Portilla, "The Norteño Variety of Mexican Culture: An Ethnohistorical Approach," in *Plural Society in the Southwest,* ed. Edward H. Spicer and Raymond H. Thompson (New York: Weatherhead Foundation, 1972), pp. 77–114.

3. Oscar J. Martínez, *Troublesome Border* (Tucson: University of Arizona Press, 1988), pp. 106–23.

4. J.Frank Dobie, *Guide to Life and Literature of the Southwest* (Dallas, Tex.: Southern Methodist University Press, 1952), pp. 13–14.

5. The idea that the border extends far into the interior of the United States and into Mexico is frequently stated by speakers at academic conferences, yet serious studies are lacking to demonstrate precisely how the border can reach so far.

6. Samuel E. Bell and James M. Smallwood, *The Zona Libre 1858–1905: A Problem in American Diplomacy,* Southwestern Studies Monograph No. 69 (El Paso: Texas Western Press, 1982).

7. Such epithets appear frequently in contemporary newspaper and magazine articles on both sides of the border.

8.   The Border Industrialization Program has generated considerable controversy both in Mexico and the United States because of its overwhelming reliance on cheap labor, especially female workers, to carry on assembly operations. See Ellwyn R. Stoddard, *Maquila: Assembly Plants in Northern Mexico* (El Paso: Texas Western Press, 1987).

9.   K.D. Kristof, "The Nature of Frontiers and Boundaries," *Annals of the Association of American Geographers* 4 (1959): 271–73; and Owen D. Lattimore, "The Frontier in History," in *Theory in Anthropology: A Sourcebook,* ed. Robert A. Manners and David Kaplaw (Chicago, Ill.: Aldine, 1968), p. 374.

10.   The government's concern over "de-Mexicanization" is illustrated by the creation in the 1970s of the National Commission for the Defense of the Spanish Language. Much of the commission's work has been concentrated in the border region.

11.   Analyses of how the northeastern United States dominated the southwestern parts of the country are found in Walter Prescott Webb, *Divided We Stand: The Crisis of a Frontierless Democracy* (Austin, Tex.: The Acorn Press, 1944); and Avrahm G. Mezerik, *The Revolt of the South and West* (New York: Duell, Sloan and Pierce, 1946).

12.   Martinez, *Troublesome Border,* pp. 133–34.

13.   *MALDEF Newsletter* (Fall, 1987), p. 3.

14.   *New York Times,* Dec. 4, 1987.

15.   See the *Findings and Recommendations of the Mexican-American Task Force on Higher Education to the Select Committee on Higher Education* (Edinburg, Tex.: Sept., 1986).

16.   The perceptions attributed to undocumented workers are based on field studies of immigration issues and illegal migration.

11 A Subregion:
The Upper Cumberland
Lynwood Montell

Regionalism is not a twentieth-century phenomenon. Regional awareness has been a part of American consciousness since before the Revolutionary War. At the Continental Congress of 1774, delegates spontaneously used such terms as *southern, middle, eastern,* and *New England* colonies. When the Constitution was drawn up, regional interests were served in the manner in which representation was fixed, export duties were banned, and the importation of slaves was provided for. Colonial settlement patterns, the journey westward across the continent, slavery and the sectional conflict, the distribution of natural resources, immigration, industrialization, urbanization, and geography all have helped to shape the cultural character of the American landscape. Broad regions, distinctive in one way or another, have resulted.[1] The process of regionalization continued apace until the last frontier—the Dry Farming Frontier—came to an end in the 1920s.[2] As pioneers traversed the American continent by ox team and wagon, by raft, flatboat, and steamboat, by railroad and on foot, they became acutely aware of geographic differences. They learned that to survive, they must recognize and adapt to the crucial differences in forest, swamp, plains, desert, and even the unfamiliar streets of giant cities that were all too often as hostile to immigrants and migrants as the worst snowstorm in Nebraska. By the time the continent was spanned, a spate of new regions had emerged: a Midwest, Great Plains, Southwest, Intermountain Basin, and Pacific Northwest were added to the nation's vocabulary and awareness as companions to the regions of the colonial period.

While such terms as *district, division, territory, section,* and *region* were and still are often used by planners to identify geographical groupings of states and counties, the terms *region* and *subregion* are now most frequently employed when the general population, scholars included, wish to identify a physical place. Often, such identification calls up fond memories, and memories evoke emotional responses to home and to the land itself. Louis Wirth recognized this aspect of regionalism as a state of mind, a way of life, a mode of collective consciousness, a social movement, and even a cult. Such a state of mind emerges, Wirth feels, to eventually produce a settled way of life, a characteristic consciousness, a sense of mutual interdependence, and a sense of common belonging.[3]

Wirth's characterizations implicitly point to a shared set of traits as the basis for defining a region's boundaries. Rupert Vance, in "The Regional Concept as a Tool for Social Research," contends that regional viability rests on a region's explicit differences from surrounding regions. Further, he feels that a "mode of homogeneous characteristics is absolutely essential if it [the region] is to possess [and maintain] identity."[4] But not even the Old South, with the dominance of the plantation system from Baltimore to Waco, could lay claim to homogeneity in the sense that Vance wrote about. Nor does the New South possess a core of characteristics that totally set it apart from neighboring regions. The southern Appalachians, for instance, have little in common with the "Chemical Coast" of Texas and Louisiana. And the Mississippi Delta between Memphis and Vicksburg has little cultural or economic affinity with the greater Atlanta megalopolis.

While I argue against regional homogeneity on the basis of economic, administrative, and political grounds, I do contend, with Louis Wirth, that there is a state of mind made possible by a composite of physical, cultural, and economic forces that molds southerners from Richmond to Houston, and Louisville to Miami, into a mental unity.

It is this state of mind that caused the poor white dirt farmer of northern Georgia to fight elbow to elbow at Shiloh with his aristocrat brother from the largest plantation along the Mobile River. It is this same state of mind that causes southerners enrolled at northern universities to feel culturally inferior to their Yankee counterpart, or, in some cases, totally exasperated with the northern mind set. Let me demonstrate the latter by quoting, in part, from an essay written by a Kentuckian when he was a graduate student at the University of Notre Dame in 1986:

Senior Bar, early last semester. A song, written by a man with a limited vocabulary, pulsates the air. Around me, Bacchus pursued elusive Aphrodite. Hormones, stirred from a light sleep, were asked to dance.

A friend and I leaned on the railing that forms a "u" around the dance floor. We talked of the value of intensity of effort. We made plans. We sparred with the future.

Two women approached. They weren't typical Notre Dame women. They weren't cute Catholics wearing color-coordinated clothes. One had coal-colored hair and wore new jeans and a sensitive smile. They asked us to dance. The request was innocent, but aggressive. My friend said "yes" with a firm voice. I said "yes" with wide eyes.

So I danced with the woman with happenstance hair—for a while. But, then, I spoke. I said only my name. But, as I am so often told at Notre Dame, I "have a Southern accent." (I must have drawn out the "i" in Gibson.)

Miss Happenstance Hair became confused. She decided to research the problem. "Just where are you from?" she asked. "Bowling Green, Kentucky," I replied.

The transformation began. Her step, once sprightly, slowed. Her smile, once sensitive, soured. I watched a rerun of the Beverly Hillbillies in her eyes. We finished a dance of obligation. We danced no more.[5]

To this point our thoughts have largely been focused on region as a composite state of mind, a mode of collective consciousness. Used in this sense, region—a physical place defined in mental constructs—may cover a large, rather amorphous area (such as the South or Midwest), or it may be a much smaller area. Poet and novelist Wendell Berry wrote of the difficulty of defining *region* in the larger sense. "In thinking about myself as a writer whose work and whose life have been largely formed in relation to one place," he mused. "I am often in the neighborhood of the word 'regional.' I find that the term very quickly becomes either an embarrassment or an obstruction," Berry continued, "for I do not know any word that is more sloppily defined in its usage, or more casually understood."[6] Berry concludes that regionalism is "local life aware of itself."[7]

The definitions supplied by Berry, Wirth, Vance, and others point out difficulties in attempting to define *region* and *regionalism* to the satisfaction of all concerned. The problem arises, it seems to me, due to the rather amorphous nature of large regions. On the following pages, I hope to demonstrate that, from the viewpoint of regional culture, that the most meaningful geographical units for scholarly investigations are subregions or folk culture areas.

I would like to illustrate the notion of a subregion by using the Upper Cumberland area of Kentucky and Tennessee as a case in point. This is both my childhood home and the focus of my research efforts since my introduction to subregional studies while I was a graduate student at Indiana University in the early 1960s.

Already interested in interdisciplinary approaches to understanding culture, I was pursuing a field of study in cultural geography to complement my interests in history and folklife studies. It was the spring term 1963; the professor was Carl O. Sauer himself. Excitement was in the air. I felt like the Apostle Paul sitting at the feet of Gamaliel, much as the many students who studied under Frederick Jackson Turner at the University of Michigan must have felt. Forty years earlier, Sauer had accompanied a small group of his students to Kentucky's Eastern Pennyroyal region to document the cultural landscape there. Their efforts were published in 1927 under the title *Geography of the Pennyroyal*.[8]

Unfortunately, this model study went largely unnoticed and passed into relative obscurity soon afterward. At Indiana in 1963, Sauer, then well into his retirement years, discussed that earlier Kentucky study and charged those of us in the seminar with the words, "If I had my academic years to live over, I'd select a small geographical area—a subregion—go there and document everything in the cultural landscape—buildings, settlement patterns, cropping practices, fences, roads and the like. Every fifteen years I'd go back to observe and record the changes that have taken place, then attempt to answer the question, 'Why?' "

Following Sauer's challenge, I chose to concentrate my attention on a small portion of the upper South, mainly because of its near proximity to Campbellsville College, where I taught and served as academic dean from 1963 to 1969, and to Western Kentucky University, where I have been since that time. This geographic area is now known, hopefully, to the academic and lay reading public as the Upper Cumberland.

Although the Upper Cumberland is located along the western margin of Appalachia, I am not an Appalachianist. I have no political axes to grind and I am not involved in social and economic reform. My commitment to regional studies per se is fixed to the extent that if I lived in another part of the country, I would outline the surrounding folk cultural area and spend considerable time investigating it.

But to say that I have no emotional attachment to the Upper Cumberland would be false and misleading. My research interests have centered on this area not only out of convenience and my commitment to regional studies, but because of personal identification with the Upper Cumberland. I was born on the extreme western edge of Kentucky's Upper Cumberland, and I continue to have a strong feeling of loyalty to and identification with the area. That's where I was born and that's where I will be buried among six generations of my ancestors. I can show you the spot designated as my final resting place. Some people do not understand this strong compulsion to be buried with prior generations. As I pointed out my burial plot and tried to explain this decision to a graduate student in 1976, she blurted out, "How can you bear to talk about your death and burial? That just freaks me out!"

I mention my personal background because I wish to show how the experience of growing up in the Upper Cumberland helped to mold my scholarly career. My family got its first battery-powered radio in 1938, when I was seven years old. We had to use battery sets, as there was no electricity to be had until 1947 for those of us who lived more than one mile from the main road. Once we got that first radio, it was placed in the kitchen, where essentially all family social activities took place. Our life-style changed significantly. No longer did I stop on the way home from school to let Dewey Wright's cows out through the rails of the fence that I prankishly disassembled twice daily. Instead, I ran the two miles from school each day to get home by 3:00 p.m. in time to hear "Ann Ford, a Woman Looks at the News," followed by "Stella Dallas" at 3:15. My afternoon soaps were rounded out by "Portia Faces Life," "Just Plain Bill," and "The Lone Ranger."

Before my family acquired its first radio, only two families in the community had them. Now that I look back on those years, I realize that the heads of both families were pensioned veterans of World War I. One of the fondest memories of my childhood was going to one or the other of these two homes on Saturday nights to hear the Grand Ole Opry. Every family in the community was gathered there for the same reason. These were heavy social occasions. The men and women sat talking in low voices among themselves while listening to the voice of George D. Hay, the Solemn Ole Judge, introducing the Opry singing acts. The kids played outdoors until dark and then came in to bundle down on the only bed in the room. Their one ambition in those days was to stay awake until the Grand Old Opry signed off at midnight. I for one never made it.

Those were the days of cultural isolation and economic stagnation in the region. Steamboats had ceased to run the Upper Cumberland in 1930, there were no railroads to speak of in the thirty-county bistate area, eighteen-wheelers or their early counterparts were still to come, and there were no paved roads, only graveled arteries, that connected the county seat towns until the late thirties and early forties. In my childhood mind, a Dodge automobile was designed to dodge the mudholes that greeted one at every turn in the road. During the periods of rain, my brother and I walked bare-foot through the mud with shoes in hand to meet the high school bus, which was paid for by private subscription.

In those days family and neighbors swapped stories, both to ward off boredom and, however unconsciously, to teach the youngsters present something about their local heritage. People of the Upper Cumberland still clung to beliefs in omens of death and the attendant manifestations of non-malevolent supernatural creatures, which was the topic of my second book.[9] It was not at all uncommon to hear stories about the spirits of dead relatives returning to visit the scenes known to them during their lifetime on earth. Those of us who were children during the lean years of the 1930s recall with considerable fondness what it was like to sit around the fireplace or stove on long winter evenings, or at Sunday afternoon gatherings, and listen to parents, grandparents, and other relatives and neighbors engage in tale-swapping sessions. These narrative sessions might recount, for example, the time that Granny saw the apparition of Uncle Andrew, or when Grandpa passed by the spot where the old home stood and heard the cries of Little Jimmy, who had perished inside the burning structure, or when the appearance of a wraith at the front gate signified the death of Mama's brother in the prime of his life. Many of these people, adults and children alike, believed in the ghosts and haunts mentioned in the stories. The existence of family legends describing real occurrences involving personal acquaintances served to reinforce such belief.

Like no other folktale genre, death omen narratives characterize and help to define the Upper Cumberland subregion. In short, people there believed that when some part of the natural universe acted in a strange manner, someone in the family or community was marked for death. I recall vividly how the sudden appearance of twenty-four doves portended the death of my great-grandmother at age eighty-eight in 1939. As an eight-year-old, I had gone with my parents and two siblings to visit Granny. She had been ill for several years, but was no worse on that particular weekend than usual. Just at the moment when we finished eating supper, the doves flew onto the side porch and lit as if they had come for a long visit. My seventeen-year-old aunt (Granny's granddaughter) took the remains of the "pone" of cornbread and went outside to feed the doves.

I watched through the window as she walked in the midst of the uncommonly tame birds, and observed her as she crumbled the bread on the porch, pushing the doves aside with her feet to avoid stepping on them. My aunt came back into the house and prophesied, "Granny will die tonight."

None of the eight to ten persons in the room cautioned her against such statements. All of those present believed in such signs and watched for them, especially during periods of sickness.

About four o'clock the next morning, my father came to the bed where my brother and I were sleeping, shook us gently, and said, "Wake up boys, Granny just died."

At this juncture one can perhaps see that the way I grew up is not at all incidental to what I write about and the way I feel about the subject matter. Not only do I write about local people and local topics, I write for local people. I am always hopeful that the academic sector will accept and endorse my publications, but I am equally hopeful that the people about whom I write will be just as receptive. The goal I set out for myself years ago was to present local people and culture in the words of the people themselves. That goal was complemented by a strong desire on the part of area residents to preserve a record of the past through memory. The general absence of transportation and communication with mainstream America until recent years perhaps accounts for this cultural characteristic of the Upper Cumberland and helps to define its geographic boundaries. In this connection I am reminded of Arnold Watson, a white man, and Calvin Coe, a black, both of whom wanted their history remembered.

I had gone to Watson's home in Cumberland County, Kentucky, in 1976 to tap into his storehouse of historical recollections about rafting and steamboating on the Upper Cumberland. Watson, well into his eighties, talked with excitement while carefully weighing his words so as to provide needed detail. The interview had been allowed to run on for nearly three hours, far beyond my normal time limit for the first session with a new interviewee. I sensed the urgency of the moment even as we talked. Seeing that he was becoming overly tired, I stopped the interview by telling him that I needed to listen to the tapes in order to detect gaps in what had been said up to that point. In response to my comment that I wanted to return in the near future to talk further with him, Watson answered, with apparent urgency in his voice, "Hurry back, I'm an old man."

I did go back in two weeks and we talked again at some length. A month later he died.

Calvin Coe had been born a slave on the Coe Plantation in southern Cumberland County. He knew the reality of slave families broken up by slave sales, as some of his siblings had been auctioned off to the highest bidder; he knew of the inceptive years of the black Coe settlement begun by a group of freedmen after the Civil War; he recalled working as a rouster at local steamboat landings to earn a little cash; and he had strong, hate-filled memories of the bloody racial strife in the 1880s when a bunch of redneck whites tried to remove the black colony from their midst. Most of all, however, Calvin Coe had memories of what it had been like to raise a family of eight mixed-race children born to him and his white live-in companion. Through all of these events, the history of the Coe colony had not been recorded, for local law officials were afraid to approach the black settlement for fear of ambush.[10]

Although I never interviewed Calvin Coe, I was able to talk at length with Coe's youngest daughter in 1960. At that time, she told me of her father's avid interest in saturating her mind with historical information that would otherwise accompany him to the grave. "My daddy was already an old man when I was a little girl," she explained. "On occasion," she went on, "he would take me by the shoulders, pull me down on his lap, and say, 'Sissy, I want you to sit down, I want you to hush up, and I want you to listen. I'm going to tell you about our people. Someday, you'll want to know these things.'"

In order to place into regional perspective the experiences of Watson and Coe, as well as my own, it was necessary to define the boundaries of the

Upper Cumberland. In my 1983 book on the Upper Cumberland that bore the title *Don't Go Up Kettle Creek: Verbal Legacy of the Upper Cumberland,* the region was delineated as follows:

> Begin at Carthage, Tennessee, then draw a line northward through Red Boiling Springs, Tennessee, to Edmonton, Kentucky. Extend the line eastward through Russell Springs to Somerset, then southward to Whitley City. From there, continue to Crossville, Tennessee, then via Sparta to the starting point at Carthage. Kentucky and Tennessee make up equal parts of the region but its history transcends boundaries. The state line was not fixed at its present location, in fact, until 1804—more than 20 years after the first white settlers arrived.

Continuing with the description from the book:

> It cannot be established when or by whom this area astraddle the midpoint of the Kentucky-Tennessee state line was first called the Upper Cumberland. It likely came about in the early 1830s with the arrival of the steamboat on the river above Carthage. Many of the riverboat captains of the day worked the Cumberland both above and below Carthage; along with the warehousemen and lumbermen in Nashville, they made a rather clear distinction between the upper river and the lower river, for the upper waters were more treacherous and the cargoes were different. Nashville newspapers made frequent reference to the Upper Cumberland in the 1860s, as news about upper river boats was commonly carried on their pages. The term was employed by the Upper Cumberland Medical Society beginning in 1894; in advertisements by the Hawk's and Company general store in Celina prior to the turn of the century; and by the Hotel Celina, which was heralded as 'one of the best hotels of the Upper Cumberland' in 1906.
>
> Across the years thousands of native sons and daughters have left the area for northern industrial cities with fond expectations of returning home someday. But since the 1940s, the Dale Hollow, Wolf Creek, Center Hill, and Cordell Hull reservoirs have inundated many of the older settlements and burial grounds of the pioneers in this low mountain fastness. As a result, the term Upper Cumberland is laden with nostalgia for present and past residents of the area; signage in Tennessee's hill country and the adjacent Cumberland Plateau makes clear the inhabitants' preference that their territory be referred to by this name. The Upper Cumberland Tourist Association in Cookeville issued a directory of the Upper Cumberlands: Tennessee's Family Funland. Included is a map of Middle Tennessee

with bold demarcation around the counties which comprise the "Fabulous Upper Cumberlands." Electric and telephone cooperatives, lumber companies, federal planning and social work agencies, bookstores, banks and other institutions from Carthage to Celina to Crossville prominently display the words Upper Cumberland as part of their official names.[11]

(I might point out here that Wilbur Zelinsky in like fashion used the names of urban business firms in drawing boundaries around the vernacular regions of North America.)[12]

Once I had found popular justification for using the term *Upper Cumberland* and had established its geographical boundaries, I set about interviewing men and women of all ages and all walks of life about the area's history. As they talked about their homeland, I listened. My purpose was to determine which of the region's historical currents were commonly described by residents in their oral narrations about the past. This manner of esoteric boundary definition was responsible for *Don't Go Up Kettle Creek.*

That study, like the much earlier *Saga of Coe Ridge* (1970), was folk history; in both I essentially let the people of the area describe their own history. My latest study from the Upper Cumberland, published under the title *Killings: Folk Justice in the Upper South* (1986), examines the historical and social conditions, as well as prevailing attitudes and values, that gave rise and support to rowdy behavior and homicidal acts from the Civil War to the 1930s. As an outsider to the small study area within the Upper Cumberland, I could see and understand the geographical, political, economic, historic, and cultural factors at work in creating a subculture of violence. Nonetheless, my delineation of the area to be studied was again largely dictated along esoteric lines, as the more than fifty killings described in the book were ones that people in the area either talked about in personal terms or learned about from the graphic descriptions provided by other local residents.

Subregional cultures such as that of the Upper Cumberland often possess their own unique characteristics, thus offering scholars from all disciplines one of their most inviting research targets. We are all aware of the Hispanics in the Southwest, the Cajuns of Louisiana, the Polish in Detroit, the Irish in Boston, the cattle herdsmen in every western state, the wheat farmers of Kansas, and, now, the hill country people of the Upper Cumberland. There are countless other such cultural groups and regions in the United States. The publishing house of Duell, Sloan, and Pearce looked to such cultural areas for their popular series on American folkways in the late 1930s. A glance at the titles in that series makes it possible to map much of the nation into folk cultural areas as perceived by the editors and authors. Among the titles are *Golden Gate Country, North Star Country, Deep Delta Country, Palmetto Country, Mormon Country, Desert Country, Pinon Country, Blue Ridge Country,* and *High Border Country.* A concurrent effort to define America's subregions was the Rivers of America series issued under the general editorship of Skinner, Benet, and Carmer for Farrar and Rinehart. More recent efforts afford far better models for us, however. Hans Kurath and his associates involved in the *Linguistic Atlas of New England,* and linguist Frederic G. Cassidy, who is chiefly responsible for the *Dictionary of American Regional English,* have demonstrated that regional speech patterns can be revealed through the use of isoglosses. Folklorists and cultural geographers like Henry Glassie and Terry Jordan have used similar techniques in mapping material cultural forms such as architecture and gravestones.[13] By extension, then, we could plot the distribution of the legends of La Llorona, patterns of violence and homicidal behavior, recreational activities, or any other cultural tangible that can be isolated and studied to define subregional boundaries. For instance, cultural geographer E. Joan Wilson Miller was able to delimit an eleven-county Ozark culture region on the basis of folktales, folk speech, and other folkloric genres and, in so doing, demonstrate that oral materials can indeed contribute to an understanding of the continuum of the changing occupancy of a folk cultural area.[14]

Even though isograms can be drawn to delineate specific cultural attributes, they do not help in outlining the outer perimeters of multifaceted regions and subregions. They help only to establish the core or heartland of the culture area. By way of explanation, if, for example, we plot four different cultural tangibles through the use of contour lines, the cultural core of the geographical area so defined is situated within the heart of the area where all of the contour lines intersect. The outer perimeters of the region or subregional area defined in this manner will always be fluid, as one or more of the four cultural characteristics in question will likely be shared with people in adjacent regions. Multiregional sharing of certain attributes is a truism, whether those characteristics are physical or cultural. What I am arguing is that, given the variable nature of cultural attributes, there is no such thing as a region with rigidly defined boundaries.

Let me underscore the point that boundaries of regions and subregions must be viewed as fluid in nature. True, economists define a region along economic lines, political scientists on the basis of political patterns, linguists on the basis of language and dialect, and folklorists, sociologists, and anthropologists look at cultural patterns and attributes. But scholars from all of these academic disciplines would likely agree that the outer perimeters of their regions are virtually impossible to articulate or define. Further, they would likely agree that flexibility in defining a region is nec-

essary, as surprises constantly enter the picture once the process of interpreting data is begun. To illustrate, in my present study of gospel music in
south-central Kentucky, my initial study area of twelve counties has grown
to nineteen. And while the study area lies largely in the Upper Cumberland, it bleeds across subregional lines to include adjacent parts of Kentucky and the upper South.

My criteria for identifying the counties to be included in the gospel music research project include the prevalence of shape-note singing schools,
singing conventions, and the number of quartets that sang outside their
home churches more than four times each year. Fieldwork and archival
research enabled me to establish these criteria initially, and then to expand
the number of counties from twelve to nineteen. I began only with an approximate idea of the number of counties in Kentucky's gospel music
subregion, then altered my geographical boundary line on the basis of data
obtained in the early stages of research.

While the geographical boundaries for the gospel music project were
defined by me, the real boundaries were established between the 1890s and
the 1920s by area residents themselves, people who either accepted or rejected the shape-note musical tradition along aesthetic lines. Thus, I have
again employed the principle of esoteric boundary definition in outlining
my gospel music study area, for it was the residents themselves who,
across the years, established the perimeters of the Upper Cumberland culture area.

William E. Lightfoot recognized the significance of regions (the Upper
Cumberland) within regions (the South) when he observed that it is sometimes difficult to determine the pertinent sociocultural context of events in
which human beings interact, because the meaning of such events may
very well exist within a system of contextual concentric circles.[15] For example, the singing tradition described above took place in the South, in the
upper South, in the Upper Cumberland, and, more specifically, in Kentucky's Upper Cumberland. An additional example is afforded by the fifty
homicides described in *Killings*. They took place, in increasingly specific
terms, in the South, in the upper South, in the Upper Cumberland, in the
study area, and in a certain community. Details of the killings, although
known beyond the community, and sometimes even beyond the study area,
are not familiar to the residents of the larger Upper Cumberland subregion.
When word of the killings did spread beyond the limits of the study area,
true understanding of the homicidal acts was lost or obscured in the absence of the value-laden social context within which the acts occurred.[16]

Because people, whether rural or urban, live in particular places, there
is an urgent need to explore the relationship of land to the lore of the people
who occupy it. Howard W. Odum grasped this relationship as early as the

late 1930s, when he wrote that "regionalism implies . . . the natural origins and quality of all folk-life and culture."[17] Folklorist J. Frank Dobie, in the early years of the century, astutely recognized that lore helped to delineate region. Likewise, Roger Welsch and William Ferris have fruitfully pursued this relationship of land and lore in recent years on the Great Plains and in the Mississippi Delta.[18] The process of studying bodies of lore that display esoteric or subregional qualities appears to hold considerable promise for those contemporary social scientists who are interested in region and the process of regionalization. Further, my own experience in studying a relatively small area intensively over a long period of time has demonstrated, at least to me, the validity of examining folk cultural regions in terms of the boundaries that the residents themselves perceive.

Notes

1.   See Falmer Mood, "The Origin, Evolution, and Application of the Sectional Concept, 1750–1900," in *Regionalism in America,* ed. Merrill Jensen (Madison: University of Wisconsin Press, 1952), pp. 5–98. Richard M. Dorson addressed the impact these historical and geographical determinants of region had on the nature of regional folklore in *Buying the Wind: The Regional Folklore in the United States* (Chicago, Ill.: University of Chicago Press, 1964).

2.   For an overview of the Dry Farming Frontier and the end of an era, consult Barbara Allen, *Homesteading the High Desert* (Salt Lake City: University of Utah Press, 1987), pp. 114–46.

3.   Louis Wirth, "The Limitations of Regionalism," in *Regionalism in America,* ed. Jensen, p. 391.

4.   Rupert B. Vance, "The Regional Concept as a Tool for Social Research," in *Regionalism in America,* ed. Jensen, p. 123.

5.   Alan Gibson, "In Defense of a Southern Accent," ms., 1986, p. 1.

6.   Wendell Berry, *Continuous Harmony: Essays Cultural and Agricultural* (New York: Harcourt Brace Jovanovich, 1972), p. 63.

7.   Ibid., p. 67.

8.   Carl O. Sauer, *Geography of the Pennyroyal: A Study of the Influence of Geology and Physiography Upon the Industry, Commerce, and Life of the People* (Frankfort: The Kentucky Geological Survey, 1927).

9.   William Lynwood Montell, *Ghosts Along the Cumberland: Deathlore in the Kentucky Foothills* (Knoxville: University of Tennessee Press, 1975).

10. Fuller details of these events may be obtained by consulting my *Saga of Coe Ridge: A Study in Oral History* (Knoxville: University of Tennessee Press, 1970).

11. William Lynwood Montell, *Don't Go Up Kettle Creek: Verbal Legacy of the Upper Cumberland* (Knoxville: University of Tennessee Press, 1983).

12. Wilbur Zelinsky, "North America's Vernacular Regions," *Annals of the Association of American Geographers* 70 (1980): 1–15.

13. See for example, Henry Glassie, *Folk Housing in Middle Virginia: Structural Analysis of Historic Artifacts* (Knoxville: University of Tennessee Press, 1975); and Terry G. Jordan, *Texas Graveyards: A Cultural Legacy* (Austin: University of Texas Press, 1982).

14. E. Joan Wilson Miller, "The Ozark Culture Region as Revealed by Traditional Material," *Annals of the Association of American Geographers* 58 (1968): 51–77.

15. William E. Lightfoot, "Regional Folkloristics," in *Handbook of American Folklore,* ed. Richard M. Dorson (Bloomington: Indiana University Press, 1983), p. 185.

16. For an elaboration on these ideas see ibid., pp. 184–92.

17. Howard W. Odum, *American Regionalism: A Cultural Approach to National Integration* (Gloucester, Mass.: Holt, Rinehart, and Winston, 1938), p. 4.

18. See Roger Welsch, *Shingling the Fog and Other Plains Lies* (Lincoln: University of Nebraska Press, 1972); and William Ferris, *Blues from the Delta* (Garden City, N.Y.: Anchor Press/Doubleday, 1978).

12 Spatial Integration: The Argument for Context

Glen E. Lich

"... the strong and refined essence of a continent ..."
—Isak Dinesen

I became conscious of regional studies on my way from Munich to Vienna when friends prevailed upon me to accompany them to a production of *Anatevka* in the old Bavarian Royal Theatre. Because it was raining, I accepted the invitation and came thereby to an important intersection that night where—for me—the world and the village came together.

I return to that juncture of world and village—global and local—because being there contributes vision, breadth, and strength. As Emerson worried a century and a half ago in "The American Scholar," we today ponder the consequences of an education that does not produce complete and engaged human beings. "The State of Society," Emerson wrote in 1837, "is one in which the members have suffered amputation from the trunk, and strut about so many walking monsters—a good finger, a good neck, a stomach, an elbow, but never a man." Emerson admonished that "man is not a farmer, or a professor, or an engineer, but he is all. Man is priest, and scholar, and statesman, and producer, and soldier." [1]

Those thoughts remain central. Amid arguments about cultural literacy and the holistic development of students, regional studies afford concrete yet *interdisciplinary* approaches to the ideal education that is both means and end, both substance and method, both a study of self and a study of what surrounds self. [2] Students, teachers, and universities can benefit from this organizing model. Indeed, if regional studies can "accommodate all researchers interested in the concept of region, from the smaller biocultural regions on the one hand to the larger, multinational regions on the other," [3] then the broad, comparative, and integrative qualities in the preceding essays suggest ways in which universities can connect curricula and build bridges to the world outside academia.

Concept

At Baylor, the start of a regional studies program in 1986 was greeted by the president as "an exciting concept" that "captured the imagination of faculty in many areas of the university." [4] With the general charge *to study, interpret, and document the perspectives which Texas derives from its position as the meeting place of several distinct regions,* the developing program also formulated the objectives of being able *to fund and administer research projects* designed to increase knowledge and understanding of both theoretical and applied regional issues; *to utilize human resources and the intellectual materials available through libraries, museums, and other repositories* in order to gather information; *to contribute to the fund of knowledge* available to scholars and the public through the program's research, exhibits, and publications; *to cooperate and interact* with other regional studies programs in order to share experiences and enhance the significance of the regional perspective; and *to present the findings* of the program's projects to the general public, specialists, and agencies charged with shaping public policies of the state and nation.[5]

Even though this broad concept of regional studies affords rich possibilities for almost any college or university, Baylor's location, character, and history played an auspicious role in the formulation of this particular program's emphasis on comparison and application. Joel Garreau's "nine nations" of North America divides Texas into three major regions,[6] whose approximate meeting point is Waco. It follows then, that Baylor's program would from the start be essentially different from those of the Center for the Study of Southern Culture at the University of Mississippi or the Center for Great Plains Studies at the University of Nebraska at Lincoln—both in the middle of huge cultural platelets. Baylor's interstitial location requires a hold on the South, the Great Plains, the Southwest, and the Gulf of Mexico—and it encourages the study of regions comparatively, even generically.

Yet even without being guided thus by a fortunate combination of circumstances, one has little choice but to consider the term *region* as an elastic and sometimes even temporary construct, one that is derived primarily from geography and other disciplines that are able to integrate both the diachronic and the synchronic, but that at varying levels begins to differ from cultural geography and to assume some qualities of the behavioral and social sciences and the humanities. Detailed explication of the *contexts* from which or in which regions develop—either disjunctively or conjunctively—will help to establish relationships among simple and complex forms and among simple and complex levels of *regionalism*. Movement up and down the macro and micro scale of regionalism and back and forth between concepts of regions may take into account such processes as the rhetorical presentation, perpetuation, and modification of a region in and through the culture that seemingly defines it, migration into and out of regions, splitting and joining of regions, demarcation of regional boundaries, and the nature of urban and multicultural and international regions. On more concrete but no less advanced levels, the consideration of the environmental modification and the perpetuation or destruction of the region's physical basis brings scholarship back to the starting point: to the relationships of land and people and time.

Three stages of development facilitate the pursuit of such research agendas in universities. The single-subject stage develops within traditional departmental disciplines, as in regional studies in history, regional studies in geology, regional studies in literature, museum studies, or American studies. Very often, such advocacy builds networks from which study groups may form. Institutional interest may eventually lead to the establishment of programs, centers, or institutes. A third—awkward but critical—stage combines the qualities of the disciplinary depth and interdisciplinary synthesis.

The preceding essays focus on concepts, applications, perspectives, teaching, and research on the interplay of land and people. The first section moves from concepts to laboratory. The second introduces spatial and generally disciplinary approaches to the organization of knowledge. The third modifies notions advanced by the earlier essays; the study of the change of regions over time, international regions, and subregions leads to broad conclusions on the history of the concept of regionalism, its significance in Europe and North America, and its many and varied manifestations in the United States. And yet important questions linger about regionalism as a phenomenon—including the extent, on the one hand, to which regional considerations might detract from efforts to synthesize knowledge and unify thought; and the extent, on the other hand, to which such constructs relate the parts of knowledge to the whole and the parts to each other.

If, in Terry Jordan's words, "the regional concept . . . for all its shortcomings and potential traps . . . offers a useful and valuable way to come to grips with the chaotic world," scholars of regional studies should also be mindful of the need to rise above colorful and sometimes beguiling descriptions of singularity or claims of outright uniqueness. Scholars of serious studies have to work with their eyes on several regions at once in the manner suggested by Howard Lamar in order to try to understand *how* people "rationalize the landscape" and *why* "the perceived region or regional culture [is] sometimes a more powerful concept than the actual geographic region." Comparative subregional, national, international, or multicultural inquiry can be staggering, but such approaches yield insight into setting or place as a mirror of self, and such approaches, perhaps such approaches alone, advance understanding of the human bent to pluralism. For despite long-standing assumptions that concepts like region—and culture, ethnicity, and religion—lose validity as the world grows smaller, they endure with remarkable variety and vitality and continue to challenge theoreticians and practitioners in a multitude of fields. Were we to take cues from painters or writers, we would acknowledge the sense of setting as a meaningful beginning from which to approach the arts, humanities, and social and behavioral sciences. Perhaps we would not all go as far as William Faulkner, who explains that Joe Christmas has to act the way the land has taught and trained him to act, but we are remiss if we do not acknowledge some aspects of Faulkner's fundamental assumption that character equals setting equals plot. [7]

Scholars of regional studies are now at one of those forks in the road that Robert Frost describes in "The Road Not Taken." The road more often traveled is a continuation for the most part of the wide road that brings us to this junction. It is a highway leading through regional studies of America that have been largely descriptive, less frequently analytical, and almost always particularistic rather than national in scope or spirit. We have produced color and contrast, but we have limited understanding.

To continue only along the wide road traveled in the past will do little to broaden understanding, either of the parts or of the whole itself. For in the proliferation of more and more of the same things we lose the habit of looking for structures and relationships, of finding causes and effects, of comparing and contrasting. Despite what otherwise seem to be the positive attributes of this broadening of inquiry, despite the attention devoted to marginalized groups and places and cultures, we lose the ability to define, to classify, to comprehend. We are left with narration and description. We inadvertently trivialize what we study in isolation but cannot integrate.

Only the "road less traveled" leads to the generative, constructive study of regions and regionalism. Integrative, multiregional—even cooperative—approaches offer great promise if scholars "use many disciplines and many techniques to probe layer by layer and state by state," according to Lamar. If such scholars seek and find meaningful comparisons not only in time but also in place, they will, Lamar predicts, develop "one of the most effective ways we have yet attempted to understand both ourselves and our extraordinarily pluralistic nation," this commonwealth of regions. Regional studies of this sort can indeed *study* the interplay of land and people—not just punch at it, not just record it. Such studies can help to answer questions about the core culture—is there one? should there be?—because this kind of regional scholarship will begin to approximate national studies and help to organize much of what is invigorating in American education in the late twentieth century, while retaining the concreteness, manageability, and integration that we consider to be advantages of regional studies.

As Jim Wayne Miller writes, "regional perspectives can present academic disciplines as they interpenetrate and impinge on one another; issues and problems in contexts that do not dwarf the individual; and the possibility of better combinations of thought and action, knowledge and power, scholarship and citizenship. . . ." In his reconnaissance of the hitherto less traveled road, Miller suggests furthermore that the concept of region offers opportunities of "studying without separating what nature, history, and culture have put together." He arrives at the conclusion that "the local and global, regional and national, the particular and the universal, are not antithetical concepts; rather, they complement each other," especially if scholars approach "the life of regions as a medium of expression—not as the message itself."[8]

Diderot and Emerson and Frost would all three approve. And so would many educators and public leaders concerned about the "disconnected" university's ability to teach a "connected" concept of the world. As former Delaware governor Russell W. Peterson argues in "Education for the Professional Generalist," "people enter the most influential positions in our society ill-prepared for the breadth of their assignments." The jobs of future presidents, corporate executives, journalists, and civic leaders "call for highly skilled generalists, people who understand such things as the place of Homo sapiens in the biosphere; the interdependence of all people and nations; and how the world's economic, political, social, and management systems operate."[9] Regional studies can open onto global perspectives, and they can do much to help people to see themselves in new ways, acquire a sure footing in a discipline, establish connections with the "other" in time and place, and learn how to put knowledge to work.

Applications

The regional studies concept, which affords a tangible and appealing way of dealing with such complexity, assumes that disciplines and the languages those disciplines employ can be integrated spatially. In many regards, the concept can be based on a rather traditional area studies model with a strong added emphasis on interdisciplinarity.

The application of this approach to regional issues can result in highly responsive, flexible, and reliable analysis—coupled with the kind of bridge and network and consensus building that results from the consortial approach encouraged by the complexity of regional studies. The ability of this kind of regional studies to inform the general public, specialists, and agencies charged with shaping public policies of state and nation may have been what the author of *The Wisconsin Idea* (1912) had in mind when he wrote idealistically of the university as a kind of "fourth branch of government" capable of drawing together the public, policymakers, and scholars in studies of policy—a concept that led, in the case of the program at Baylor, to the development of a center for teams of faculty and students in various departments and colleges at the university and that cooperates with other research centers both at Baylor and elsewhere.[10] An interuniversity consortium inaugurated in 1987 and supported by the Texas Committee for the Humanities under the statewide initiative of "Preparing for Texas in the Twenty-First Century" became for the Baylor program the first of a series of such projects, which have brought together the global and the regional and which have appealed to various audiences. And, likewise, the concept has demonstrated what it means both procedurally and methodologically *to study a region.*[11]

Subsequent projects have taken the program at Baylor a step further toward developing the concept of "the spatial integration of knowledge." "Region North America: Canada, United States, Mexico" is part of a massive, multidisciplinary study of the application of economic models to define regional boundaries and interchange. Against the backdrop of the free trade accord of 1987, the center launched an international study—drawing in scholars of the Pacific Rim as well as of the European Community and Africa—on the formation of such international regional trade blocs; on scenarios that show relations between countries forming trade areas, in this instance, Canada, the United States, and Mexico; and on how the pieces of the North American continent interconnect as an international region and separate into national and subnational parts.

International trade theory, according to the principal investigator for "Region North America," "through the 'Law of Comparative Advantage' points to the potential benefits to consumers and producers of the removal of barriers to free trade and the expansion thereby of market boundaries. However, the political, cultural, social, geographical, educational, and institutional barriers to free trade have often left economists frustrated by the differences between theory and the reality of what they perceive to be 'artificial' barriers to market forces. Only when many of the dimensions of an issue are simultaneously examined can the feasibility of a concept as complex as a North American trade region be understood realistically."[12]

Learning to *see* things in this way is the first step toward *teaching* in this way. The educational objective assumes that a *spatial approach to learning* can challenge the university community to see interconnections of knowledge, issues, and actions as these matters relate to a specific place or region, whether the Southwest, New England, or North America, thus giving students and teachers a world of knowledge that more closely resembles the world in which we live. The ongoing research program for "Region North America" is intended to show culture "in action" and to open for public discourse some important considerations of what it means to be a "neighbor" in a world where telecommunications and computers put a banker in Houston "right down the hallway" from a financier in Montreal and "across the street" from an investor in Mexico City. In looking at the shift from spatial to functional in the concepts of *neighbor* and *community*, this work deromanticizes but also strengthens the notion of the global village.

Another long-term, comparative project, a twenty-year series entitled "The Natural Regions of Texas: Land, History, and Culture" was formulated by two geologists. Starting with the blackland prairie, the physical region dominant in Central Texas—the one where three of Garreau's "nine nations of North America" meet—and continuing through ten eighteen-month cycles, a series of conferences, field trips, exhibits, proceedings, and guidebooks will teach how to recover, collect, record, interpret, and extend an understanding of self, setting, history, and future. In its examination of the natural landscape and cultural geography of Texas, this work places a strong emphasis on putting ideas about the use of resources into practice, as well as on place studies.

According to one of the geologists, "In the present world of splintered science and humanities, knowledge has been converted into a giant *Trivia* game played by tens of thousands of participants, each with a single fact. Players have become increasingly isolated as the game gets bigger. A fundamental purpose of the Blacklands study is to bring some sense of reality to a tiny part of this knowledge by *specializing* on the generalities of a small but definable part of the complex world.

"The increasing separation of science and the humanities," the geologist continued, "has been destructive to both science and the humanities. From the standpoint of the humanities, the very human world of our experience is far more comprehensible when we understand something of its natural foundation. Likewise, the natural sciences become far more meaningful to those who study nature when they begin to recognize the immense impact of the natural world on humans and of humans on the natural world." [13]

Through regional studies programs universities can take active roles in regional development, policy formulation, and public outreach, as well as research and education. Matching the benefits that the university community derives from involvement in regional affairs are two immediate and invaluable benefits that accrue to the region. The first is that universities can help to record, define, develop, and impart a sense of place, or even to "make" a place out of what is not generally perceived to be a region. Universities can help to articulate the *shared* in shared interests, find the *common* in common agendas, and foster the *dialogic* and the *cooperative* in regional solutions. The second is that universities are the strongest repositories of interdisciplinary depth of knowledge and likewise of experience in analysis, interpretation, and programming—all of which can be focused on regional issues. These are the two thrusts of applied regional studies: definition and action.

The application of this concept in the classroom can encourage the development of students who will have a broad perception of the relationships between the unique and general features of situations and who are sensitive to the tension between the local and the universal, between the specific and the general. Such students can develop unusually high analogic, comparative, contextual, descriptive, interpretive, and synthetic skills.[14] They should be able to conceptualize, assuming adequate disciplinary grounding, and to generalize from evidence or from parts to whole; they would have insight into seeing self as other and other as self. In a metaphor, they should be able to build the whole house—maybe not right away, but eventually. Implicit in all such studies, then, is an assumption of praxis and the suggestion that one can "go global" from these beginnings: that thus grounded, some students can go on to become architects and general contractors rather than plumbers or carpenters or roofers.

The discourse of such three-dimensional and highly dynamic learning does not lead in straight lines, or even in zigzags, from discipline A to discipline B, but rather proceeds (or winds) into structures and through metadisciplines in what seems like anything but an orderly and efficient manner. And yet there is order, and there is efficiency—although both are of a higher and more arduous sort than that of single disciplines, for the world is chaos and each discipline blinds us to much reality even as it helps us to define reality. The regional model frames chaos in a different way than do the disciplines that blank out the biggest parts of reality on the basis of subject, distinguishing characteristics, or qualities. Regional studies reduces the *quantity* but not the complexity of chaos. In that sense its approach is fundamentally spatial, implying boundaries and masses and description before it speaks of definitions and chronologies and differentiae. But the "disciplines" are all present in the regional approach—indeed, not only present but also visible to a far greater degree than, let us say, geography and economics tend to be when we study history.

What follows is the development of a regional studies program that *complements* the existing curricula of departments, institutes, and areas of concentration—but that is not a "stand-alone" curriculum. Piecemeal as some aspects of higher education in the United States are today, the pieces *are* there at most universities and colleges. Integration is the primary issue. Another reason for developing courses as augmentations to existing curricula is an assumption that breadth needs to be attended—often preceded—by the depth that comes through grounding in the disciplines. But some specialized courses eventually become necessary: one on regional theory *per se,* for example, to facilitate the integration of such thinking into other courses and thus broaden the regional perspective among teachers in the departments, lower the age at which regional awareness is introduced to students, and thereby put teachers and students in touch with tangible aspects of the global view; and another to teach methods for the *management* of chaos—how to call a truce with fluid, multidimensional life and how to select, organize, and link knowledge; how to make layers of signification for description, for analysis, for interpretation, for prediction; and how to write, how to speak, how to act, even though one could be overwhelmed by the many dimensions of reality.

The *spatial approach to learning* can help to erase, or reduce to realistic size, what are artificial and often unnecessary divisions of the knowledge that describes and helps us to understand the world. Such an approach can help to develop in students broad perceptions of the relationships between the concrete and the abstract and, if understanding translates into praxis, should produce students more inclined toward active involvement in the world and better prepared for involvement in it because they would be able to discuss large issues in terms of relatively localized specifics and see themselves in the context of a time and place. These exciting, yet highly realistic thoughts address persistent problems—making connections, developing commitment, and seeing applications—that trouble primary, secondary, and higher education in the United States. But the regional method, more homespun than radical and always more technique than substance, is not a replacement as much as it is an enhancement of a curriculum of "subjects" that give discipline and depth to education. But learning "subjects" alone, without context or application, will not teach participation.

Problems and Promise

Too often, challenges like that implicit in regional studies to the concept of a single dominant culture suggest only a replacement of the whole with a multiplicity of small parts. Can we not, however, produce an integrated view of the parts related—if not explicitly compared—to the whole? Would we, if we engaged in regional studies in ways that acknowledge the broader contexts of region and that also acknowledge the powerful criticism that regionalism gives to the national *culture,* not have a clearer understanding once again of what makes a *national culture?*

The "unique, colorful, and true to life" approach that has stigmatized much of regional studies, particularly in Texas, might be more appropriately described as pop culture than as the *study* of regions and regionalism. As Louis Wirth wrote many years ago in an essay in *Regionalism in America,* still a definitive text on regional studies in this country, "the regional idea . . . can lead to the falsification of the facts. It can become a futile effort to squeeze life into a rigid mold, and it can become a vain gesture to retard the integration of life on a wider and more inclusive scale." There is no mystique in things regional; it is, in fact, hard to imagine things that do *not* partake of the regional: of what Wirth describes as a "spatial or a real approach to social phenomena": "If we do not mean by the term 'region' to call attention to the fact that we are looking at life in terms of the space dimension and the interest in location and position which that implies, then the term 'region' has no intelligible meaning whatsoever." It is a mixed blessing, Wirth concludes, that "regionalism is not one thing but many things": a fact of nature, a fact of culture, an administrative and problem-solving strategy, a social movement, a political force, something other than community (which is based on interdependence) or society (which is based on consensus), a tool of research, "a counterpoise to gigantism, to uniformity, to standardization, and to over-centralization," and even a cult—"seminal ideas" like regional studies, being, Wirth asserts, "so rare that when we meet them in the scientific world we tend to embrace them with more than justifiable enthusiasm."[15] Defining regionalism and defining regional studies, one concludes, can be grueling but rewarding, because the process of definition is a mode of discourse that can tell a great deal about relationships between the local and the global in general and about the human definition of the world in which we live: about the *fictions* people narrate to explain the chaos.

In an essay about why we read fiction, Robert Penn Warren, practitioner and interpreter of literary regionalism, may give some insight not only into why we read but also into this strongly personal appeal of regionalism, which is both its strength and weakness. "When we read as we say to 'escape,'" he writes, "we seek to escape not *from* life but *to* life, to a life more satisfying than our own drab version. Fiction gives us an image of life—sometimes of a life we actually have and like to dwell on, but often and poignantly of one we have had and do not have now, or one we have never had and can never have."[16] This impulse brings us back to regionalism: the spirit that defines and divides, that puts self in the center of the universe and answers to important questions within reach, that brings us again and again to that juncture of the world and the village.

Despite Wirth's warning about claiming too much for regional studies, it does seem entirely safe to conclude that while regional studies are not new, the so-called new and *contexted* approaches to regional studies, which combine the disciplines, which are undertaken with an aim toward explanation and interpretation instead of only description (important as that is), and which are also undertaken *comparatively,* give ample promise of creating a way of trying to understand reality that is more than the sum of its disciplinary parts. This is perhaps not a new way of thinking about reality—Wirth would throw up his hands if we said that—but it is a *wise* one,

the employment of which can have synergistic effect upon the institutions
of education, upon those educated and those educating, and upon regions.

Notes

The author acknowledges the assistance of Michael Steiner at California State
University at Fullerton; Kent Keeth, director of the Texas Collection; Thomas
L. Charlton, director of the Institute for Oral History; and David Stricklin,
lecturer in oral history at Baylor University. Versions of this paper were read
at the North Louisiana Folklife Conference at Northwestern State University
of Louisiana in 1988 and at the universities of Ludwigsburg and Mainz in the
Federal Republic of Germany in 1988. Parts of this paper have been published in Lakehead University Centre for Northern Studies, *Proceedings of
the First Annual Conference of the Association for Northern Studies* (Thunder
Bay, Ontario: Lakehead University, 1991). They are reprinted here with permission.

1. From "The American Scholar," in *Ralph Waldo Emerson: Essays
    and Lectures*, ed. Joel Porte (New York: Library of America,
    1983), p. 54.
2. By *interdisciplinary* I mean—in the words of a publication of the
    Association for Integrative Studies—that "a variety of disciplines
    are coordinated from a higher level by a sense of purpose." *Mul-
    tidisciplinary,* used later, describes "a one-level, multi-goal ap-
    proach with a variety of disciplines offered simultaneously but
    without explicit cooperation among the disciplines." See Erich
    Jantsch, "Towards Interdisciplinarity and Transdisciplinarity in
    Education and Innovation," in *Interdisciplinarity: Problems of
    Teaching and Research in Universities,* ed. Léo Apostel, Guy
    Berger, Asa Briggs, and Guy Michand (Paris: Organization for
    Economic Cooperation and Development, 1972), pp. 97–121.
3. Lynwood Montell and Barbara Allen, letter dated Jan. 24, 1986.
4. Herbert H. Reynolds, letter dated Mar. 5, 1986.
5. Adopted by the Regional Studies Council, Feb. 2, 1987.
6. Joel Garreau, *The Nine Nations of North America* (Boston:
    Houghton Mifflin, 1981).
7. William Faulkner, *Light in August* (New York: Random House,
    1932), p. 231.
8. Jim Wayne Miller, "Anytime the Ground Is Uneven: The Out-
    look for Regional Studies and What to Look Out For," in *Geog-
    raphy and Literature: A Meeting of the Disciplines,* ed. William
    E. Mallory and Paul Simpson-Housley (Syracuse, N.Y.: Syra-
    cuse University Press, 1987), pp. 15, 17.

9.   Russell W. Peterson, "Education for the Professional Generalist,"
      in *Rethinking the Curriculum,* ed. Nancy Clark (Westport,
      Conn.: Greenwood, 1990).

10.   Charles McCarthy, quoted in LaVern J. Rippley, "Charles Mc-
      Carthy and Frederic C. Howe: Their Imperial German Sources
      for the Wisconsin Idea in Progressive Politics," *Monatshefte* 80
      (1988): 75; see also Charles McCarthy, *The Wisconsin Idea*
      (New York: Macmillan, 1912).

11.   See also Michael Steiner and Clarence Mondale, *Regions and
      Regionalism in the United States: A Source Book for the Human-
      ities and Social Sciences* (New York: Garland, 1988). The publi-
      cation that resulted from the future studies project sponsored by
      the Texas Committee for the Humanities is *The Humanities and
      Public Issues,* volume III of a five-volume series entitled *Prepar-
      ing for Texas in the 21st Century: Building a Future for the Chil-
      dren of Texas,* ed. James F. Veninga and Catherine Williams
      (Austin: Texas Committee for the Humanities, 1990).

12.   Thomas M. Kelly and Glen E. Lich, quoted from Glen E. Lich,
      Preface, *Region North America: Canada, United States, Mexico,*
      ed. Glen E. Lich and Joseph A. McKinney (Waco, Tex.: Baylor
      University, 1990), p. viii. See also Glen E. Lich and Joseph A.
      McKinney, eds., *Free Trade and the United States-Mexico Bor-
      derlands: An Impact Study for the Joint Economic Committee,* 15
      January 1991.

13.   From a text by O. T. Hayward, member of the Regional Studies
      Council and professor of geology; see "Blacklands: The Soil and
      the Soul," *Waco Tribune Herald,* Nov. 19, 1989.

14.   The curriculum committee of the Regional Studies Council for-
      mulated these and additional objectives during meetings in 1989;
      members of the committee included Alta N. Lane (Department
      of Home Economics and head of the committee), Dudley Burton
      (Institute of Environmental Studies), and Stanley Campbell (De-
      partment of History); Glen E. Lich (director of regional studies)
      was an *ex officio* member of the committee.

15.   Louis Wirth, "The Limits of Regionalism," in *Regionalism in
      America,* ed. Merrill Jensen (1951; rpt. Madison: University of
      Wisconsin Press, 1965), pp. 381, 384–85, 386–87, 391, 392,
      and 393.

16.   Robert Penn Warren, "On Reading Fiction," reprinted in the
      Chronicle of Higher Education, Oct. 4, 1989, p. B64. See also
      Texas College English 22.1 (1989): 12–15.

About the Contributors

S USAN H. A RMITAGE is the director of the American Studies Program and professor of history at Washington State University in Pullman. She is the former director of the Women's Studies Program, and she specializes in western American women's history and women's oral history. Her research interest in feminist revisions of western history is reflected in numerous articles and in an anthology, *The Women's West* (1987), coedited with Elizabeth Jameson.

F REDERIC G. C ASSIDY is the chief editor of the *Dictionary of American Regional English,* a former Fulbright fellow, and professor emeritus of English and linguistics at the University of Wisconsin in Madison. With research interests in American and Caribbean linguistics, he is the author of *A Method for Collecting Dialect; The Development of Modern English; Jamaica Talk;* and *Dictionary of Jamaican English.* Cassidy is a former president of the American Dialect Society, the Society for Caribbean Linguistics, and the American Name Society.

W ILLIAM R. F ERRIS is the director of the Center for the Study of Southern Culture and professor of anthropology at the University of Mississippi. He has produced a number of documentary films from *Mississippi Blues* to *Painting in the South,* and he has written or edited numerous books, including *Blues from the Delta; Images of the South: Visits with Eudora Welty and Walker Evans; Local Color; Afro-American Folk Arts and Crafts;* and *Folk Music and Modern Sound.* Ferris is also co-editor of the *Encyclopedia of Southern Culture.*

C HARLES H AMM is the Arthur R. Virgin Professor of Music at Dartmouth College. A former president of the American Musicological Society and twice chair of the International Association for the Study of Popular Music, he has written such books as *Contemporary Music and Music Cultures, Yesterdays: Popular Song in America, Music in the New World,* and *Afro-American Music, South Africa and Apartheid.* He has received the Woodrow Wilson, Fulbright, Guggenheim, and Rockefeller Foundation awards, and he is editor of the North American volume of *The Universe of Music: A History,* a multi-volume global history of music sponsored by the International Music Council.

179

SAMUEL S. HILL is professor of religion at the University of Florida. A specialist in modern Western religious movements and the history of Western religion, he has written widely on religion in American culture, including the *Handbook of Denominations in the United States; Southern Churches in Crisis; The South and the North in American Religion; The New Religious-Political Right in America* (coauthor); and the *Encyclopedia of Religion in the South* (editor). Hill is past president of the southern section of the American Academy of Religion.

TERRY G. JORDAN is the Walter Prescott Webb Professor of History and Ideas, Department of Geography, at the University of Texas at Austin. A former Woodrow Wilson fellow and specialist in the cultural geography of Anglo-America and its European origins, Jordan is a former president of the Association of American Geographers. His publications include textbooks and such scholarly works as *German Seed in Texas Soil: Immigrant Farmers in Nineteenth-Century Texas; Texas Log Buildings: A Folk Architecture; Trails to Texas: Southern Roots of Western Cattle Ranching;* and *American Log Buildings: An Old World Heritage.*

HOWARD R. LAMAR is the Sterling Professor of American History at Yale University and former dean of Yale College. Specializing in the history of the American West, family history, and comparative frontier history, Lamar has written and edited numerous works, including *Dakota Territory: A Study of Frontier Politics; Far Southwest, 1846–1912: A Territorial History; Reader's Encyclopedia of the American West; Trader on the American Frontier: Myth's Victim;* and *The Frontier in History: North America and South America Compared.*

GLEN E. LICH is the newly appointed Secretary of State Professor of Multicultural and German-Canadian Studies at the University of Winnipeg in Canada and is a visiting professor of regional studies at Baylor University. He holds an appointment also as a senior research fellow at the Center for Socioeconomic Research at the University of Coahuila in Saltillo, Mexico. Lich is the author or editor of articles and books on folk life, migration, area studies, literature, and biography. His most recent books are *Texas Country: The Changing Rural Scene* (a collection of essays coedited with Dona Reeves-Marquardt); *Fred Gipson at Work; The Humanities and Public Issues;* and *Region North America: Canada, United States, Mexico* (coedited with Joseph A. McKinney).

ANN R. MARKUSEN is professor of urban planning and policy development at Rutgers University and is Director of the Project on Regional and Industrial Economics. She is a specialist in interregional growth and urban/regional policy, state and local economic planning, and the economic aspects of gender. Markusen has coauthored or edited *The Rise of the Gunbelt: The Military Remapping of Industrial America; Profit Cycles, Oligopoly and Regional Development; Silicon Landscapes; High-Tech America: The What, How, Where and Why of the Sunrise Industries;* and *Regions: The Economics and Politics of Territory.*

OSCAR J. MARTÍNEZ is professor of history at the University of Arizona and former director of the Center for Inter-American and Border Studies at the University of Texas at El Paso. His research has focused on the social and economic history of the U.S.-Mexican border region, including the Chicano population in the Southwest. His publications include five books and numerous articles and book chapters. He recently authored *Troublesome Border* and edited *Across Boundaries: Transborder Interaction in Comparative Perspective.* Martínez is a former president of the Association of Borderlands Scholars and has held leadership positions in the Latin American Studies Association and the National Association for Chicano Studies.

LYNWOOD MONTELL is professor of folk studies at Western Kentucky University. He is the author of numerous articles and seven books, including *The Saga of Coe Ridge: A Study in Oral History* and *Killings: Folk Justice in the Upper South.* Former coordinator of the Center for Intercultural and Folk Studies, Montell has created degree programs in folk studies, Afro-American studies, and Latin American studies.

WILBUR ZELINSKY is professor of geography at Pennsylvania State University at University Park. His research interests include population and cultural geography, social and historical geography, cartography, geographic bibliography, and geography and social policy. Zelinsky is the author of *Nation into State: The Shifting Symbolic Foundations of American Nationalism; A Bibliographic Guide to Population Geography; Prologue to Population Geography;* and *The Cultural Geography of the United States.* He is a former president of the Association of American Geographers.

Regional Studies was composed into type on a Linotron 202 phototypesetter in ten point Times Roman with two points of spacing between the lines. Gill Sans was selected for display. The book was designed by Cameron Poulter, typeset by Graphic Composition, Inc., printed offset by Thomson-Shore, Inc., and bound by John H. Dekker & Sons, Inc. The paper on which this book is printed carries acid-free characteristics for an effective life of at least three hundred years.

TEXAS A&M UNIVERSITY PRESS : COLLEGE STATION